Graded exercises in
Advanced level mathematics

Graded exercises
in mechanics

Ann Kitchen
Geoff Wake

CAMBRIDGE
UNIVERSITY PRESS

PUBLISHED BY THE PRESS SYNDICATE OF THE UNIVERSITY OF CAMBRIDGE
The Pitt Building, Trumpington Street, Cambridge, United Kingdom

CAMBRIDGE UNIVERSITY PRESS
The Edinburgh Building, Cambridge CB2 2RU, UK
40 West 20th Street, New York, NY 10011-4211, USA
10 Stamford Road, Oakleigh, VIC 3166, Australia
Ruiz de Alarcón 13, 28014 Madrid, Spain
Dock House, The Waterfront, Cape Town 8001, South Africa

http://www.cambridge.org

First published 2001

Printed in the United Kingdom at the University Press, Cambridge

Typeface *Times*   System *3B2*

A catalogue record for this book is available from the British Library

ISBN 0 521 64686 3 paperback

ACKNOWLEDGEMENTS

The authors and publishers are grateful to the following Examination Boards for permission
to reproduce questions from past examination papers:

AEB	Associated Examining Board (now AQA)
AQA	Assessment and Qualifications Alliance
Edexcel	Edexcel Foundation
MEI	Mathematics for Education and Industry (validated by OCR)
NEAB	Northern Examinations and Assessment Board (now AQA)
OCR	Oxford, Cambridge and RSA Examinations
OCSEB	Oxford and Cambridge Schools Examination Board (now OCR)
UCLES	University of Cambridge Local Examination Syndicate (now OCR)
WJEC	Welsh Joint Education Committee

Contents

Introduction

This book provides carefully graded questions in mechanics that start with the very simple and progress to the very difficult. The questions are divided by chapter into topics covering those at present demanded by A level specifications for mechanics modules. Each chapter is divided into four levels of questions: basic, intermediate, advanced and revision. Working through the chapters will build up confidence in tackling examination questions. The questions themselves have been designed to be drawn as far as possible from everyday situations. The importance of mathematical modelling is stressed in the emphasis on real-world situations. Some questions have fully worked solutions to help with the understanding of key topics. In addition, while many of the questions require a numerical answer, there are a good number which require a fluency in algebra. These will be especially useful in providing extra revision for pure mathematics. Not all formulae are provided in examinations. Remember that it is worth learning all formulae used within a specification, even those given in the formulae book, as it will save time in examinations.

Basic questions will give you routine practice. They will help you to remember formulae and to understand the principle behind the particular piece of theory. They will not bring in any other theory.

Intermediate questions offer a greater challenge. They will often involve more than one stage of working and may involve theory met earlier in the book. Some of the questions here are of a standard found in the AS modules of several boards.

Advanced questions are more challenging and are designed to be as close to examination questions as possible. They will require several stages of working.

Revision questions give extra practice that can be used just before the examination. These sections end with several questions from past papers.

Answers are given for all questions (except proofs, definitions and some diagrams). Questions marked with an asterisk (*) have full worked solutions and are intended to help you understand key topics.

Some topics are in the specifications for one or two awards only. These are marked with a †. Students who are not studying for these awards should omit the questions concerned.

1
Motion in one dimension

Acceleration, velocity and displacement; the use and interpretation of graphs; the use of differentiation and integration; the use of the equations of motion for constant acceleration; motion where acceleration is a function of time

Take the acceleration due to gravity as $g\,\mathrm{m\,s^{-2}}$ where $g = 9.8$.
Give answers to three significant figures unless otherwise stated.

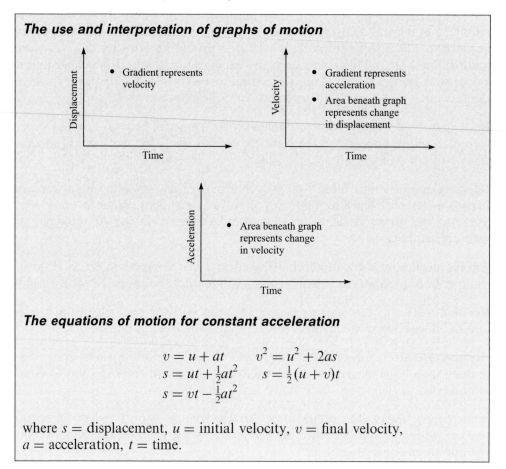

The use and interpretation of graphs of motion

Displacement / Time
- Gradient represents velocity

Velocity / Time
- Gradient represents acceleration
- Area beneath graph represents change in displacement

Acceleration / Time
- Area beneath graph represents change in velocity

The equations of motion for constant acceleration

$$v = u + at \qquad v^2 = u^2 + 2as$$
$$s = ut + \tfrac{1}{2}at^2 \qquad s = \tfrac{1}{2}(u + v)t$$
$$s = vt - \tfrac{1}{2}at^2$$

where s = displacement, u = initial velocity, v = final velocity, a = acceleration, t = time.

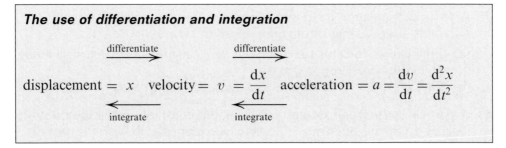

Basic

1 A boy drops a stone into a well. He hears a splash 3.5 seconds after the stone is released. How far below the point of release of the stone is the water surface?

*2 A stone is thrown vertically upwards with an initial speed of $10\,\mathrm{m\,s^{-1}}$.
   (a) Find the maximum height above the point of projection that the stone reaches.
   (b) Find the total time it takes for the stone to return to the point from which it was projected.

3 A particle moves along a horizontal straight line with an acceleration of $2\,\mathrm{m\,s^{-2}}$. At time $t = 0$ it passes a point O with a velocity of $1\,\mathrm{m\,s^{-1}}$.
   (a) Find the velocity of the particle 5 seconds after it passes O.
   (b) Find how far the particle has moved in this time.

4 At time $t = 0$ a particle passes the origin O travelling along a horizontal straight line with a speed of $10\,\mathrm{m\,s^{-1}}$. It has a constant acceleration of $-2\,\mathrm{m\,s^{-2}}$.
   (a) Find how far away from O the particle is when it comes to rest.
   (b) Find the time that elapses between the particle being at O and returning there.

5 A jogger runs in a straight line from home for 4 kilometres at constant speed for 20 minutes. She completes the return journey in a further 20 minutes in two stages:
   stage 1   for 10 minutes at a constant speed of $4\,\mathrm{m\,s^{-1}}$,
   stage 2   the rest of the journey at a constant speed of $u\,\mathrm{m\,s^{-1}}$.
   (a) Find u.
   (b) Sketch a *velocity*–time graph for the jogger's entire journey.

6 A train is travelling on a horizontal straight section of track at $80\,\mathrm{km\,h^{-1}}$ when its brakes are applied. The train then decelerates at $0.5\,\mathrm{m\,s^{-2}}$.
   (a) Find how long the train takes to come to rest.
   (b) Find how far the train travels in coming to rest.

7 A particle, moving in a straight horizontal line, has velocity, v m s^{-1}, t seconds after passing through an origin O, where $v = 3t - 1$.

    (a) Find expressions for the displacement, x metres, of the particle from O, and its acceleration a m s^{-2}.

    (b) Sketch graphs to show how x, v and a vary with time.

8 A particle starts from rest and travels under constant acceleration until it reaches a velocity of 20 m s^{-1}. The particle immediately starts to travel under constant deceleration until it is stationary. The particle accelerates for 10 seconds and decelerates for 20 seconds.

    (a) What is the total distance travelled?

    (b) How far is the particle from its start position when it first reaches a speed of 10 m s^{-1}?

9 A juggler throws her clubs vertically in the air so they reach a maximum height of 3.2 metres above her hand.

    (a) How fast must she throw them?

    (b) For how many seconds is each club in the air?

Intermediate

1 A girl drops a ball from rest vertically downwards from a tall tower.

    (a) Find how far the ball travels in the first second, and its speed at the end of this time.

    (b) Find how far the ball travels in the 2nd second and its speed at the end of this time.

The girl throws a second ball vertically downwards with initial speed u m s^{-1} so that after 1 second it has travelled the same distance as the first ball did in the first 2 seconds of its motion.

    (c) Find u.

2 A ball travelling in a straight line passes through a point O with an initial speed of u m s^{-1} and deceleration of a m s^{-2}.

    (a) Find how long it is before the ball first comes to rest.

    (b) Find the distance travelled by the ball between the two instances that it is at O.

3 A particle travels with constant acceleration along a straight line ABC. It passes point A with velocity 2 m s^{-1}. Two seconds later the particle passes B with velocity 5 m s^{-1}.

    (a) Find the acceleration of the particle.

    (b) Find the distance between A and B.

The point C is 8 metres from B along ABC.

    (c) Find how long the particle takes to travel from B to C.

    (d) Find the velocity of the particle when it is at C.

4 A ball is thrown vertically into the air from a point 1.5 metres above the ground, with a speed of $20\,\mathrm{m\,s}^{-1}$. Find the length of time that elapses between the ball's release and when it hits the ground.

5 An aircraft at take-off can be assumed to have a constant acceleration of $2.5\,\mathrm{m\,s}^{-2}$. To lift off the ground it needs to have a speed of $75\,\mathrm{m\,s}^{-1}$.

(a) Find how far the aircraft needs to travel to reach a speed at which it can lift off, assuming that it starts from rest.

(b) Find how long the aircraft takes to reach this speed.

6 A car accelerates uniformly from rest to reach a speed of $25\,\mathrm{m\,s}^{-1}$ in time T seconds. It then travels at constant speed for $4T$ seconds, after which it decelerates uniformly to stop after a further $2T$ seconds.

(a) Sketch a speed–time graph for the motion of the car.

(b) Given that the car travels a total of 3850 metres, find T.

7 A ball is thrown vertically upwards with a speed of $6\,\mathrm{m\,s}^{-1}$. A second ball is dropped t seconds later from the same spot. They meet when the second ball has fallen through 11 metres.

(a) Find t.

(b) Which ball is travelling faster?

8 An object is thrown vertically upwards with speed u near the Earth's surface.

(a) Find, in terms of u and g, the greatest height through which the object rises.

The same object is thrown vertically upwards near the surface of the Moon, where the acceleration due to gravity may be taken to be $\dfrac{g}{6}$. The object rises through the same height as that in part (a).

(b) Find its initial speed, v, in terms of u.

9 A particle moves in a straight line so that its acceleration, $a\,\mathrm{m\,s}^{-2}$, is given by $a = 4 - 0.2t$, for $0 \le t \le 20$, where t is the time in seconds after the particle passes through origin O. When $t = 0$ the velocity of the particle is $-40\,\mathrm{m\,s}^{-1}$.

(a) Find t when the particle has zero velocity.

(b) Find its acceleration at that time.

*10 A particle moves in a straight line. Its displacement, x metres, from an origin O at time t seconds, is given by $x = -t^2 + 7t - 10$.

(a) Find the displacement of the particle when $t = 0$.

(b) Find t when the particle is first at O.

(c) Find its velocity and acceleration at that time.

11 Over the first 5 seconds of a 100 metre race, the acceleration, $a\,\mathrm{m\,s}^{-2}$, of a sprinter starting from rest, who runs in a straight line, can be modelled by $a = 1 - 0.1t$.

(a) Find the speed of the sprinter at the end of the first 5 seconds.
(b) Find the distance run by the sprinter in that time.
(c) Explain why this model for the acceleration cannot be valid for the whole race given that the sprinter completes the course.

Advanced

1 A ball is thrown vertically upwards with a speed of $10\,\mathrm{m\,s}^{-1}$. For how long is the ball more than 2 metres above its point of projection?

2 A body moving in a straight line with constant acceleration $a\,\mathrm{m\,s}^{-2}$ has an initial velocity of $u\,\mathrm{m\,s}^{-1}$ at time $t = 0$. After t seconds the body has travelled a distance $x\,\mathrm{m}$ and has a velocity $v\,\mathrm{m\,s}^{-1}$.

(a) Sketch a velocity–time graph for the body.

Use your graph to show how you can arrive at the result:

(b) $x = \left(\dfrac{u+v}{2}\right)t$

(c) $v = u + at$

(d) $x = ut + \frac{1}{2}at^2$

*3 Cyclist A travels at a constant speed of $10\,\mathrm{m\,s}^{-1}$ along a straight road. At time $t = 0$ cyclist A passes cyclist B who is stationary. Thirty seconds later cyclist B sets off in pursuit of A. Cyclist B accelerates uniformly at $2\,\mathrm{m\,s}^{-2}$ until she reaches a speed of $15\,\mathrm{m\,s}^{-1}$, and catches up with A when $t = T$.

(a) Sketch a graph of the speed, $v\,\mathrm{m\,s}^{-1}$, of each cyclist plotted against time, t seconds, for the period after A passes B.
(b) Find T.

Cyclist A is travelling at $10\,\mathrm{m\,s}^{-1}$ when she applies her brakes. Her acceleration, $a\,\mathrm{m\,s}^{-2}$, during this period is given by $a = \dfrac{-t}{2}$, where t is the time in seconds after she first applies her brakes.

(c) Find an expression for the speed, $v\,\mathrm{m\,s}^{-1}$, of cyclist A, t seconds after she applies her brakes.
(d) Find:
  (i) how long it takes cyclist A to brake from $10\,\mathrm{m\,s}^{-1}$ to rest,
  (ii) how far cyclist A travels in this period.

4 A particle has velocity $-2\,\mathrm{m\,s}^{-1}$ as it moves in a straight line and passes through point O. The acceleration of the particle t seconds after it passes through O is $a\,\mathrm{m\,s}^{-2}$ where $a = 1 + 0.5t$.

  (a) Find an expression for the velocity, $v\,\mathrm{m\,s}^{-1}$, of the particle t seconds after it passes through O.

  (b) Find the displacement of the particle from O when it first comes to rest.

5 A particle moves so that its displacement, x metres, t seconds after it passes through an origin O, moving in a straight line, is given by $x = t^3 - 5t^2 + 6t$.

  (a) Find the two times, other than $t = 0$, that the particle is at O.

  (b) Find an expression for the velocity of the particle.

  (c) Find when the velocity of the particle is $-2\,\mathrm{m\,s}^{-1}$ and find its acceleration at these times.

6 A car accelerates from rest at traffic lights along a straight road so that after t seconds its acceleration, $a\,\mathrm{m\,s}^{-2}$, is given by:

$$a = 1 + 0.1t \quad 0 \le t \le 2$$
$$a = 3 \quad\quad\quad 2 \le t \le 5$$
$$a = 0 \quad\quad\quad 5 < t$$

  Find the velocity, $v\,\mathrm{m\,s}^{-1}$, and distance, s metres, of the car from the traffic lights when

  (a) $t = 2$,

  (b) $t = 5$,

  (c) $t = 10$.

7 A ball is projected vertically upwards from a point 4 metres above the ground, with speed $v\,\mathrm{m\,s}^{-1}$. It reaches the ground after 4 seconds.

  (a) What was its initial speed?

  (b) How far has it travelled?

Revision

1 A sprinter completes 100 metres in 11.5 seconds. His motion takes place in a straight line and may be considered to consist of two parts. In the first part he accelerates uniformly for 2 seconds; in the second part he runs at the constant speed he has reached for the remaining 9.5 seconds.

  (a) Sketch a speed–time graph for the sprinter's motion.

  (b) Find the constant speed at which the sprinter runs in the second part of the motion.

2 A stone is dropped from rest into a well. It takes 2.5 seconds to hit the water. How far does the stone fall before it hits the water?

3   A girl throws a ball into the air so that it leaves her hand travelling vertically upwards with a speed at $15\,\mathrm{m\,s^{-1}}$ at a point 1 metre above the surface of the ground. Find:

(a) the maximum height the ball reaches above the ground,
(b) the time it takes the ball to hit the ground.

4   A lift accelerates uniformly upwards at $a\,\mathrm{m\,s^{-2}}$ until it reaches a constant speed of $v\,\mathrm{m\,s^{-1}}$. It decelerates uniformly at $1.5a\,\mathrm{m\,s^{-2}}$ before coming to rest at a floor.

(a) Draw a sketch graph of speed plotted against time for the journey of the lift between two floors.
(b) For the situation where the lift travels 50 metres between floors, and takes 3 seconds to reach a maximum speed of $5\,\mathrm{m\,s^{-1}}$, find the time taken for the whole journey.

5   A train travels along a straight section of track between two stations A and B. The train starts from rest at A and accelerates uniformly at $0.25\,\mathrm{m\,s^{-2}}$ for 80 seconds. It then travels at constant speed until its brakes are applied and it decelerates uniformly at $0.5\,\mathrm{m\,s^{-2}}$ until it comes to rest in station B.

(a) Find the speed of the train over the section of the journey where it travels at constant speed.
(b) Sketch a speed–time graph of the train's journey between A and B.
(c) Find the length of time for which the brakes are applied to bring the train to rest in station B.
(d) The stations A and B are $5400\,\mathrm{m}$ apart. Find the total time taken by the train to travel between A and B.

6   A particle moves along a straight line through O. At time t seconds the acceleration of the particle is $a = 2(t-1)\,\mathrm{m\,s^{-2}}$. At $t = 0$ the particle has a velocity of $-1\,\mathrm{m\,s^{-1}}$ as it passes through O. Find:

(a) an expression for the velocity of the particle at time t,
(b) an expression for the displacement of the particle from O at time t,
(c) the exact times at which the velocity of the particle is zero,
(d) the total distance travelled by the particle in the first 2 seconds.

7   A particle moves along the x-axis. Its velocity, $v\,\mathrm{m\,s^{-1}}$, t seconds after passing the origin, O, is given by $v = 15 - 2t - t^2$. Find:

(a) the displacement of the particle from O when it is instantaneously at rest,
(b) the acceleration of the particle when it returns through O,
(c) the total distance travelled by the particle in the first 9 seconds of its motion.

8 A ball is thrown vertically upwards with a speed of $10\,\mathrm{m\,s^{-1}}$. A second ball is dropped from the same position, T seconds later. The two balls meet 15 metres below the point of projection. Find T.

9 A small ball is projected vertically upwards with a speed of $15\,\mathrm{m\,s^{-1}}$. One second later another ball is projected vertically upwards from the same point with a speed of $10\,\mathrm{m\,s^{-1}}$. Find where the two balls meet.

10 A particle, P, travels along a straight line so that t seconds after being at rest at O its velocity $v\,\mathrm{m\,s^{-1}}$ is given by $v = t(2 - 3t)$.
   (a) Find t when the acceleration of P is zero.
   (b) T seconds after leaving O the particle stops instantaneously. Find:
       (i) T,
       (ii) the distance of the particle from O at this instant.

11 A particle is projected vertically upwards from a point O with speed u. When this particle reaches its greatest height a second particle is projected upwards from O with speed $\dfrac{u}{2}$.

   (a) Find, in terms of u and g, the time after the projection of the second particle that collision occurs.
   (b) Find where the two particles collide.

12 A cyclist starts from rest and moves in a straight line. She has constant acceleration of $0.5\,\mathrm{m\,s^{-2}}$ for 15 seconds and then travels with constant speed for a further 45 seconds. At this point the cyclist applies her brakes to decelerate uniformly to rest. The total distance travelled is 500 metres. Find the total time of the cyclist's journey.

13 A particle P moves in a straight line in such a way that, at time t seconds, its acceleration $a\,\mathrm{m\,s^{-2}}$ is given by

$$a = 6t - 3t^2, \quad t \geq 0$$

When $t = 0$, P is at rest at O.
   (a) Calculate the velocity of P when $t = 2$.
   (b) Find the time when P is next at rest.
   (c) Find the distance from O to the point where P is next at rest.
   [Edexcel]

14

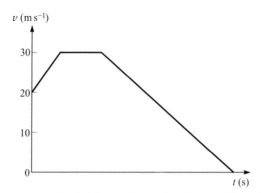

A car travelling on a straight road accelerates uniformly at $a\,\text{m}\,\text{s}^{-2}$ from its initial speed of $20\,\text{m}\,\text{s}^{-1}$ until it reaches a speed of $30\,\text{m}\,\text{s}^{-1}$. The car travels at this speed for $600\,\text{m}$ and then decelerates uniformly at $\frac{1}{2}a\,\text{m}\,\text{s}^{-2}$ until it comes to rest. The (t, v) graph for the motion is shown above. Show that the time spent decelerating is six times as long as the time spent accelerating.

The total distance travelled by the car from time $t = 0$ until it comes to rest is $2900\,\text{m}$. Calculate

  (i) the time for which the car is accelerating,
 (ii) the value of a,
(iii) the speed of the car $40\,\text{s}$ before it comes to rest.

[OCR]

2 Projectiles

The use of vector methods; the use of equations of motion under gravity

For all projectiles assume that the only force acting is constant and due to gravity. Take the acceleration due to gravity as $g\,\mathrm{m\,s^{-2}}$ where $g = 9.8$. Give answers to three significant figures unless otherwise stated.

You may be able to answer the questions in this chapter by either or both of two methods:

- using vectors
- using the equations of motion for constant acceleration.

Use the method which you are used to; when solutions are given to basic and intermediate questions they include both methods. The revision section has a number of questions which use only vector techniques.

Projectile motion is considered in two directions: vertical and horizontal. In the vertical direction the particle accelerates downwards at $g\ \mathrm{m\ s^{-2}}$, and the equations of motion for constant acceleration can be applied.
In the horizontal direction there is no acceleration, so the speed of the particle is constant.

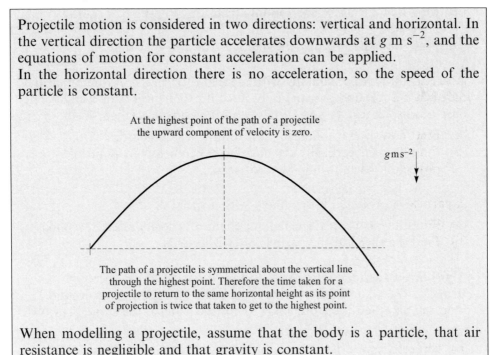

At the highest point of the path of a projectile the upward component of velocity is zero.

$g\,\mathrm{m\,s^{-2}}$

The path of a projectile is symmetrical about the vertical line through the highest point. Therefore the time taken for a projectile to return to the same horizontal height as its point of projection is twice that taken to get to the highest point.

When modelling a projectile, assume that the body is a particle, that air resistance is negligible and that gravity is constant.

Basic

1 A particle is projected vertically upwards with a speed of $10\,\mathrm{m\,s^{-1}}$ from a height of 1 metre above the ground.

   (a) Find the time the ball takes to reach its greatest height above the ground.

   (b) Find the greatest height of the ball above the ground.

2 A ball is dropped down a well. The surface of the water is 15 metres below the point from which the ball is released. The ball is released from rest.

   (a) Find how long the ball takes to reach the water surface.

   (b) Find the speed of the ball just as it reaches the water surface.

*3 A small rubber ball rolls off a desk at a height of 0.75 metres above a horizontal floor. The ball can be considered to be moving horizontally with speed $5\,\mathrm{m\,s^{-1}}$ when it reaches the edge of the desk.

   (a) Find the time for which the ball is in the air.

   (b) Find how far horizontally the ball travels in that time.

4 A boy throws a ball horizontally with a speed of $20\,\mathrm{m\,s^{-1}}$ from the top of a cliff.

   (a) Find how far away horizontally from the boy the ball is after 2 seconds.

   (b) Find how far vertically the ball has fallen in that time.

5 A dart is thrown horizontally with a speed of $20\,\mathrm{m\,s^{-1}}$. Assume that the dart is a particle and that the only force it experiences is its weight. The dart travels 2.5 metres horizontally and then hits a dartboard.

   (a) Find how long it takes the dart to hit the dartboard.

   (b) Find how far vertically the dart has fallen below its point of projection when it hits the dartboard.

6 A particle is projected horizontally with a speed of $25\,\mathrm{m\,s^{-1}}$.

   (a) Find the particle's vertical component of velocity after 2 seconds.

   (b) Find the speed of the particle after 2 seconds.

7 A girl throws a stone into a well so that it has an initial speed of $10\,\mathrm{m\,s^{-1}}$. The water in the well is 50 m below the point of projection. Find the time that the stone takes to hit the water if the stone is thrown:

   (a) vertically downwards,

   (b) vertically upwards.

8 A ball is kicked from a horizontal playing field so that it initially has a speed of $15\,\mathrm{m\,s}^{-1}$ at an angle of $30°$ above the horizontal. Find:

(a) the time the ball takes to reach its greatest height,

(b) the horizontal distance it travels before bouncing.

9 Jack throws a ball so that it has an initial speed of $10\,\mathrm{m\,s}^{-1}$ at an angle of $45°$ above the horizontal as shown in the diagram. The ball leaves Jack's hand at a height of 1 m above the horizontal ground. Find the horizontal distance of the ball from its point of projection when the ball lands.

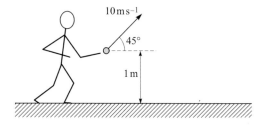

10 A projectile has an initial speed of $20\,\mathrm{m\,s}^{-1}$ at an angle of $60°$ above the horizontal. Find the distance of the projectile from O, its point of projection, after 2 seconds.

11 A tennis player serves a ball over a horizontal surface so that, when the ball leaves his racket at a height of 2.7 metres above the ground, it is travelling horizontally with a speed of $40\,\mathrm{m\,s}^{-1}$. Find the horizontal distance that the ball travels to its first bounce.

Intermediate

1 A particle is projected at a speed of $4.9\,\mathrm{m\,s}^{-1}$ at an angle of $45°$ to horizontal ground.

(a) Show that the time taken for the particle to reach its maximum height above the ground is $\dfrac{1}{2\sqrt{2}}$ seconds.

(b) Find the maximum height that the projectile reaches above the ground.

*2 A golf ball is hit so that it leaves horizontal ground with a speed of $19.6\,\mathrm{m\,s}^{-1}$ at an angle of $45°$ to the horizontal.

(a) How long does it take to reach its highest point?

(b) What height does it reach?

(c) Find its range (the horizontal distance between its take-off and landing points).

3 A ball is kicked from a point on horizontal ground with a speed of $14.7\,\mathrm{m\,s^{-1}}$ at an angle of $30°$ with the ground.

   (a) Find how long it takes the ball to return to the ground.

   (b) Find how far the ball has travelled away from the point at which it was kicked when it first lands.

4 A golfer hits a ball at a speed of $35\,\mathrm{m\,s^{-1}}$ at an angle of $25°$ above the horizontal. The ball lands at a point on the horizontal golf course 95.8 metres away.

   (a) Find the time for which the ball is in the air.

   (b) How long after being hit does the ball pass through its highest point?

   (c) Find the maximum height the ball reaches above the golf course.

5 A ball is kicked from a point on horizontal ground with a speed of $15\,\mathrm{m\,s^{-1}}$ at an angle of $60°$ above the horizontal. The ball hits a vertical wall 5 metres away. The situation is shown in the diagram.

   (a) Find how long it takes the ball to hit the wall.

   (b) Find how high above the ground the ball is when it hits the wall.

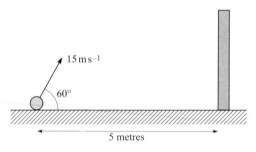

               5 metres

6 A ball is thrown vertically into the air. It takes 2 seconds to reach its highest point. Find the speed with which it was thrown.

7 A ball is thrown horizontally with a speed of $12\,\mathrm{m\,s^{-1}}$ from the top of a cliff. It lands in the sea 100 metres below.

   (a) Find how long it takes to land in the sea.

   (b) How far it is from the base of the cliff at that point?

   (c) Sketch a graph showing (i) the path of the ball according to your model and (ii) its likely actual path.

   (d) State any assumptions you made to simplify this situation.

8 A ball rolls over the edge of a cliff with a horizontal speed of $10\,\mathrm{m\,s^{-1}}$. The top of the cliff is 20 metres from a horizontal beach below. Find the distance of the ball from the base of the cliff when it first bounces.

9 A ball is kicked from a point which is 5 metres horizontally from the base of a wall. The ball has a speed of $15\,\mathrm{m\,s^{-1}}$ in a direction making $45°$

with the horizontal when it is kicked. Find the height of the wall if the ball just clears it.

10 In modelling the motion of a beachball it is decided to model the ball as a particle projectile.

(a) What assumptions have been made?
(b) Which of these are justified?
(c) Is the range of the ball calculated using this model likely to be an overestimate or underestimate.

11 A particle is projected from horizontal ground, reaches a height of 10 metres and lands back on the ground a distance 30 metres from its point of projection. Find its initial velocity.

12 A particle leaves the ground at an angle of 25° to the horizontal. What must its initial speed be if it is to reach a maximum height of 8 metres before falling back to earth?

Advanced

*1 A ball leaves a horizontal playing field at $30\,\mathrm{m\,s^{-1}}$. What possible angles of projection can be used if the ball is to land 60 metres away?

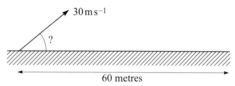

2 A girl hits a ball with a bat so that it takes 2 seconds to reach its highest point. At that moment the ball is 20 metres horizontally away from the point at which it was hit.

(a) Find the ball's speed at the instant that it was hit.
(b) Find, to the nearest degree, the angle above the horizontal at which the ball was hit by the girl.

3 Claire throws a cricket ball with a speed of $19\,\mathrm{m\,s^{-1}}$ at an angle of 15° above the horizontal.

(a) State any assumptions you make to simplify this situation.
(b) If her partner catches it at the same height, how far apart must they be?
(c) Her partner misses the ball completely and it lands 22 metres away from Claire. Find the height above the ground from which it was thrown.

4 Sonia hits a tennis ball horizontally at a speed of $30\,\mathrm{m\,s^{-1}}$. It just passes over the net, 92 cm above the court, and lands on the other side. The distance between Sonia and the net is 12 metres. The ball can be modelled as a particle.

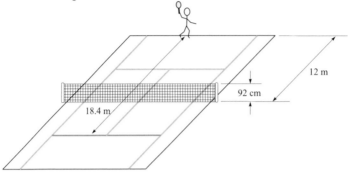

(a) Calculate the initial height of the tennis ball.
(b) Find the time during which the ball is in the air, from when it is hit until it first hits the ground.
(c) Show whether or not the ball lands inside the service line 18.4 metres away from Sonia.

5 A football is kicked from a point A on horizontal ground so that it leaves the ground at an angle of $32°$. It just clears a vertical wall of height 4 metres. It can be modelled as a particle at A when $t = 0$. If A is 10 metres from the wall:

(a) find the initial speed of the ball,
(b) discuss the assumptions made in modelling this situation.

6 David throws a cricket ball at an angle of $3°$ below the horizontal. Its initial height is 2.2 metres above the ground and it hits the ground after 0.6 seconds. The ground is horizontal. Assume the ball can be modelled as a particle.

(a) Calculate the speed of projection.
(b) Calculate the horizontal distance travelled by the ball in this time.

*7 A boy aims a paint ball at a wall as shown. The boy stands 12 metres from the wall and throws the ball so that it leaves his hand with a speed of $15\,\mathrm{m\,s^{-1}}$ at an angle ϕ with the horizontal, where $0° \le \phi \le 30°$. Investigate the relationship between ϕ and possible release heights if the ball is to hit the wall at a height of 1 metre.

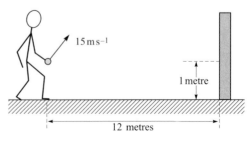

8 A ball is thrown from shoulder height (1.5 metres) to land on the ground 9 metres away from your feet. The ball is thrown with a speed of $9\,\mathrm{m\,s^{-1}}$.

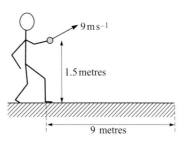

(a) State any assumptions you make to simplify this situation.

(b) What angles of projection could have been used?

(c) The ball is actually a beachball of diameter 0.5 metres. Which of your assumptions are not valid in reality? Give reasons for your answer.

9 A particle is projected from a point O with an initial speed $u\,\mathrm{m\,s^{-1}}$ at an angle of θ above the horizontal. Take x- and y-axes aligned horizontally and vertically respectively and O as the origin. Show that the equation of the path of the projectile is:

$$y = x\tan\theta - \frac{gx^2}{2u^2}\sec^2\theta$$

10 A particle is projected up an inclined plane from point A with a speed of $23\,\mathrm{m\,s^{-1}}$ at an angle of $30°$ to the horizontal. The plane makes an angle of $15°$ with the horizontal. The particle lands on the plane at B. Find the distance AB.

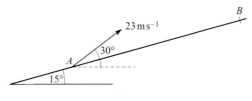

Revision

Sections A and C may be tackled using any method; section B uses vector methods.

SECTION A
Questions in this section may be tackled using any method.

1 A boy drops a stone from a bridge. After 1.5 seconds the boy sees a splash.

(a) How far did the stone fall?

(b) What assumptions have you made when modelling this situation?

2 A ball rolls off the edge of a desk. When it leaves the desk it is travelling horizontally with a speed of $2\,\mathrm{m\,s^{-1}}$. The ball takes 0.5 seconds to hit the horizontal floor.

(a) How high above the floor is the surface of the desk?

(b) Find the vertical component of the ball's velocity when it first hits the floor.

(c) Find the speed of the ball when it first hits the floor.

(d) Find the horizontal distance that the ball travels from the edge of the desk until it first hits the floor.

3 A golf ball is hit at a speed of $40\,\text{m\,s}^{-1}$ at an angle of $15°$ above the horizontal fairway.

(a) Find the length of time that the ball is in the air.

(b) Find the horizontal range of the ball.

4 Jenni hits a ball horizontally so that it has a speed of $30\,\text{m\,s}^{-1}$ and is at a height of 2.5 metres above a horizontal surface when it leaves her tennis racket.

(a) Find the length of time that the ball is in the air before it first bounces.

(b) Find the horizontal distance that the ball travels in that time.

5 Samina throws a ball from a height of 1 metre above horizontal ground so that it has a speed of $15\,\text{m\,s}^{-1}$ and is travelling at an angle of $30°$ above the horizontal when it is released.

(a) Find the greatest height that the ball reaches above the ground.

(b) Find the maximum distance that the ball travels horizontally before it first bounces.

6 Les kicks a ball so that it leaves the horizontal ground with a speed of $25\,\text{m\,s}^{-1}$ at an angle of $40°$ above the horizontal. The ball hits a wall after half a second.

(a) Find the height of the ball above the ground when it hits the wall.

(b) Find the speed of the ball when it hits the wall.

7 Asmat throws a ball for his dog. The ball is 0.2 metres above horizontal ground and has a speed of $9\,\text{m\,s}^{-1}$ at $20°$ above the horizontal when it leaves Asmat's hand. The dog is 0.3 metres high and 4 metres away from Asmat. It leaps into the air and catches the ball.
Find how high the dog must leap.

SECTION B

Questions in this section should be answered using vector techniques. Take the x- and y-axes as horizontal and vertically upwards respectively. Assume that the acceleration due to gravity is $\begin{pmatrix} 0 \\ -9.8 \end{pmatrix}\,\text{m\,s}^{-2}$.

*1 A particle is projected with initial velocity $\mathbf{u}\,\text{m\,s}^{-1}$, where $\mathbf{u} = 10\mathbf{i} + 12\mathbf{j}$ and $\mathbf{i}$ and $\mathbf{j}$ are unit vectors aligned horizontally and vertically upwards respectively. Its acceleration is $\mathbf{a}\,\text{m\,s}^{-2}$ where $\mathbf{a} = -9.8\mathbf{j}$.

    (a) Find the time the particle takes to reach its highest point.

    (b) The displacement **r** metres of the particle is given by $\mathbf{r} = x\mathbf{i} + y\mathbf{j}$ at time t seconds.

        (i) Find **r** after 2 seconds.

        (ii) Find y when $x = 15$.

        (iii) Find the magnitude and direction of the particle's velocity when $x = 15$.

2 A particle leaves the horizontal ground with velocity $\begin{pmatrix} 3 \\ 8 \end{pmatrix}$ m s^{-1}.

Find the maximum height reached by the particle.

3 A particle is fired from an origin, O, on horizontal ground with a velocity of $\begin{pmatrix} 25 \\ u \end{pmatrix}$ m s^{-1}. It reaches its highest point after 4 seconds.

Find u and the displacement of the particle from O at its highest point.

4 A particle leaves an origin, O, on horizontal ground with velocity $\begin{pmatrix} 4 \\ 6 \end{pmatrix}$ m s^{-1}.

    (a) Find the displacement of the particle from O after t seconds.

    (b) What is the maximum height above the ground reached by the particle?

    (c) Find the particle's height when $t = 0.5$ seconds and calculate its distance from the origin when it falls back to the same height above the ground.

5 A particle is projected horizontally from an origin at the top of a cliff 125 metres above a flat sea. It passes through the point $\begin{pmatrix} 20 \\ -25 \end{pmatrix}$ metres.

Find the horizontal distance travelled by the particle and its speed of impact when it hits the sea.

6 A particle leaves an origin with velocity $\begin{pmatrix} a \\ 6 \end{pmatrix}$ m s^{-1}. It reaches its highest point when it is 2.5 metres from the origin. Find a and hence its initial speed.

7 A particle is projected from an origin so that it passes through the points $\begin{pmatrix} 7 \\ 9 \end{pmatrix}$ metres and $\begin{pmatrix} 21 \\ 9 \end{pmatrix}$ metres. Find its initial velocity.

SECTION C
Questions in this section may be tackled using any method.

1 A golf ball is projected from a point O on horizontal ground with speed $40\,\mathrm{m\,s^{-1}}$ at an angle of $30°$ above the horizontal. The ball just clears the top of a vertical tree in its plane of motion. The base of the tree is 18 m from O.

(a) Show that the ball reaches the top of the tree after approximately 0.52 s.

(b) Find:
  (i) the height of the tree, in metres, correct to one decimal place.
  (ii) the distance from O, in metres, correct to one decimal place, of the ball when it first strikes the ground,
  (iii) the time, in seconds, correct to two decimal places, taken by the ball to reach the point where it is moving at an angle β above the horizontal where $\tan \beta = \frac{1}{2}$.

[WJEC]

2 A firework commonly used in displays is the 'mortar shell'. This is projected from a tube and explodes when high in the air. In order to model the motion of a shell, it may be regarded as a particle projected from ground level over horizontal ground. Air resistance may be neglected.

In parts (i) to (iii) each shell is projected with a speed of $35\,\mathrm{m\,s^{-1}}$.

(i) How high does a shell go when projected vertically?
(ii) A shell projected at $75°$ to the horizontal explodes 4 seconds after projection. How high is the shell when it explodes? Is it rising or falling at this instant?

For safety reasons, the shell must be at least 50 m above the ground when it explodes.

(iii) For a shell projected at $80°$ to the horizontal, find the earliest and latest times after it is projected that the shell can explode.

Suppose now that a shell is projected with an initial speed and at an angle such that it reaches its maximum height of H metres after T seconds.

(iv) Show that $H = 4.9T^2$.

Two shells are projected at the same time but with *different* initial speeds and angles of projection.

(v) Explain why the result in part (iv) means that, if the two shells explode at the top of their trajectories at the same time, then they do so at the same height.

[OCR]

3 A popular attraction at school fairs is 'Splat the Rat'. The 'rat' is a small object which slides down a board AC as shown in the diagram. The top part, AB, of the board is covered so that the player cannot see the first part of the motion. The rat has a constant acceleration of $6.7 \, \text{m s}^{-2}$ while it is on the board.

The rat is released from rest at A and slides through 1.5 metres before reaching C.

(i) Show that the speed of the rat at C is $4.5 \, \text{m s}^{-1}$.

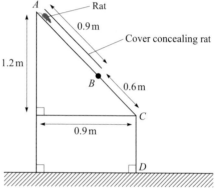

The aim of the game is to hit (splat) the rat with a stick when it comes into view. Referring to the diagram, the rat must be hit between B and C, a distance of $0.6 \, \text{m}$.

(ii) Show that the length of time for which the rat can be hit is 0.15 seconds, correct to 2 decimal places.

(iii) The board is mounted on a frame with dimensions as shown in the diagram. Calculate the horizontal and vertical components of velocity of the rat at C.

Not many players win a prize so the organisers decide that the rat may also be hit while it is dropping from C to the ground. On one occasion the rat is not hit and goes on to hit the ground. The rat takes 0.1 seconds to fall to the ground from C. The air resistance on the rat is negligible.

(iv) How far from D does the rat land?

(v) Calculate the distance CD.

[MEI]

3

Resultant and relative velocity

Resultant velocity; relative velocity; interception; closest approach

Take the acceleration due to gravity to be $g\,\mathrm{m\,s}^{-2}$ where $g = 9.8$.
Give answers to three significant figures unless otherwise stated.

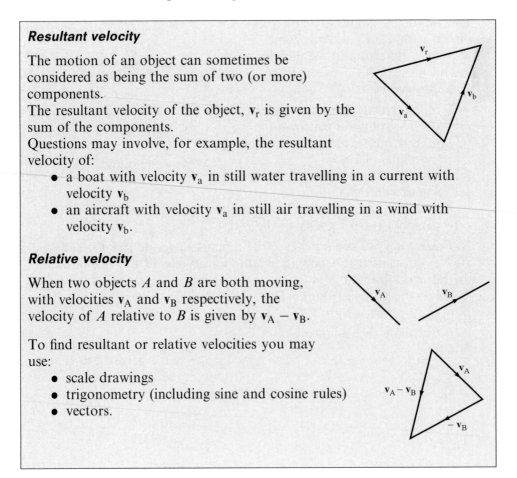

Resultant velocity

The motion of an object can sometimes be considered as being the sum of two (or more) components.
The resultant velocity of the object, $\mathbf{v_r}$ is given by the sum of the components.
Questions may involve, for example, the resultant velocity of:
- a boat with velocity $\mathbf{v_a}$ in still water travelling in a current with velocity $\mathbf{v_b}$
- an aircraft with velocity $\mathbf{v_a}$ in still air travelling in a wind with velocity $\mathbf{v_b}$.

Relative velocity

When two objects A and B are both moving, with velocities $\mathbf{v_A}$ and $\mathbf{v_B}$ respectively, the velocity of A relative to B is given by $\mathbf{v_A} - \mathbf{v_B}$.

To find resultant or relative velocities you may use:
- scale drawings
- trigonometry (including sine and cosine rules)
- vectors.

Closest approach

If the velocity of A relative to B is $\mathbf{v}_A - \mathbf{v}_B$ and you know the positions of A and B at a certain instant, you can find their closest distance of approach by finding the perpendicular distance from B to the path of A relative to B.

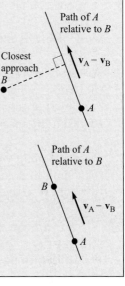

Interception

Two objects A and B will be at the same point at some instant if the path of A relative to B passes through B.

Basic

1   A toy car travels along a track on the deck of a ship with a speed of $4\,\mathrm{m\,s^{-1}}$. The ship is travelling due north with a speed of $5\,\mathrm{m\,s^{-1}}$. Give the resultant velocity of the toy car if it runs:

(a) from north to south,
(b) from west to east,
(c) from south-west to north-east.

*2   A model boat with a speed of $0.4\,\mathrm{m\,s^{-1}}$ in still water is steered due north across a river that flows with speed $5\,\mathrm{m\,s^{-1}}$ from west to east between parallel banks that are 20 metres apart. Find:

(a) the time taken by the boat to cross the river,
(b) the distance travelled by the boat.

3   A girl can swim in still water at $1.5\,\mathrm{m\,s^{-1}}$. She swims across a river that flows at $2\,\mathrm{m\,s^{-1}}$ and is 75 m wide. Find the distance she travels if she crosses the river in the shortest time possible.

4   A swimmer is heading directly across a river which has a current of $4\,\mathrm{km\,h^{-1}}$ parallel to its banks. Her speed through the water is $2\,\mathrm{km\,h^{-1}}$.

(a) Find her resultant velocity.
(b) The river is 25 metres wide. How far downstream does she land?

5 A model plane is flying at 40 km h^{-1} through the air. Its resultant velocity is 20 km h^{-1} due south. There is a wind blowing from east to west. What is the speed of the wind?

6 A crop-spraying plane can spray water out of its water jets with a speed of 10 m s^{-1}. The water jets are perpendicular to the plane. If the plane can fly at speeds of between 30 m s^{-1} and 40 m s^{-1}, find the possible range of resultant speeds of the water jets as they leave the sprays.

7 Rain is falling vertically downward with a speed of 8 m s^{-1}. A passenger travelling in a car thinks the rain is falling at an angle of $25°$ with the horizontal. How fast is the car travelling?

8 A man can row his boat at 3 m s^{-1} in still water. He wants to cross a straight river flowing at 4 m s^{-1} between parallel banks at 40 m apart. Find the distance that he would row if he took the quickest possible route.

9 A river flows at 5 m s^{-1} from east to west between parallel banks that are 300 metres apart. A canoeist paddles at a speed of 1.5 m s^{-1} through still water.

  (a) State the direction in which the canoeist must head to cross the river in the shortest possible time.
  (b) Find the time taken and the actual distance travelled.

*10 A passenger on a ship travelling at 10 m s^{-1} in a north-easterly direction observes a second ship that appears to be travelling at 4 m s^{-1} in a southerly direction. Find the true velocity of the second ship.

11 A wind of 10 km h^{-1} is blowing from the south across a lake. The resultant velocity of a yacht sailing on this lake is 8 km h^{-1} on a bearing of $045°$. Find the direction of the wind relative to the yacht.

12 One ship is travelling with a velocity $6\mathbf{i} + 4\mathbf{j} \text{ m s}^{-1}$. Another ship appears on the horizon sailing with a velocity of $8\mathbf{i} - 12\mathbf{j} \text{ m s}^{-1}$. Find the velocity of the second ship relative to the first.

Intermediate

1 At noon, two ships A and B are such that B is 5 km due north and 5 km due west of A. B is sailing at $v_B \text{ m s}^{-1}$ due east and A is sailing due north at $v_A \text{ m s}^{-1}$ as shown in the diagram on the next page.

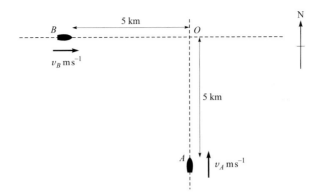

The paths of A and B intersect at O. Find the velocity of B relative to A and the position of B when A is at O if:

(a) $v_A = 10$, $v_B = 15$;   (b) $v_A = 15$, $v_B = 20$.

2 Three fish are swimming horizontally in a stretch of river as shown in the diagram. Their speeds and their directions of motion in still water are indicated. If the river flows at $0.5\,\mathrm{m\,s^{-1}}$ from right to left, find:

(a) the resultant velocity of each fish,
(b) the velocity of fish C relative to fish B.

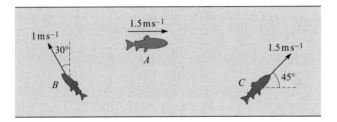

*3 Two model aircraft are flying on a still day at the same height. At time $t = 0$ the aircraft A is 100 m due north of aircraft B and is flying due east with a constant speed of $3\,\mathrm{m\,s^{-1}}$. Aircraft B is flying with a constant speed of $4\,\mathrm{m\,s^{-1}}$ on a bearing of θ.

(a) Given that the two aircraft collide, find θ, in degrees.
(b) Find t when the collision occurs.

4 John is standing on the deck of a cross-channel ferry which is travelling due south at a speed of 15 knots. He sees another ferry in the distance which appears to be travelling south-west at 5 knots. Find the actual velocity of the second ferry.

5 Sion swims across a river 20 m wide flowing at $0.5\,\mathrm{m\,s^{-1}}$. She swims at $0.8\,\mathrm{m\,s^{-1}}$ in still water. How long will it take her to reach the opposite bank if she swims so that she:

(a) reaches the other side as quickly as possible,
(b) reaches the bank directly opposite her point of entry?

6 A bird is flying through the air at $15\,\mathrm{m\,s^{-1}}$ due south. There is no wind. It sees another bird directly ahead of it, 100 metres away, which appears to be flying on a bearing of $30°$ at a speed of $10\,\mathrm{m\,s^{-1}}$. The two birds are flying at the same height above the ground.

(a) What is the velocity of the second bird through the air?
(b) What is the closest they get to one another?

7 Two girls, Pat and Jemima, are walking with the same constant speed at right angles to each other. They start 50 metres apart and after 10 seconds Jemima crosses Pat's path 10 metres in front of her. With what speed are the two girls travelling?

8 A runner travelling along a straight section of road thinks that the wind is coming from a point $40°$ clockwise from his direction of travel. On his return at the same speed the wind appears to be blowing at right angles to his direction of travel. If he is running with a speed of $8\,\mathrm{m\,s^{-1}}$ find the magnitude and direction of the wind relative to the ground.

*9 At a certain instant a boat A is $5\,\mathrm{km}$ due north of boat B. From boat B the boat A appears to be moving on a bearing of $135°$ with constant speed $2\,\mathrm{m\,s^{-1}}$. Find, to the nearest minute, the time that elapses until the boats are closest together and their distance apart at that time.

Advanced

1 At 1 p.m. two ships A and B are observed from a coastguard station C. A is $10\,\mathrm{km}$ west of C sailing at a steady speed of $15\,\mathrm{km\,h^{-1}}$ on a bearing of $060°$. B is $3\,\mathrm{km}$ due north of C sailing on a bearing of $270°$ with constant speed $10\,\mathrm{km\,h^{-1}}$. The situation is shown in the diagram.

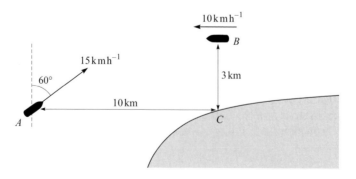

(a) Find the velocity of A relative to B.
(b) Show that the closest approach of the two ships is $0.249\,\mathrm{km}$.

2   A small balloon filled with water is released from rest at a height of
    4 metres above the point from which a crossbow fires a small dart. The
    crossbow is 20 metres horizontally from the point of release of the
    balloon as shown in the diagram. The velocity of the dart at release is
    $25\,\mathrm{m\,s^{-1}}$ at θ above the horizontal. If the balloon and dart are released at
    the same instant and the dart bursts the balloon find,

    (a) θ, giving the angle in degrees,
    (b) the time taken for the dart to reach the balloon.

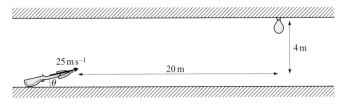

3   At noon, ship P is travelling with constant velocity $7\mathbf{i} + 6\mathbf{j}\,\mathrm{km\,h^{-1}}$ where
    $\mathbf{i}$ and $\mathbf{j}$ are unit vectors acting due east and north respectively. At this
    time, ship Q is due east of P and travelling with constant velocity
    $-5\mathbf{i} + 15\mathbf{j}\,\mathrm{km\,h^{-1}}$. The shortest distance between the two ships is $2\,\mathrm{km}$.
    Find:

    (a) the distance that the ships are apart at noon,
    (b) the time when the ships are closest together.

4   Two aircraft P and Q are flying on straight paths at the same vertical
    height. Their flight paths make an angle of $70°$ with one another and
    cross at a point O. Aircraft P, travelling at $200\,\mathrm{m\,s^{-1}}$, passes O first, two
    minutes before Q. Aircraft Q is travelling at $250\,\mathrm{m\,s^{-1}}$.

    (a) How far from O is Q when P passes O?
    (b) What is the velocity of Q relative to P?
    (c) What is the shortest distance between the planes and how far are
         they both from O when this occurs?

5   Two straight roads cross at right angles. Julie, running towards the
    junction at a speed of $8\,\mathrm{m\,s^{-1}}$, is 480 metres from the crossroads when
    she sees Anna running along the other road towards the junction at a
    speed of $6\,\mathrm{m\,s^{-1}}$. They both continue running without slowing down.

    (a) What is the magnitude of Julie's velocity relative to Anna?
    (b) Find the two possible values of Anna's distance from the crossroads
         when Julie first sees her, if the nearest they get to each other is
         150 metres.

6   At noon, boat A is $4\,\mathrm{km}$ due east of boat B. To a passenger on boat B,
    boat A appears to have constant speed $3\,\mathrm{m\,s^{-1}}$ and to be travelling on a
    bearing of $300°$.

(a) Find the time, to the nearest minute, at which the boats are closest together and their distance apart at that time.
(b) Find the length of time, to the nearest minute, for which the boats are within 3 km of each other.

7 A ship, A, is moving due north with constant speed 5 km h^{-1}. A second ship, B, is 5 km away on a bearing of $210°$. Ship B has a steady speed of 15 km h^{-1} and sails on a bearing of $060°$. Find the length of time, to the nearest minute, for which the ships are within 4 km of each other.

8 At a certain instant A is at the point with position vector $(2\mathbf{i} + \mathbf{j})\,\text{m}$ and is moving with constant velocity $(-\mathbf{i} + \mathbf{j})\,\text{m s}^{-1}$. At the same instant B is at the point with position vector $(\mathbf{i} - \mathbf{j})\,\text{m}$ moving with constant velocity $1.5\mathbf{j}\,\text{m s}^{-1}$.

(a) Find as a vector, $\mathbf{r}$, the displacement of B relative to A at time t.
(b) Find when A and B are closest together and their distance apart at that instant.

9 An aircraft is flying between two airports A and B that are a distance d apart. The aircraft can fly with speed v in still air. A wind blows with speed u making an angle θ with the direction AB. The aircraft is flown so that its resultant velocity is directed along AB. For the case where $\theta = 60°$ and $u = \dfrac{v}{4}$ show that the total time for the aircraft to fly from A to B and back again is given by $2.08\,\dfrac{d}{v}$.

10 Two cyclists are riding on a disused airfield. Ben is travelling with a velocity of $(-4\mathbf{i} + 5\mathbf{j})\,\text{m s}^{-1}$ and Mary is travelling with velocity $(6\mathbf{i} + 2\mathbf{j})\,\text{m s}^{-1}$ relative to the ground. At time $t = 0$ Ben has position vector $50\mathbf{i} + 50\mathbf{j}\,\text{m}$ relative to Mary.

(a) How far apart are they after 2 seconds?
(b) What is the closest they get to each other?
(c) How long does it take for this to occur?

11 A branch railway line runs due south and the main railway line runs south-east.
Two railway trains, P and Q, both travelling at 30 m s^{-1}, are approaching the point where the lines cross. P is on the main line and is 12 km from the junction, and Q is on the branch line and is 8 km from the junction. If the speeds of the trains do not alter, find:

(a) the closest they get to one another,
(b) the time at which this occurs.

Revision

1 A car on a motorway is heading due north at $30\,\mathrm{m\,s^{-1}}$. A motorbike travels on a minor road that crosses the motorway, heading from west to east at $20\,\mathrm{m\,s^{-1}}$. Find the velocity of the motorbike relative to the car.

2 A model boat can travel at $2\,\mathrm{m\,s^{-1}}$ in still water. Its owner steers it across a river that flows at $0.5\,\mathrm{m\,s^{-1}}$ between parallel banks that are $25\,\mathrm{m}$ apart so that the boat ends up at a point directly opposite its starting point. Find:
   (a) the direction in which the owner should steer the boat,
   (b) the time taken by the boat to cross the river.

3 A passenger on an aircraft flying due west at $650\,\mathrm{km\,h^{-1}}$ spots a second aircraft below her that appears to be travelling at $400\,\mathrm{km\,h^{-1}}$ due north. Find the true velocity of the second aircraft giving its magnitude and bearing.

4 Aircraft A has speed $200\,\mathrm{m\,s^{-1}}$ and flies due north. Aircraft B has speed $250\,\mathrm{m\,s^{-1}}$ and flies on a bearing 045°. Find the velocity, giving its magnitude and bearing, of:
   (a) A relative to B,
   (b) B relative to A.

5 Aled can throw a rugby ball with a speed of $7\,\mathrm{m\,s^{-1}}$.
   (a) What is the ball's actual velocity if he throws it straight ahead when he is running at a speed of $6\,\mathrm{m\,s^{-1}}$?
   (b) Aled wants the ball to reach a friend who is level with him and running with the same velocity.
      (i)   In what direction should he aim the ball?
      (ii) What will its actual velocity be relative to the ground?

6 A car is travelling along a horizontal road with a speed of $35\,\mathrm{m\,s^{-1}}$. Rain is being blown by the wind so it falls with a speed of $5\,\mathrm{m\,s^{-1}}$ at an angle of 30° with the vertical. Find the apparent speed and direction of the rain to the driver of the car:
   (a) if the wind blows directly towards the car,
   (b) if the wind blows directly away from the car.

7 A walker is travelling along a horizontal road with a speed of $u\,\mathrm{m\,s^{-1}}$. Rain is falling at an angle of 10° to the vertical with a speed of $9\,\mathrm{m\,s^{-1}}$. The rain appears to the walker to be falling straight down. Find u, the speed of the walker.

8 A ship is sailing due east at $4\,\mathrm{m\,s^{-1}}$. A power-boat has a velocity relative to the ship of $15\,\mathrm{m\,s^{-1}}$ in a direction of 045°. Find the velocity of the power-boat, giving its magnitude and bearing.

9 At noon, ship P is due east of ship Q and is sailing at a steady speed of $10\,\mathrm{km\,h^{-1}}$ on a bearing of 30°. Ship Q sails at a steady speed of $12.5\,\mathrm{km\,h^{-1}}$ on a bearing so that the two ships eventually meet. Find the bearing on which ship Q sails.

10 Two straight roads cut at an angle of 60° at point O. Two cyclists, one on each road, are travelling towards O. If their speeds are $16\,\mathrm{m\,s^{-1}}$ and $10\,\mathrm{m\,s^{-1}}$ and they are 35 metres and 20 metres respectively from the crossroads, find:
(a) the relative velocity of the second rider to the first,
(b) the distance between the riders when the second rider reaches the crossroads.

11 A stone is thrown with a horizontal velocity of $10\,\mathrm{m\,s^{-1}}$ from the top of a tower of height h m. At the same instant a stone is thrown from the foot of the tower with speed $20\,\mathrm{m\,s^{-1}}$ at an angle of 60° above the horizontal. Find:
(a) the height of the tower if the stones collide after $\sqrt{3}\,$s,
(b) the distance of the stones from the foot of the tower when they collide.

12 At time $t = 0$, A is at O and B is at the point with position vector $(5\mathbf{i} + 5\mathbf{j})$ metres referred to O. A has constant speed $2\,\mathrm{m\,s^{-1}}$ in the direction of the vector $\mathbf{j}$. B has constant speed $3\,\mathrm{m\,s^{-1}}$.
Given that A and B collide, find the time at which the collision occurs.

13 Two straight roads intersect at right angles at O. A cyclist on each road is 200 m from O at time $t = 0$. One of the cyclists travels with a constant speed of $4\,\mathrm{m\,s^{-1}}$ towards O, the other with a constant speed of $5\,\mathrm{m\,s^{-1}}$ towards O. Find the time, t seconds, when the cyclists are closest together.

14 At noon, the position vectors, relative to a fixed origin, of two aircraft A and B are $(50\mathbf{i} + 30\mathbf{j} + 10\mathbf{k})$ km and $(-10\mathbf{i} + 70\mathbf{k})$ km respectively. Aircraft A is moving with constant velocity $(-200\mathbf{i} + 60\mathbf{j})\,\mathrm{km\,h^{-1}}$ and aircraft B is moving with constant velocity $(160\mathbf{i} + 240\mathbf{j} - 60\mathbf{k})\,\mathrm{km\,h^{-1}}$.
(a) Write down the position vectors of the two aircraft at time t hours after noon.
(b) Show that the vector representing the line AB is given by $(-60 + 360t)\mathbf{i} + (-30 + 180t)\mathbf{j} + (60 - 60t)\mathbf{k}$ km.
(c) Show that the planes do not collide.
[WJEC]

15

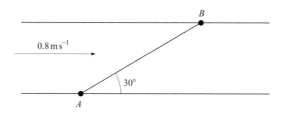

A swimmer can move through still water at $1.2\,\mathrm{m\,s^{-1}}$. She swims in a straight line in a river flowing at $0.8\,\mathrm{m\,s^{-1}}$.

She travels from the point A to the point B, so that her resultant velocity makes an angle of $30°$ to the downstream bank, as shown in the diagram.

(a) Sketch an appropriate triangle of velocities.
(b) Use either a scale drawing or trigonometry to find the magnitude of her resultant velocity.

[AQA]

4 | Momentum

Momentum; instantaneous impulse; conservation of momentum; inelastic impact; impulsive tension; elastic impact (excluding *e*, the coefficient of restitution)

Take the acceleration due to gravity as $g\,\mathrm{m\,s}^{-2}$ where $g = 9.8$.
Give answers to three significant figures unless otherwise stated.

Momentum

The momentum of a body is the product of its mass and its velocity

$$\text{momentum} = m\mathbf{v}$$

Momentum has both magnitude and direction. If mass is measured in kilograms and velocity in metres per second, momentum is measured in newton seconds ($\mathrm{N\,s}$).

Impulse

The impulse on a body is equal to the change in momentum produced.

If two objects collide then they exert equal and opposite impulses on each other.

The **principle of conservation of linear momentum** states that, if two bodies collide, their total momentum remains constant.

Impulsive tension

If two moving bodies are joined by a light inextensible string which becomes taut, then the total momentum of the system remains unchanged. However, the momentum of each body is changed in the direction of the string.

Basic

*1 Two particles A and B move towards each other along a straight line. A has mass $4m$ and speed $2u$; B has mass $2m$ and speed $4u$. After collision, A moves in the opposite direction to its previous motion with speed u. Find the velocity of B after the collision.

2 Two particles P and Q each have the same mass. P is moving on a smooth horizontal surface with speed $5\,\mathrm{m\,s^{-1}}$ when it collides with the stationary particle Q. After the collision both move along the original line of motion of P, and Q has three times the speed of P. Find the speed of each ball.

3 A toy train engine of mass 20 grams moves along a straight horizontal section of track with speed $2.5\,\mathrm{m\,s^{-1}}$. It collides with a stationary carriage of mass 15 grams, and immediately after the collision both move off together with the same speed $v\,\mathrm{m\,s^{-1}}$. Find v.

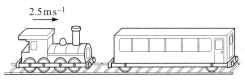

2.5 m s⁻¹

4 A gun of mass 6 kg is horizontal when it fires a bullet of mass 30 g. The bullet leaves the gun with a speed of $350\,\mathrm{m\,s^{-1}}$. Find the initial speed of recoil of the gun.

5 Two small model railway trucks A and B of mass 25 grams and 30 grams respectively are placed on a length of track on a level surface. A is projected towards B with a speed of $0.4\,\mathrm{m\,s^{-1}}$. The two trucks couple together on impact. Find the *exact* speed of the trucks immediately after impact:

(a) if B is initially at rest,
(b) if B is travelling towards A with a speed of $0.2\,\mathrm{m\,s^{-1}}$,
(c) if B is travelling away from A with a speed of $0.2\,\mathrm{m\,s^{-1}}$.

6 A car of mass 1200 kg is travelling with speed $25\,\mathrm{m\,s^{-1}}$ when it is brought to rest by a crash barrier. Find the impulse exerted by the barrier on the car.

7 Water leaves a hose with circular cross-section of area $2\,\mathrm{cm^2}$ at a speed of $5\,\mathrm{m\,s^{-1}}$. Find the momentum of the water that leaves the hose each second. (1 litre of water has a mass of 1 kg.)

8 A ball A, of mass 0.5 kg, is moving at $2\,\mathrm{m\,s^{-1}}$ when it collides with a stationary ball, B, of mass 0.2 kg. After the collision the speed of A is $0.5\,\mathrm{m\,s^{-1}}$ and it moves in the same direction as previously. Find the speed of B after the collision.

9 Two toy railway trucks, each of mass 100 grams, are free to move on a straight horizontal section of track. One truck is moving at a speed of $0.5\,\mathrm{m\,s^{-1}}$ when it collides with the other which is stationary. At the collision the trucks become coupled and then move off together. Find:

(a) the speed at which the two trucks move off,
(b) the impulse that each truck experiences at the collision.

10 A rock of mass $5m\,\mathrm{kg}$ slides with speed $8\,\mathrm{m\,s^{-1}}$ over a smooth horizontal sheet of ice. It collides with a stationary stone of mass m kg. After the collision the two stick together and move with constant speed $v\,\mathrm{m\,s^{-1}}$ in the direction of motion of the rock. Find:

(a) v,
(b) the impulse experienced by the stationary stone.

11 A girl of mass 50 kg stands at rest on a skateboard of mass 10 kg. The girl leaps off the skateboard so that at the instant she leaves she has a velocity of $2\,\mathrm{m\,s^{-1}}$ in a horizontal direction. The skateboard moves in the opposite direction to the girl. Find its speed.

Intermediate

*1 A stone of mass 200 grams is dropped from rest down a well. When the stone has fallen 25 metres it hits the surface of the water. Its velocity after impact is one-tenth of its velocity just before it hits the water. Find:

(a) the momentum of the stone just before it hits the water,
(b) the impulse the stone experiences from the water.

2 Three particles A, B, C lie in a horizontal straight line. Particles B and C are at rest and particle B has mass m.

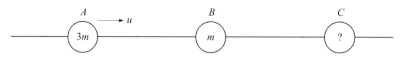

Particle A, of mass $3m$, travels with speed u and collides with B so that they coalesce and travel on to collide with C. Following this collision all three particles have now coalesced and travel in the same straight line with speed $\dfrac{u}{2}$. Find the mass of particle C.

3 Particle A, of mass M, is moving at speed v when it collides with a particle B, of mass $2M$, which is moving towards A along the same straight line with speed $\dfrac{v}{2}$. A is brought to rest by the collision. Find:

(a) the speed of B after the collision,
(b) the impulse experienced by each particle.

4 Two modules will dock together to form a spaceship. Before this, each module is moving at constant speed in the same straight line. Module A has a mass of 2500 kg and is moving at $4\,\mathrm{m\,s^{-1}}$; module B is moving at $2\,\mathrm{m\,s^{-1}}$. After docking the combined spaceship moves at a speed of $2.5\,\mathrm{m\,s^{-1}}$. Find the mass of module B.

5 A block of mass M lies at rest on a smooth horizontal plane. A pellet of mass kM is fired horizontally, with speed u, at the block so that it becomes lodged in the block and both move off together with speed v. Find k such that v is $\frac{1}{250}$th of u.

6 Beth is playing hockey. A ball of mass m kg travels directly towards her with a speed of $15\,\mathrm{m\,s^{-1}}$. Beth hits it so that it travels back along its path in the opposite direction with a speed of $20\,\mathrm{m\,s^{-1}}$. The magnitude of the impulse applied by the hockey stick to the ball is 5.39 N s. Find the mass of the ball.

7 An ice hockey puck of mass 160 grams is hit directly at the goalkeeper. It rebounds off her pad, travelling back along the same line of motion but with only a quarter of its initial speed. The magnitude of the impulse between the goalkeeper's pad and the puck is 4 N s. Find the initial speed of the puck.

8 A supermarket trolley is standing at rest on a horizontal surface. It is free to move. A small child of mass 25 kg who is running along at $3\,\mathrm{m\,s^{-1}}$ jumps onto the trolley. They both move off at a speed of $2\,\mathrm{m\,s^{-1}}$. Assume that the initial direction of motion of the child and the final direction of motion of the child and trolley are the same.

(a) Find the mass of the trolley.

(b) The trolley then crashes into a barrier and comes to an abrupt stop. Find the magnitude of the impulse which acts on the trolley during its impact with the barrier.

Advanced

1 An astronaut of mass 65 kg is on a space walk and is stationary relative to her spacecraft at a distance 10 metres away from it.
She throws a spanner of mass 0.5 kg away from her at a speed of $1\,\mathrm{m\,s^{-1}}$ so that she moves directly towards the spacecraft. Calculate how long it will take the astronaut to reach the spacecraft. Comment on your answer.

2 An object of mass m kg is dropped from rest h metres above horizontal ground and rebounds to a height kh metres, where $k \le 1$. Show that the impulse I N s exerted on the object by the ground is given by
$I = m\sqrt{2gh}(1 + \sqrt{k})$.

3 A ball of mass 750 grams falls from rest at a height of 2 metres above horizontal ground. It rebounds to a height of 1.5 metres. Find the impulse exerted by the ground on the ball.

4 Two particles A and B of masses $2m$ and m respectively are connected by a light inextensible string and lie at rest on a smooth horizontal plane. Particle A is given a velocity u directly away from B. Once the string becomes taut, the particles travel with the same velocity. Find, in terms of m and u:

(a) the final speed of the system,
(b) the magnitude of the impulse in the string when it tightens.

5 Particles A and B of masses 500 grams and 200 grams respectively are connected by a light inextensible string which passes over a small, smooth light pulley. Particle B lies at rest on the floor and particle A is dropped from rest so that it falls through a distance of 0.5 metres before the string tightens and both particles move together with speed $v\,\mathrm{m\,s^{-1}}$. Find:

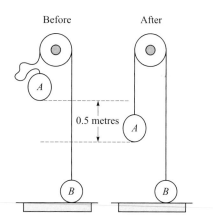

(a) the impulse given to B when the string becomes taut in terms of v,
(b) the impulse given to A when the string becomes taut in terms of v,
(c) the value of v.

6 Jane lobs a tennis ball of mass $m\,\mathrm{kg}$ up into the air.
Peter then hits it so that the direction of its motion directly after impact is at right angles to its motion just before impact. The speed of the ball just before the impact is $25\,\mathrm{m\,s^{-1}}$ and the speed just after impact is $30\,\mathrm{m\,s^{-1}}$.
Find the magnitude of the impulse which acts on the ball in terms of m.

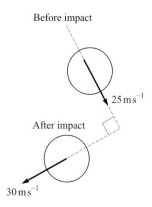

7 A hailstone of mass 3 grams is travelling with speed $22\,\mathrm{m\,s^{-1}}$ at an angle of $30°$ to the vertical when it hits the roof of a stationary car. The roof can be modelled as a horizontal flat plane. The hailstone bounces off the roof. The horizontal component of velocity of the hailstone is unchanged but the vertical component after the impact is now $5\,\mathrm{m\,s^{-1}}$.

(a) Find the impulse given to the hailstone by the roof of the car.

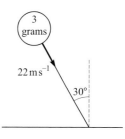

(b) The maximum impulse that the roof can give without becoming dented is 0.1 N s vertically upwards. Find, to the nearest gram, the maximum mass of a hailstone, with velocities as described above, that can hit the car roof without denting it.

*8 Two model railway trucks A and B of masses m and M respectively approach each other along a horizontal section of track. They are both travelling with speed $v\,\mathrm{m\,s^{-1}}$. They fail to couple on impact and after impact each moves in the opposite direction to its original motion. A returns along the track with a speed of $1.5v\,\mathrm{m\,s^{-1}}$.
Explain why $M < 2.5m$ if this is to be possible.

9 Particles A and B, of masses $3m\,\mathrm{kg}$ and $2m\,\mathrm{kg}$ respectively, are attached, one to each end of a light inextensible string of length $5a\,\mathrm{m}$. The whole system is on a smooth horizontal floor with B initially a distance $3a\,\mathrm{m}$ due south of A. The particle A is projected across the floor with initial speed $u\,\mathrm{m\,s^{-1}}$ moving west.

(a) Find the velocity with which particle B begins to move immediately after the string becomes taut.

(b) Calculate the magnitude of the velocity of A immediately after the string becomes taut.

Revision

1 Two particles, A of mass m and B of mass $2m$, move directly towards each other on a smooth horizontal plane. A moves with speed $4u$ and B with speed u. After collision, B moves with speed $2u$ in the opposite direction to its original direction of motion. Find:

(a) the velocity of A immediately after the collision,

(b) the impulse A receives during the collision.

2 A toboggan of mass $70\,\mathrm{kg}$ slides down a smooth slope. It collides with a bystander of mass $60\,\mathrm{kg}$ who falls onto the toboggan and is carried along by it. The speed of the toboggan immediately before impact is $18\,\mathrm{m\,s^{-1}}$. What is its speed immediately after the collision? (Assume the bystander is stationary at the moment of impact.)

3 A boy throws a sticky ball of mass $0.4\,\mathrm{kg}$ at a coconut of mass $2\,\mathrm{kg}$ on a coconut shy. The ball sticks to the coconut and they both fly off with a speed of $2\,\mathrm{m\,s^{-1}}$.
Find the speed of the sticky ball just before impact.

4   In a game of bowls, a wood of mass 0.8 kg, moving at $3\,\mathrm{m\,s}^{-1}$, collided with a stationary wood such that the whole motion took place in a straight line. The speed of the wood which was moving was reduced to $1\,\mathrm{m\,s}^{-1}$ by the collision and the other wood moved off at $1.8\,\mathrm{m\,s}^{-1}$ as a result. Find the mass of the wood that was initially stationary.

5   Two particles A and B move towards each other along a straight line. Particle A has mass m and speed $5\,\mathrm{m\ s}^{-1}$. Particle B has mass km, where k is a constant, and speed $2\,\mathrm{m\,s}^{-1}$.

   (a) In the case where both particles are brought to rest at collision, find k.
   (b) In the alternative case where both particles move with speed $2\,\mathrm{m\,s}^{-1}$ after the collision, find the largest possible value of k.

6   Two particles A and B, of masses 2 kg and 3 kg and speeds $u\,\mathrm{m\,s}^{-1}$ and $4\,\mathrm{m\,s}^{-1}$ respectively, are moving along the same line. They are both travelling in the same direction. A collides with B and they set off together with a speed of $6\,\mathrm{m\,s}^{-1}$. Find u.

7   A man drops a heavy steel hammer of mass 3 kg onto one of his shoes from a height of 1.5 metres. What impulse must his shoe be able to withstand without deformation if he is not to be injured?

*8   A pile driver has a block of mass 8000 kg. It is dropped on to a pile from a height of h metres and rebounds to a height of 3 metres. The impulse exerted on the pile by the block is 132 000 N s. Find h to the nearest metre.

9   Particles A and B, of masses 1 kg and 1.5 kg respectively, are connected by a light inextensible string which passes over a small, smooth light pulley. Particle B lies at rest on the floor. Particle A is dropped from rest so that it falls through a distance of 2 metres before the string tightens and both particles begin to move at the same speed. Find:

   (a) the speed of B immediately after the string becomes taut,
   (b) the impulse given to A when the string becomes taut.

10 Mary lobs a tennis ball of mass 0.058 kg up into the air. Afzal then hits it so that the direction of its motion directly after impact is at right angles to its motion just before impact. The speed of the ball just before the impact is $25\,\mathrm{m\,s}^{-1}$. The magnitude of the impulse which acts on the ball is 1.5 N s. Find the speed of the ball just after the impact.

11 The diagram shows three particles, A, B and C, of masses 3 kg, 1 kg and 2 kg respectively, lying at rest in a smooth horizontal channel. A is projected towards B with speed $5\,\mathrm{m\,s}^{-1}$; after colliding with B it continues in the same direction with a reduced speed of $3\,\mathrm{m\,s}^{-1}$. B then collides with C, after which its direction of motion is reversed and its speed is $1\,\mathrm{m\,s}^{-1}$. When A and B collide again, A continues in the same direction and its speed is reduced to $1.4\,\mathrm{m\,s^{-1}}$. The table shows the velocities, in $\mathrm{m\,s^{-1}}$, of A, B and C at various stages.

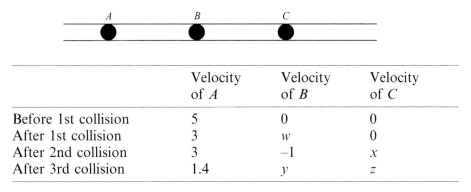

	Velocity of A	Velocity of B	Velocity of C
Before 1st collision	5	0	0
After 1st collision	3	w	0
After 2nd collision	3	-1	x
After 3rd collision	1.4	y	z

Neglecting air resistance, find the values of w, x, y and z.
State, with a reason, whether there is a fourth collision.
[UCLES]

12 A particle A of mass m is moving along a straight line with constant speed $4u$. It collides with a particle B of mass $2m$ moving with constant speed u along the same line and in the same direction as A. Immediately after the collision the particles continue to move in the same direction, and the speed of B is twice the speed of A.
Find:
(a) the speed of A immediately after the collision,
(b) the impulse exerted by B on A, stating clearly its magnitude and direction.
[Edexcel]

13 Particles A and B, each of mass m kg, are attached, one to each end of a light inextensible string of length $2a$ m. The whole system is on a smooth horizontal floor with B initially a distance a m due south of A. The particle B is projected across the floor with initial speed $u\,\mathrm{m\,s^{-1}}$ moving east.
(a) Find the velocity with which the particle A begins to move immediately after the string becomes taut.
(b) Calculate the magnitude of the velocity of B immediately after the string becomes taut.
[WJEC]

5 | Forces at a point

Equilibrium of concurrent coplanar forces; triangle of forces; vector representation of forces; resolution of forces

Take the acceleration due to gravity as $g\,\mathrm{m\,s}^{-2}$ where $g = 9.8$.
Give answers to three significant figures unless otherwise stated.

A set of forces acting on a particle can be reduced to a single force. This is called the **resultant force**.

If the resultant force is zero then the forces are said to be in **equilibrium**.

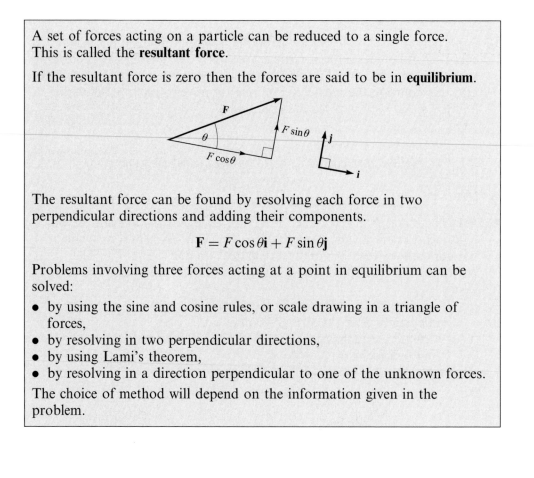

The resultant force can be found by resolving each force in two perpendicular directions and adding their components.

$$\mathbf{F} = F \cos \theta \mathbf{i} + F \sin \theta \mathbf{j}$$

Problems involving three forces acting at a point in equilibrium can be solved:

- by using the sine and cosine rules, or scale drawing in a triangle of forces,
- by resolving in two perpendicular directions,
- by using Lami's theorem,
- by resolving in a direction perpendicular to one of the unknown forces.

The choice of method will depend on the information given in the problem.

Basic

1 Express each force shown as a vector in terms of perpendicular unit vectors **i** and **j** aligned as indicated.

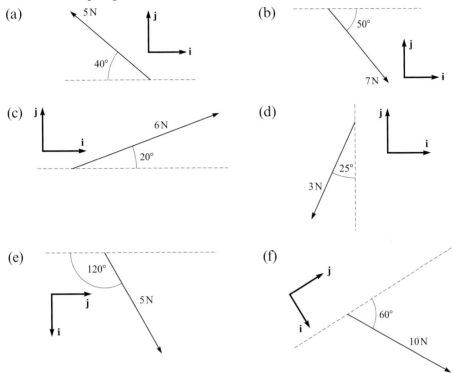

(a)

(b)

(c)

(d)

(e)

(f)

2 For each of the coplanar systems of forces shown, find the resultant, giving its magnitude and describing clearly its direction.

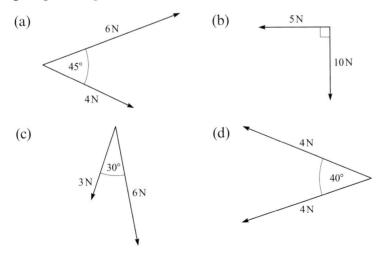

(a)

(b)

(c)

(d)

3 For each of the coplanar systems of forces shown, find the resultant in the form $a\mathbf{i} + b\mathbf{j}$

(a) 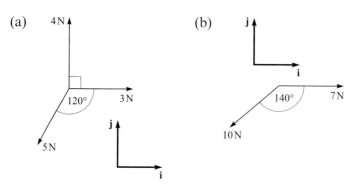 (b)

*4 Forces of magnitude 4 N, 6 N and 8 N are in equilibrium. Find, to the nearest degree, the angles between the forces.

5 Forces of magnitude 14 N, 21 N and 28 N are in equilibrium. Find, to the nearest degree, the angles between the forces.

6 An object of weight 200 N is suspended by two light strings each of which makes an angle of 20° with the vertical as shown in the diagram.
Find the tension in each string.

7 A mass of m kg is suspended by two light inextensible strings of equal length. Each string makes an angle of 15° with the vertical. The situation is shown in the diagram.
The tension in each string is 3.1 newtons.
Find m.

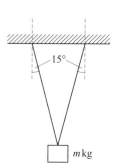

8 Four forces, **P**, **Q**, **R** and **S**, act at a point. They are in equilibrium.
$\mathbf{P} = 6\mathbf{i} - 4\mathbf{j}$ newtons, $\mathbf{Q} = 2\mathbf{i} - 3\mathbf{j}$ newtons,
$\mathbf{R} = -3\mathbf{i} + r\mathbf{j}$ newtons and $\mathbf{S} = s\mathbf{i} + 4\mathbf{j}$ newtons.
Find the values of r and s.

9 Four forces, **L**, **M**, **N** and **R**, acting at a point are in equilibrium.
$\mathbf{L} = 2\mathbf{i} - \mathbf{j}$ newtons, $\mathbf{M} = -12\mathbf{i} - 3\mathbf{j}$ newtons and $\mathbf{N} = -3\mathbf{i} + 4\mathbf{j}$ newtons.
Find the magnitude of **R**.

10 Three forces, **P**, **Q** and **R**, act at a point.
P = 9**i** − 4**j** newtons and **Q** = 3**i** − **j** newtons. Given that the forces are in equilibrium, find **R**.

Intermediate

1 Express each force shown as a vector in terms of perpendicular unit vectors **i** and **j** aligned as indicated.

(a)   (b)

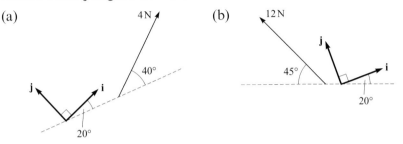

2 For each of the following coplanar systems of forces shown, find the resultant in the form $a\mathbf{i} + b\mathbf{j}$.

(a)   (b)

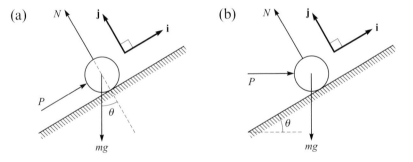

*3 An object of weight 50 N is suspended at B by two light strings. One string, AB, makes an angle of 30° with the horizontal and the tension in it is T_1; the other, BC, makes an angle of 45° with the horizontal and has tension T_2. The situation is shown in the diagram.
Find the tension in each string.

4 A body of weight 10 N is suspended by a light inextensible string. A horizontal force P N pushes the body so that the string makes an angle of 40° with the vertical as shown in the diagram.
Find P.

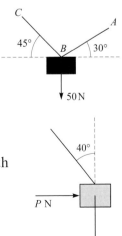

5 An object of weight 20 newtons is at rest on a smooth plane which is inclined at an angle of 30° to the horizontal. The object is kept in equilibrium by applying a horizontal force of magnitude $P\,\text{N}$. The diagram shows the forces acting on the object.

Find P, and the normal reaction force, N.

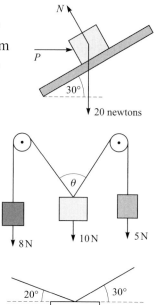

6 The diagram shows three masses joined by light and inextensible strings that pass over two smooth pulleys that are on the same level. The system hangs freely in equilibrium. The masses have weights 10 N, 5 N and 8 N. Find the angle θ.

7 Two children, Dario and Mia, lift a parcel of mass 20 kg off the floor using two ropes. Dario's rope is inclined at 20° to the horizontal; Mia's is inclined at 30° to the horizontal.

Model the ropes as being light and inextensible and the parcel as a particle. The situation is shown in the diagram.

Find the tension in each rope.

Advanced

1 A cablecar of mass 2500 kg is suspended on a cable between two points A and B. It is clamped firmly to the cable. Large driving pulleys at A and B move the cable so that the cablecar travels from A to B. The cablecar can be modelled as a particle fixed to a light inextensible string at P. The car is stationary at a point on the cable where $AB = 110$ metres, $AP = 92$ metres and $PB = 36$ metres. AB makes an angle of 25° with the horizontal as shown in the diagram.

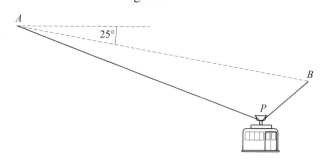

(a) Explain what is meant by 'modelled as a particle'.
(b) Find the angles that AP and PB make with the horizontal.
(c) Find the tension in AP and PB to the nearest kN.

*2 Andrew and Peter are playing near some
quicksand when Andrew falls in and is
unable to extricate himself. A safety rope is
hanging on a metal pole which is firmly
fixed in the ground. Peter unties the rope
and, throwing one end to his friend, tells
him to tie it round his waist. Peter then tries
to pull Andew out. However he can not pull
hard enough. This situation is shown in
diagram (a).

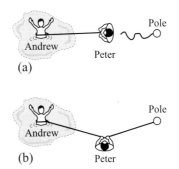

Peter ties his end of the rope to the pole
and, holding firmly to the middle of the
rope, pulls in a direction perpendicular to the line between Andrew and
the pole. This is shown in diagram (b).

Explain why, as long as the pole does not break, Peter now has a much
better chance of pulling Andrew out of the quicksand.

3 Sean is filling carrier bags of toys for a charity appeal.
He must make sure that each bag does not weigh more
than 50 N.

He has borrowed three spring balances, each of which
can weigh up to 30 N. He and Mark use two of the
balances, holding them so that they each make an angle
of 30° to the vertical as shown. He finds that the
reading on each of them is 25 N.

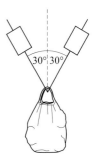

(a) Calculate the weight of the bag to the nearest
newton.
(b) What would the reading on each balance be, to the
nearest newton, if the bag weighs 49 N?
(c) Mark says that it would be better just to hang one
balance from the other and then hang the bag on the bottom.
Explain what the result of this would be.

4 A builder is hauling up a heavy bucket of weight 400 N using a pulley
and rope. One end of the rope is fixed to a hook on the ceiling and the
rope then passes through the handle of the bucket, up round a pulley
that is also fixed to the ceiling, and then down to the builder. The pulley
and hook are 2 metres horizontally apart. Initially the hook and pulley
are 5 metres above the handle of the bucket. The rope can be taken to be
light and inextensible. The angle between the two sections of the rope
either side of the handle is 2α as shown and is measured in degrees.

The bucket handle can be modelled as smooth and the weight of the builder is 850 N.

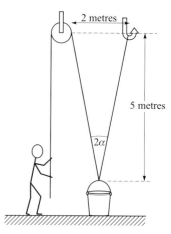

(a) What is meant in mechanics by the word 'smooth'?

(b) Sketch a graph to show the tension in the rope, T newtons, against α. Explain the nature of your graph in the region $\alpha = 90°$.

(c) Calculate the greatest distance the builder can raise the bucket off the floor.

5 A man is using a power drill to make some holes in the floor. He has plugged the drill into the power socket and left the flex trailing over the carpet.

The flex is 3 metres long and the distance between the drill and the power socket is 2.5 metres. His small son runs across the room and trips over the flex midway between the drill and the socket.

The boy exerts a constant force of 50 N on the flex. Calculate the tension in the flex at the instant that it becomes taut.

6 A particle, P, of weight W is suspended from two light inextensible ropes. The other ends of the ropes are fixed to two points A and B which lie in a straight horizontal line. Strain gauges at the tops of the ropes show that the tensions in AP and BP are $5T$ and $6T$ respectively. The angles between AP and BP and the vertical are α and $30°$ respectively.

(a) Find α.

(b) Find an *exact* expression for W in terms of T.

(c) What is meant by 'light inextensible' in mechanics?

(d) If the weight of the rope is significant, is the expression for W an overestimate or an underestimate? Give your reasons.

7 A light inextensible string passes over a pulley system as shown in the diagram. The pulleys can be modelled as light and friction free. A load of weight W is suspended from D, the midpoint of a light bar that connects two of the pulleys.

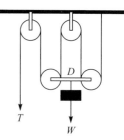

A force T is applied to the end of the rope as shown.

(a) Find T in terms of W.

(b) Each pulley actually has a weight of $0.1W$. Find a revised expression for T in terms of W.

Revision

1 For each of the coplanar systems of forces shown, find the resultant, giving its magnitude and describing clearly its direction.

(a)   (b)

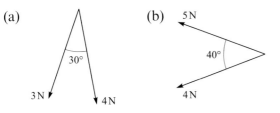

2 Three forces, P, Q and R, act at a point. They are in equilibrium. If the ratio of the magnitudes of the forces is $2:2:3$ find the angles between the forces P and Q, Q and R, R and P.

3 Three wires lead out from the top of a telegraph pole. Each wire has a tension of 200 newtons. The wires can be modelled as being horizontal. The forces are in equilibrium.

(a) Find the angle between the wires.

(b) A sparrow comes and sits on one of the wires and the tension in it increases by 20 newtons. Explain how this affects the tension in the other wires if they are to remain in equilibrium.

4 A lamp of mass 0.8 kg is suspended by two light inextensible wires above a certain point. The wires make angles of $40°$ and $30°$ with the horizontal as shown in the diagram. Find the tension in each wire.

5 A particle of weight 20 newtons hangs from a light inextensible string. It is pulled to one side by a horizontal force of 5 newtons so that the string makes an angle of α with the vertical as shown in the diagram.
Find:

(a) the tension in the string,

(b) α, given in degrees.

6 Three volunteers are trying to remove a broken sign post. They tie three ropes to it and pull as hard as they can. The two side ropes make angles of $20°$ and $30°$ with the centre rope. All three ropes lie in the same horizontal plane.

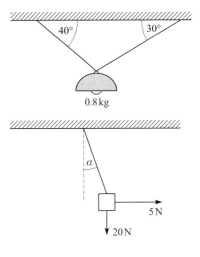

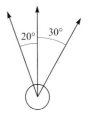

The three volunteers, A, B and C, can exert forces of 600 N, 700 N and 850 N respectively.

(a) (i) Which volunteer should hold which rope in order to maximise the pull on the post?

    (ii) Find, to the nearest newton, the magnitude of the resultant force in this case.

(b) What is the least pull the volunteers can exert if they hold on to different ropes? Give your answer to the nearest newton.

7 A hanging flower basket H, of weight 50 N is held in equilibrium by two light inextensible strings. One string is attached to a fixed point A and this string makes an angle of 60° with the vertical; the other string is attached to a fixed point B and this string makes an angle of θ with the vertical, as

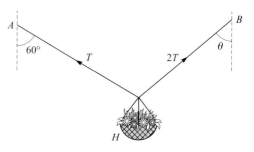

shown in the diagram. Given that the tension in the string attached to A is T and the tension in the string attached to B is $2T$, find the values of θ and T.

[OCR]

8 A removal man wants to lift a large packing case into a window at the top of a building. He ties a rope to the case and tries to pull it up. However the packing case is quite large and so it drags against the side of the building. He fixes another rope to the packing case and asks a friend to pull on the rope to keep the case away from the building.
The friend is to pull his rope so that the centre of the case is 1 metre from the building and his rope makes an angle of 45° with the vertical as shown in the diagram.
The packing case has weight $\mathbf{W}$ and the ropes can be modelled as being light and inextensible. The top of the packing case is a distance x m below the window. The tensions in the two ropes are $\mathbf{P}$ and $\mathbf{Q}$ as shown. The rope between the window

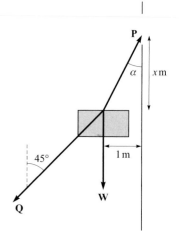

and the packing case makes an angle of α with the vertical as shown.

(a) Find expressions for $\cos \alpha$ and $\sin \alpha$ in terms of x.

(b) Find expressions for $\mathbf{P}$ and $\mathbf{Q}$ in terms of $\mathbf{W}$ and x.

(c) Use these expressions to explain why x must be greater than 1 if the other conditions are to be met.

(d) Both ropes have the same breaking strain of **4W**. State which rope
will break first and give the value of x when this occurs.

9 Three forces, with magnitudes and
directions as shown in the diagram, act in a
horizontal plane at the point A. The
resultant of the three forces has magnitude
14 N and acts in the direction of the force
of magnitude X newtons. Find θ and X.
[UCLES]

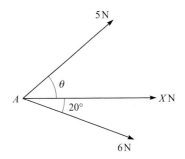

6

Force models

Static friction; tension in elastic strings and springs; gravitational force[†]

Take the acceleration due to gravity to be $g\,\mathrm{m\,s^{-2}}$ where $g = 9.8$.
Take the universal gravitation constant to be $G\,\mathrm{N\,m^2\,kg^{-2}}$ where $G = 6.67 \times 10^{-11}$.

Static friction acts along the surface of contact in a direction that will prevent motion.

$$F \leq \mu N$$

where F is the force due to friction, N is the normal reaction between the two surfaces and μ is the coefficient of static friction. μ depends on the nature of the two surfaces in contact.

The **tension in an elastic string or spring** can be modelled as obeying Hooke's law. This states that $T = kx$ where k is the spring stiffness and depends on the length of the spring or string and the material that it is made from and x is the extension or compression from its natural length. The tension of an elastic string may also be given in the form

$$T = \frac{\lambda x}{l}$$

where λ is the modulus of elasticity,
x is the extension of the string,
and l is the natural length of the string.

Gravitational force[†] is the force acting between two bodies.

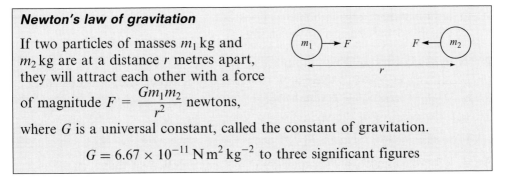

Newton's law of gravitation

If two particles of masses m_1 kg and m_2 kg are at a distance r metres apart, they will attract each other with a force of magnitude $F = \dfrac{Gm_1m_2}{r^2}$ newtons,

where G is a universal constant, called the constant of gravitation.

$$G = 6.67 \times 10^{-11} \, \text{N m}^2 \, \text{kg}^{-2} \text{ to three significant figures}$$

Basic

1   Find the maximum frictional force that can act when a block of mass 4 kg rests on a rough horizontal surface and the coefficient of static friction between the block and the surface is 0.8.

2   A box of mass 17.5 kg lies at rest on a horizontal surface where the coefficient of static friction between the box and the surface is 0.8. A boy pushes the box with a horizontal force of 140 N. Determine whether the box remains at rest or accelerates along the surface.

*3   A block of mass 4 kg lies so that it is on the point of slipping down a rough plane which is inclined at an angle of 25° to the horizontal. Find the coefficient of static friction between the block and the plane.

4   A parcel of mass 8 kg lies at rest on a plane rough surface which is hinged along one edge. The surface makes an angle of $\theta°$ with the horizontal, as shown in the diagram. The coefficient of static friction between the parcel and the surface is 0.9.

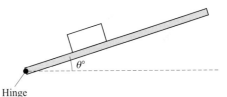

(a)   Find the friction force that acts when $\theta = 20$.
(b)   Find θ when the parcel just starts to slide.

5   A particle is just on the point of sliding down a rough plane that makes an angle of 60° with the horizontal, although a force of 25 N acts up the slope attempting to stop the particle from sliding. The coefficient of static friction between the particle and the plane is 0.75. Find the mass of the particle.

6   A light spring has an elastic constant $100 \, \text{N m}^{-1}$. A mass of 2 kg is suspended freely from the spring. Find its extension to the nearest centimetre.

7 A light elastic string with elastic constant $125\,\mathrm{N\,m^{-1}}$ is stretched by 25 cm. Find the tension in the string.

8 A light elastic string has modulus of elasticity 20 N and natural length 0.5 m. It has one end fixed and attached to the other end is a mass of 0.25 kg which hangs freely. Find:

(a) the tension in the string,

(b) the extension of the string.

9 A light elastic string with modulus 50 N is stretched so that it has a tension of 20 N. Find the extension of the string as a fraction of its natural length, $l\,\mathrm{m}$.

10 A light spring has a constant $50\,\mathrm{N\,m^{-1}}$. The spring is compressed by 12.5 cm. Find the thrust in the spring.

11 A light elastic string with modulus 25 N and natural length 0.2 m is fixed at one end to a point on a smooth slope that makes an angle of 25° with the horizontal. The other end of the string is attached to a mass of 5 kg and remains in equilibrium as shown in the diagram. Find, to the nearest centimetre, the extension of the string.

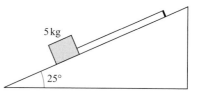

12† Two particles, each of mass 1000 kg, are 1 m apart. Calculate the magnitude of the gravitational force of attraction between them.

13† Assume that the Earth is a sphere of radius 6.4×10^6 metres. Its mass is 6.0×10^{24} kg. Use this information to find the weight of a mass of 1 kg at the surface of the Earth.

14† Calculate the force of attraction between the Earth and the Sun. Assume that both the Earth and the Sun are particles a distance 1.50×10^8 km apart and that the Earth has a mass of 5.98×10^{24} kg and the Sun has a mass of 1.99×10^{30} kg.

Intermediate

*1 A large crate of mass 25 kg is at rest on a rough horizontal surface. The coefficient of static friction between the block and the surface is 0.45. A girl pushes the crate with a force of $P\,\mathrm{N}$ acting at an angle of 12° to the horizontal as shown. The crate is just about to slide. Find P.

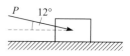

2 A suitcase of mass 20 kg is placed on a conveyor belt so that it can be loaded into an aircraft hold. When the belt is stationary and at an angle of 35° to the horizontal the suitcase just starts to slide down the belt.

    (a) Find the coefficient of static friction between the belt and the suitcase.

    (b) Find the force that needs to be applied up the line of greatest slope of the conveyor belt so that the suitcase just starts to move up the belt.

3 A crate of mass 30 kg is on a horizontal floor where the coefficient of static friction between the crate and the floor is 0.7. A man wraps a rope around the crate so that he can pull the crate along the floor. Find the minimum force which the man should apply if the rope makes an angle of 60° with the vertical, as shown in the diagram, so that the crate should just start to move.

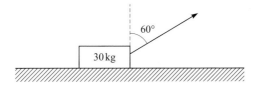

4 An object of mass 5 kg is at rest on a sloping rough surface that makes an angle of 45° with the horizontal. The coefficient of static friction between the object and the surface is 0.6. A horizontal force, P N, acts on the object, as shown in the diagram. Find P if:

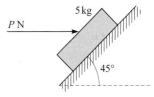

    (a) the object is just on the point of sliding down the slope,

    (b) the object is just on the point of sliding up the slope.

5 A block of mass 3 kg lies at rest on a rough horizontal surface. The coefficient of static friction between the block and the surface is 0.9. Find the maximum force P N that can be used to push the block without it moving when:

    (a) P is applied horizontally,

    (b) P is applied so that it makes an angle of 70° with the vertical as shown in the diagram.

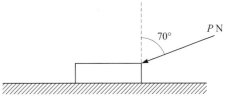

6 A piece of elastic of length 0.4 m is cut from a roll of elastic which has modulus 24 N. The elastic is fixed at one end and a mass of 0.1 kg hangs freely from the other end. A second piece of elastic, of length *l* m, is cut from the roll. This is used to hang a mass of 0.15 kg so that when fixed at the same horizontal level as the first piece both masses hang at the same distance beneath their points of support as shown in the diagram. Find *l*.

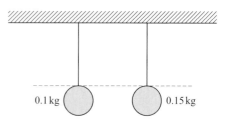

7 A light elastic string has a natural length *l* and modulus of elasticity λ. It is fixed at one end and hangs freely in equilibrium supporting a mass *m*. A second light elastic string has a natural length 1.5*l* and modulus of elasticity $\frac{3}{4}\lambda$. If this second string is also fixed at one end and hangs freely in equilibrium supporting a mass *M* such that the extension of each string is the same, find *M* in terms of *m*.

8 A light elastic string has a natural length of 50 cm. The string has one end attached to a point *A* and the other to a point *B*, which are both on the same horizontal level a distance 60 cm apart. A particle of mass 750 g is attached to the midpoint of the string and hangs in equilibrium 10 cm below the level of *AB*, as shown in the diagram. Find the modulus of elasticity of the string.

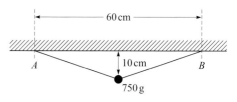

9 A particle of mass 2.5 kg is attached to one end of a light elastic string of natural length 1 m. The other end of the string is held fixed so that the string hangs freely in equilibrium and is extended by 10 cm. This extension is increased to 20 cm by pulling the particle to one side with a horizontal force, *P* N. Find:

(a) *P*,
(b) the angle that the string makes with the vertical.

10 A mass of 2 kg is attached to one end of a light elastic string of natural length 50 cm and modulus 5*g* N. The other end of the string is fixed and the mass hangs freely in equilibrium.

(a) Find the extension of the string.
(b) The mass is now pulled to one side by a horizontal force, *P* N, so that the extension is trebled. Find:
    (i) the angle that the string makes with the vertical,
    (ii) *P*.

11[†] Two particles, each of mass 1000 kg, are 1 cm apart.

(a) Calculate the magnitude, FN, of the gravitational force of attraction between them.

(b) If the distance between the particles is doubled, find the new gravitational force in terms of F.

(c) If the mass of each particle is doubled and the distance between them remains 1 cm, find the new gravitational force in terms of F.

(d) State one configuration of this type where the gravitational force between masses will be $\dfrac{F}{2}$.

12[†] Assume that the Earth is a sphere of radius 6.378×10^6 metres, and that the acceleration due to gravity at the Earth's surface is $g\,\mathrm{m\,s^{-2}}$ where $g = 9.8$.

(a) Use this information to find the mass of the Earth.

(b) Calculate the distance above the Earth's surface of a point where the acceleration due to gravity is half of its value at the Earth's surface.

13[†] Two identical masses, each of 1 tonne, are supported by two light inextensible strings, each of length 5 metres and a distance 10 centimetres apart, so that the masses hang on the same horizontal level. Find the angle that each string makes with the vertical by taking account of the force of attraction between the two masses.

14[†] Model the Earth as a sphere of radius 6.378×10^6 m. When an object of mass m kg is weighed at the top of Mount Everest (height 8849 m) it appears to weigh less than it does at the surface of the Earth. The acceleration due to gravity at the top of Mount Everest, g', is smaller than the acceleration due to gravity at the Earth's surface, g. Find g' in terms of g.

15[†] Calculate the force of attraction on an object of mass 1 kg at the surface of the Moon, assuming that the Moon is spherical with radius 1.74×10^6 m and its mass is 7.35×10^{22} kg. Use your result to explain why it is often quoted that the Moon's gravity is one-sixth that of the Earth's.

Advanced

1 A box is pulled along a rough horizontal surface at constant speed by a rope that makes an angle of $30°$ with the horizontal. The tension in the rope is one-half of the weight of the box. Show that $\mu = \dfrac{\sqrt{3}}{3}$.

2 Two identical small rings of mass m are threaded onto a rough horizontal wire. The coefficient of static friction between the rings and the wire is $\frac{4}{5}$. A third ring of mass $3m$ is threaded onto a smooth, light

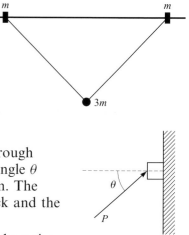

inextensible string of length l. This is
attached to each of the rings on the
wire, and the system is in equilibrium
with the third ring hanging below the
wire. The situation is shown in the
diagram. The two rings on the wire are
on the point of sliding. Find, in terms
of l, the distance between the two rings.

3 A block of mass m is held at rest against a rough
vertical wall with a force P that acts at an angle θ
with the horizontal, as shown in the diagram. The
coefficient of static friction between the block and the
wall is μ.

(a) For the case where the block is just on the point
of sliding down the wall show that
$$P = \frac{mg}{\sin\theta + \mu\cos\theta}.$$
(b) For the case where the block is just on the point of sliding up the
wall:
  (i)   find P in terms of m, g, μ and θ,
  (ii) if $\mu = \frac{1}{2}$, show that $\theta > 26°$.

4 A ring of mass 1.5 kg is threaded onto a rough horizontal rod. A light
inextensible string is attached to the ring and is pulled with a force of 8 N
at an angle of 45° to the rod so that the ring just begins to slide along
the rod. The situation is shown in Figure 1.

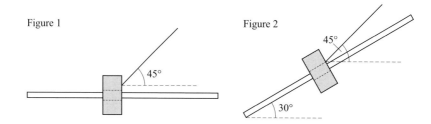

Figure 1   Figure 2

(a) Find the coefficient of static friction between the ring and the rod.

The rod is now tilted so that it is at 30° to the horizontal as shown in
Figure 2.

(b) Find the force that now needs to be applied to the ring by the string
so that the ring is on the point of sliding up the slope.

*5 A light elastic string of length l has modulus λ. A second elastic string
has length $\frac{2}{3}l$ and modulus $\frac{1}{3}\lambda$. The strings are joined end-to-end in such
a way that you may assume that none of their length is lost. Find, in
terms of λ and g, the mass m that the combined string would need to
support hanging freely in equilibrium if the total extension was to be half
of their total unstretched length.

6 A light elastic string, of natural length l, has
modulus $5mg$. The string is fixed at one end and the
other supports a mass m.
The mass is pulled to one side by a horizontal force
of magnitude $\dfrac{mg}{2}$.

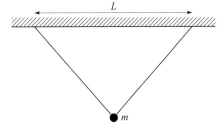

   (a) Find the angle that the string makes with the
        vertical.
   (b) Show that the string is extended by $\frac{\sqrt{5}}{10}l$.
   (c) Find the horizontal distance by which the mass is displaced in terms
        of l.

7 A light elastic string has a natural
length l. One end is attached to a
fixed point and a particle of mass m
is attached to the other which hangs
freely in equilibrium so that the
string is extended by $\dfrac{l}{10}$.

   (a) Find the modulus of elasticity of the string.
   (b) A second identical string is attached to the particle and each has its
        free end attached to the same horizontal level above the particle, a
        distance L apart, so that the system hangs in equilibrium as shown in
        the diagram. If the extension of each string remains $\dfrac{l}{10}$, find the exact
        value of L in terms of l.

8† A planet A has a mass M and is at a certain instant a distance d from a
second planet B which has a mass $4M$. An asteroid at this same instant is
in a position which is on the direct line AB, such that the resultant of the
forces of attraction due to A and B is zero. Find, in terms of d, the
distance of the asteroid from B.

Revision

*1 A wooden block, of mass m, rests on a rough
plane that is inclined at an angle θ to the
horizontal, as shown in the diagram. The block is
just on the point of slipping. Show that
$\mu = \tan\theta$.

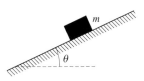

2 A large wooden crate, of mass m kg, is at rest on a rough horizontal surface. The crate is pulled by a rope that is inclined at an angle θ to the horizontal, as shown in the diagram. The rope is pulled with a force of P newtons.

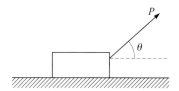

The coefficient of static friction between the crate and the surface is 0.6.

Find, in terms of m, g and θ, the minimum value of P to just move the crate.

3 A parcel, of mass 15 kg, is on a rough slope that is inclined at an angle of 20° to the horizontal. The coefficient of static friction between the parcel and the slope is 0.2. The parcel is just about to slide down the slope although it is held by a horizontal force P newtons. The situation is shown in the diagram. Find P.

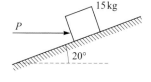

4 A man just starts to move a large box of weight 400 newtons along rough horizontal ground when he pushes with a horizontal force of 300 newtons.

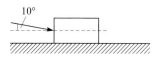

(a) Find the coefficient of static friction between the box and the ground.

On another occasion the man pushes the box with a force of P newtons at angle of 10° downwards to the horizontal as shown in the diagram.

(b) On this occasion find the force P that the man needs to apply to just get the box to move.

5 A slipway for launching boats consists of a rough straight track inclined at an angle of 10° to the horizontal. A boat of mass 300 kg is pulled down the slipway by means of a rope which is parallel to the slipway. When the tension in the rope is 500 N, the boat moves down the slipway with constant speed.

(a) Find, to 2 significant figures, the coefficient of friction between the boat and the slipway.

Later the boat returns to the slipway. It is now pulled up the slipway at constant speed by the rope which is again parallel to the slipway.

(b) Give brief reasons why the magnitude of the frictional force is the same as when the boat is pulled down the slope.

(c) Find, in newtons to 3 significant figures, the tension in the rope.

[Edexcel]

6 A light elastic string of unstretched length 0.4 m has a mass of 0.3 kg attached to one end. The other end of the string is held fixed and the system hangs freely in equilibrium so that the mass is 0.5 m below the fixed end. Find the modulus of elasticity of the string.

7 A light spring of stiffness $200 \, \mathrm{N \, m^{-1}}$ has one end fixed on a horizontal surface. On the other end sits a mass of 0.5 kg so that the spring is compressed. The situation is shown in the diagram. Find, in centimetres, the amount by which the spring is compressed.

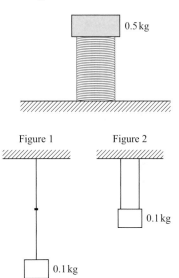

0.5 kg

8 A single elastic string, AB, of length 15 cm extends by 2 cm when a mass of 0.1 kg hangs freely from end B of the string while the other end, A, is held firmly fixed.

(a) Find the elastic constant of the string.
(b) Two of these elastic strings are joined together so that none of the length is lost, as shown in Figure 1. Find the distance of the mass below the point of suspension.

Figure 1

Figure 2

0.1 kg

0.1 kg

On another occasion two of the strings are attached to the mass as in Figure 2.

(c) Find the distance of the mass below the points of suspension.

9 A light elastic string of natural length 25 cm and modulus 50 N is fixed at one end to a point O on a rough plane that makes an angle $\sin^{-1} \frac{3}{5}$ with the horizontal. A block of weight 5 N is attached to the other end of the string and the block is at rest on the plane with the string parallel to the line of greatest slope. The coefficient of friction between the block and the slope is $\frac{3}{4}$. Given that the block is placed in a position so that it is just about to slide up the slope, find the extension of the string.

10 A smooth bead B of mass 0.6 kg is threaded on a light inextensible string whose ends are attached to two identical rings each of mass 0.4 kg. The rings can move on a fixed straight horizontal wire. The system rests in equilibrium with each section of the string making an angle θ with the vertical as shown in the diagram.

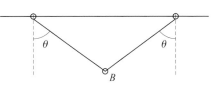

θ θ

B

   (i) Find the magnitude of the normal contact force exerted on each ring by the wire.

  (ii) Find, in terms of θ, the magnitude of the frictional force on each ring.

 (iii) Given that the coefficient of friction between each ring and the wire is 0.3, find the greatest possible value of θ for the system to be in equilibrium.

[OCR]

11[†] Find the force of attraction between the Sun and the planet Pluto assuming that the mass of the Sun is 2.0×10^{30} kg, the mass of Pluto is 1.3×10^{22} kg and that Pluto is in circular orbit about the Sun with radius 5.9×10^{12} m.

12[†] The force of attraction between two bodies each of equal mass has magnitude F newtons. If the distance between the two bodies is halved and the mass of each is doubled find, in terms of F, the magnitude of the force of attraction between them now.

13[†] Find the distance from the centre of the Earth at which the force acting on a 1 kg mass is 1 newton. You may take the mass of the Earth to be 5.98×10^{24} kg.

7 | Newton's second law

Motion due to a constant force on a body; motion of connected particles

Take the acceleration due to gravity as g m s^{-2} where $g = 9.8$.
Give answers to three significant figures unless otherwise stated.

Newton's second law states that the resultant force on a body is equal to the rate of change of momentum of that body.

$$\mathbf{F} = \frac{d(m\mathbf{v})}{dt}$$

For a body of constant mass this means that the resultant force on the body is equal to the product of its mass and its acceleration.

$$\mathbf{F} = m\frac{d\mathbf{v}}{dt} = m\mathbf{a}$$

The resultant force acting on a body and the acceleration of the body are in the same direction.

A constant resultant force acting on a body of constant mass produces a constant acceleration.

Motion of a system of connected particles

The forces acting on each particle must be considered separately and the equation $\mathbf{F} = m\mathbf{a}$ applied to each particle in turn.

Basic

1   A car of mass 1200 kg is decelerating at 2.5 m s^{-2} while travelling along a horizontal road. Find the resultant horizontal resistive force acting on the car.

2 A toboggan of weight 100 N slides down a
smooth icy slope that makes an angle of 30°
with the horizontal. The toboggan can be
modelled as a particle. Find the acceleration
of the toboggan.

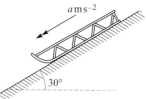

3 A toy hangs freely from a light inextensible
string attached to the roof of a car. When the car accelerates away from
traffic lights the string makes an angle of 5° with the vertical through the
point of suspension of the string. You may assume there are no resistive
forces on the toy. Find the acceleration of the car.

4 A particle of mass 0.2 kg is subject to a constant force of 5 N which acts
in a straight line.

  (a) Find the acceleration of the particle.
  (b) Find the speed of the particle after 10 seconds if it moves from rest.
  (c) Find the distance the particle has moved after 10 seconds.

5 A child of mass 40 kg is in a lift that moves vertically between floors.
Find the normal contact force between the child and the floor of the lift
when:

  (a) the lift is accelerating upwards at $2.5\,\mathrm{m\,s^{-2}}$,
  (b) the lift is accelerating downwards at $1\,\mathrm{m\,s^{-2}}$.

6 A coin is flicked in a straight line up a slope that makes an angle of 25°
with the horizontal. The coefficient of friction between the coin and the
slope is 0.4. Assuming that the coin can be modelled as a particle, find
the deceleration of the coin.

*7 A cable is raising a load vertically so that it accelerates at $2\,\mathrm{m\,s^{-2}}$. The
cable has a tension of 250 N. Find the mass of the load.

8 A block is held at rest on a rough slope that is inclined at an angle of
40° to the horizontal. The coefficient of friction between the block and
the slope is 0.25. The effect of air resistance can be ignored.
Find:

  (a) the acceleration of the block when it is released,
  (b) the distance travelled down the slope by the block in the first
        5 seconds.

9 A wooden block of mass 4 kg slides down a slope that makes an angle of 45° with the horizontal. The coefficient of friction between the block and the slope is 0.4. Find the acceleration of the block.

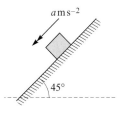

10 A particle of mass 2 kilograms is acted upon by three forces, $\mathbf{F}_1 = 2\mathbf{i} + 3\mathbf{j}$ newtons, $\mathbf{F}_2 = 4\mathbf{i} - 4\mathbf{j}$ newtons, $\mathbf{F}_3 = 4\mathbf{i} + 7\mathbf{j}$ newtons. Find the magnitude of its acceleration.

11 A particle of mass 0.5 kg is acted upon by three forces, $\mathbf{F}_1 = \mathbf{i} + 3\mathbf{j}$ newtons, $\mathbf{F}_2 = -5\mathbf{i} + 4\mathbf{j}$ newtons, and $\mathbf{F}_3$ newtons. Its acceleration is $2\mathbf{i} + 5\mathbf{j}$ m s^{-2}. Find $\mathbf{F}_3$.

Intermediate

1 A car of mass 800 kg tows a trailer of mass 200 kg along a horizontal road. A driving force of 500 N is produced by the engine and there is no resistance to motion. Find the tension in the tow-bar.

2 A mass of 400 grams is connected to another mass of 500 grams by a light inextensible string which passes over a smooth light pulley. The system is held with the string taut and then released. Find the acceleration of the system.

3 Two forces of magnitudes 4 N and 5 N act on a particle of mass 2 kg. The forces act in such a way that there is an angle of 120° between them as shown in the diagram. Find the acceleration of the particle, giving its magnitude and its direction in relation to the 4 N force.

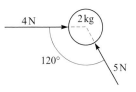

4 A book of mass 0.25 kg is just at the point of slipping on a horizontal table. The table is in a train which is accelerating at 2 m s^{-2} along a horizontal section of track. Find the coefficient of friction between the book and the table.

5 A car of mass 1000 kg tows a caravan of mass 600 kg. The car and caravan travel along a horizontal section of road. The car produces a driving force of 500 N and experiences a resistive force of 150 N; the caravan experiences a resistive force of 100 N. Find:

(a) the acceleration of the car and trailer,
(b) the tension in the tow-bar.

*6 Two particles are connected by a light inextensible string that passes over a smooth light pulley. One of the particles has mass 0.25 kg, the other mass m kg, where $m > 0.25$. The system is released from rest with the string taut and the masses accelerate at $2\,\mathrm{m\,s^{-2}}$.
Find:

(a) the tension in the string,
(b) m.

7 A crate of mass 250 kg is pulled along a rough horizontal surface by a rope inclined at an angle of 30° above the horizontal. The coefficient of friction between the crate and the surface is 0.4. All other resistive forces can be ignored.
The crate is accelerating at $1.5\,\mathrm{m\,s^{-2}}$. Find the tension in the rope.

8 A toboggan of mass 25 kg is pulled across a horizontal surface by a rope that is horizontal. The toboggan accelerates at $0.2\,\mathrm{m\,s^{-2}}$ and the coefficient of friction between it and the surface is 0.1. All other resistive forces can be ignored.

(a) Find the tension in the rope.
(b) On another occasion the same acceleration is achieved but the rope is inclined at an angle of 30° above the horizontal. Find the tension in the rope on this occasion.

9 A hot air balloon has a total weight of 3000 N and is accelerating upwards at $0.5\,\mathrm{m\,s^{-2}}$. The drag on the balloon due to air resistance can be ignored.

(a) Find the lift force, L N, experienced by the balloon.
(b) If the lift force is increased by 500 N, find the resulting acceleration of the balloon.

10 A mass of 3 kg is held at rest on a smooth plane inclined at an angle of 30° to the horizontal.

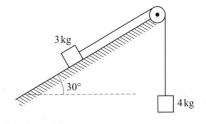

The 3 kg mass is connected to a mass of 4 kg, by a light inextensible string that passes over a smooth light pulley. The system is shown in the diagram. Air resistance is negligible.

Find, when the system is released:

(a) the acceleration of the system,
(b) the tension in the string.

Advanced

1 A mass of 2 kg is held at rest on a rough plane inclined at an angle of 20° to the horizontal. The coefficient of friction between the mass and the plane is 0.25.

The 2 kg mass is connected to a mass of 5 kg, by a light inextensible string, parallel to the line of greatest slope of the plane, that passes over a smooth light pulley. The system is shown in the diagram. Air resistance can be ignored.

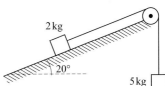

Find, when the system is released:

(a) the acceleration of the system,
(b) the tension in the string.

*2 A box of mass 25 kg is pulled up the line of greatest slope of a rough surface that makes an angle of 20° to the horizontal. The rope pulling the box is inclined at 30° to the slope, as shown in the diagram. The coefficient of friction between the box and the slope is 0.6. The box is accelerating at $1\,\text{m s}^{-2}$. Find the tension in the rope.

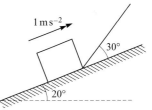

3 A heavy box of mass 100 kg is pulled over rough horizontal ground by two horizontal ropes attached to it. One of the ropes has a tension of 500 N, the other a tension of 750 N. There is an angle of 30° between the two ropes. Find:

(a) the angle that each of the ropes makes with the direction of motion of the box,
(b) the acceleration of the box if the coefficient of friction between the box and the ground is 0.75.

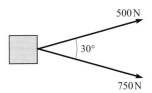

4 Two masses, *A* of 0.2 kg and *B* of 0.4 kg, are connected by a light inextensible string. Another light inextensible string is attached to *B* and this is passed over a smooth light pulley. A further mass *C* of 1 kg is attached to the free end of this string, as shown in the diagram. The masses can be modelled as particles.
The system is released from rest.
Find:

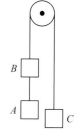

(a) the acceleration of the system,
(b) the tension in the string connecting *B* and *C*,
(c) the tension in the string connecting *A* and *B*.

5 On a model cable railway, a car of mass 250 grams is drawn up a slope of 7° from rest with an acceleration of $2 \, \text{cm s}^{-2}$. There is a resistive force equal to $\frac{1}{10}$ of its weight.

(a) Find the tension in the cable.
(b) The cable breaks. Assuming that the resistive force remains the same, describe briefly the motion that follows.

6 A mass of 2 kg is held at rest on a rough plane inclined at an angle of 20° to the horizontal. The coefficient of friction between the mass and the plane is 0.25.
A 5 kg mass is held at rest on a rough plane inclined at an angle of 40° to the horizontal. The coefficient of friction between this mass and the plane is 0.3.
The two masses are joined by a light inextensible string that passes over a smooth light pulley, fixed so that the string remains parallel to the line of

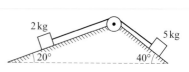

greatest slope of each of the two planes. The system is shown in the diagram. Air resistance can be ignored.
Find, when the system is released:

(a) the acceleration of the system,
(b) the tension in the string.

7 A mass of 2 kg is held on a smooth horizontal table. It is attached by light inextensible strings to two masses, one of 3 kg and one of 5 kg, which are suspended one at either side of the table. The strings pass over smooth pulleys. The system is released from rest. Find:

(a) the acceleration of the masses,
(b) the tension in each of the strings.

8 A passenger from a sinking ship is rescued from the water by a member of a helicopter rescue team. The passenger has a mass of 70 kg and the rescuer a mass of 65 kg. The rescuer is suspended part way down a light inextensible rope. The passenger is suspended from the bottom of the rope by means of a harness. Assume the rope is vertical. Once they are both clear of the water the helicopter accelerates upwards at $0.5\,\mathrm{m\,s^{-2}}$. Find the tension in:

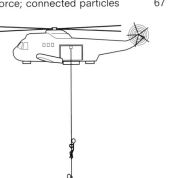

(a) the top section of the rope,
(b) the bottom section of the rope.

9 Two planes, one rough and one smooth, inclined at angles of $40°$ and $50°$ to the horizontal respectively, are placed back to back. Particles of masses 2 kg and M kg are placed on the slopes and are joined by a light inextensible string that passes over a smooth pulley as shown. The $40°$ slope has a coefficient of friction of 0.5. Air resistance can be ignored. The system is released from rest and the masses accelerate at $0.5\,\mathrm{m\,s^{-2}}$. Find:

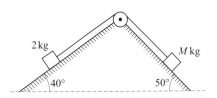

(a) the two possible values of M,
(b) the tension in the string for each case.

Revision

1 A particle of mass 5 kilograms is acted upon by three forces, $\mathbf{F}_1 = 2\mathbf{i} + 3\mathbf{j}$ newtons, $\mathbf{F}_2 = 4\mathbf{i} - 4\mathbf{j}$ newtons, $\mathbf{F}_3 = x\mathbf{i} + 7\mathbf{j}$ newtons. The magnitude of the particle's acceleration is $2\,\mathrm{m\,s^{-2}}$. Find the possible values of x.

2 A toboggan slides down an icy slope that makes an angle of $30°$ with the horizontal. The coefficient of friction between the toboggan and the slope is 0.05. All other resistive forces can be ignored. Find the acceleration of the toboggan.

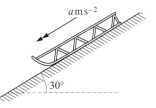

3 Two particles are connected by a light inextensible string that passes over a smooth light pulley. One of the particles has mass 0.5 kg, the other mass m kg, where $m < 0.5$. The system is released from rest with the string taut and the masses accelerate at $1\,\mathrm{m\,s^{-2}}$. Find:

(a) the tension in the string,

(b) m.

4 Two forces of magnitudes 6 N and 5 N act on a particle of mass 10 kg. The forces act in such a way that there is an angle of $120°$ between them as shown in the diagram. Find the acceleration of the particle, giving its magnitude and its direction in relation to the 6 N force.

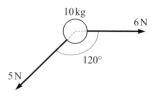

5 A car of mass 800 kg tows a trailer of mass 200 kg along a horizontal road. A driving force of D newtons is produced by the engine and there is no resistance to motion. The tension in the towbar is 125 newtons. The car and trailer can be modelled as particles joined by a light inextensible string. Find D.

6 A mass of 5 kg is held at rest on a smooth plane inclined at an angle of $40°$ to the horizontal.
The 5 kg mass is connected to a mass of 2 kg by a light inextensible string that passes over a smooth light pulley. The system is shown in the diagram. Air resistance is negligible.
The 5 kg mass is released. Find:

(a) the acceleration of the system,

(b) the tension in the string.

*7 A mass of 9 kg is held at rest on a rough plane inclined at an angle of α to the horizontal. The coefficient of friction between the mass and the plane is 0.25. The 9 kg mass is connected to a mass of 3 kg by a light inextensible string that passes over a smooth light pulley. The system is shown in the diagram. Air resistance can be ignored.
The tension in the string when the system is released from rest is 35 N. Find:

(a) the acceleration of the system,

(b) the angle α, given in degrees.

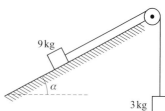

8   A mass of 2 kg is held at rest on a rough plane inclined at an angle of 20° to the horizontal. The coefficient of friction between the mass and the

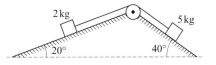

plane is 0.25. A 5 kg mass is held at rest on another rough plane inclined at an angle of 40° to the horizontal. The coefficient of friction between this mass and the plane is λ. The two masses are joined by a light inextensible string that passes over a smooth light pulley. The system is shown in the diagram. Air resistance can be ignored.

When the system is released the 5 kg mass accelerates down the slope at $2\,\mathrm{m\,s^{-2}}$. Find:

(a) λ,

(b) the tension in the string.

9   A toy train is on display in a shop. The train consists of an engine and a truck which are linked together by a short inextensible cord. The engine is of mass 600 grams and the truck is of mass 200 grams. The train runs along a straight horizontal track. The force of resistance on each part of the train is 0.2 N per 100 grams. The train is released from rest on the track and moves under a constant forward propulsive force of 1.8 N exerted by the engine.

(a) (i) Show that the acceleration of the train is $0.25\,\mathrm{m\,s^{-2}}$.

    (ii) Find the magnitude of the tension in the cord.

(b) After a few seconds the propulsive force ceases so that the train moves solely under the force of resistance. Without making any further calculations, describe the subsequent motion of the train.

[NEAB]

10   A metal block M, of mass 2 kg, is held at rest on a smooth horizontal table. The block M is connected to a wooden block W, of mass 0.1 kg, by a light inextensible string which passes over a

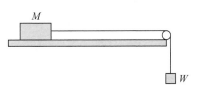

smooth light pulley fixed at the edge of the table. The block W hangs vertically, as shown in the diagram. Block M, which is 0.6 metres from the pulley, is now released. Modelling the blocks as particles and ignoring air resistance, find

(i) the tension in the string in the ensuing motion,

(ii) the speed of W immediately before M reaches the edge of the table.

[OCR]

8 | Circular motion with constant speed

Circular motion with constant speed; conical pendulum; banked tracks; motion under Newton's law of gravitation[†]

Take the acceleration due to gravity to be $g\,\mathrm{m\,s}^{-2}$ where $g = 9.8$.
Give answers to three significant figures unless otherwise stated.

A body of mass m that moves in a circle of radius r at constant speed v is acted on by a force of magnitude $\dfrac{mv^2}{r}$ perpendicular to the motion of the body, i.e. along the radius of the circle.

The angular velocity of a body travelling at a constant speed v in a circle of radius r is ω where $v = r\omega$. Angular velocity is measured in radians per second. The acceleration of the body is $r\omega^2$ towards the centre of the circle.

Newton's law of gravitation

If two particles of masses m_1 kg and m_2 kg are at a distance r metres apart, they will attract each other with a force of magnitude
$F = \dfrac{Gm_1m_2}{r^2}$ newtons, where G is a universal constant, called the constant of gravitation.

$$G = 6.67 \times 10^{-11}\,\mathrm{N\,m^2\,kg^{-2}} \text{ to three significant figures}$$

Basic

1 A particle moves on a circular path of radius 0.5 metres. It has a constant speed of $2\,\mathrm{m\,s}^{-1}$.

   (a) Find the particle's:
      (i) angular speed,
      (ii) acceleration.
   (b) Find the force acting on the particle if it has a mass of 3 kilograms. State the direction of this force.

2 A particle moves on a circular path of radius 1.5 metres, with a constant angular speed of $5\,\text{rad s}^{-1}$. Find:

    (a) the velocity,
    (b) the acceleration
of the particle, stating the direction of each.

3 A particle of mass $0.1\,\text{kg}$ has an acceleration of $4\,\text{ms}^{-2}$ while moving at constant speed in a circle of radius 2 metres.

    (a) Find the speed of the particle in surd form.
    (b) Find the centripetal force acting on the particle, giving its direction.

*4 A car of mass $800\,\text{kg}$ travels on a bend in a horizontal road. Assume that the car is moving at a constant speed of $24\,\text{m s}^{-1}$ on a circular path of radius 80 metres. Find:

    (a) the angular speed of the car in rad s^{-1},
    (b) the acceleration of the car,
    (c) the frictional force acting on the car toward the centre of its circular path.

5 A car moves on a horizontal circular path of radius 25 metres with constant speed $15\,\text{m s}^{-1}$. It can be modelled as a particle. Find:

    (a) the acceleration of the car,
    (b) the time taken by the car to make one complete revolution of the circle.

6 Find the acceleration, due to the rotation of the Earth, of a person standing on the equator. Assume that the Earth is a sphere of radius 6.4×10^{6} metres.

7 The path of a particle referred to a fixed origin is described by position vector $\mathbf{r} = 3\cos\left(\frac{\pi}{2}t\right)\mathbf{i} + 3\sin\left(\frac{\pi}{2}t\right)\mathbf{j}$ metres, where $\mathbf{i}$ and $\mathbf{j}$ are perpendicular unit vectors. Find:

    (a) the radius of the circular path of the particle,
    (b) the magnitude of the velocity of the particle,
    (c) the magnitude of the acceleration of the particle,
    (d) the time taken by the particle to make one complete revolution.

8 A dog runs round a circular path in a horizontal field. The dog's motion can be represented by the vector equation
$\mathbf{r} = 10\cos(0.4t)\,\mathbf{i} + 10\sin(0.4t)\,\mathbf{j}$ m, relative to a fixed point O, where $\mathbf{i}$ and $\mathbf{j}$ are unit perpendicular vectors.
Find

    (a) the radius of the path,
    (b) the velocity, in vector form, of the dog's motion,

(c) the acceleration, in vector form, of the dog's motion,
(d) the dog's speed,
(e) the magnitude of the dog's acceleration.

9 A fairground wheel has a diameter of
20 metres. It rotates at a constant speed so
that it makes one complete revolution every
30 seconds.
Each rider can be assumed to be a particle a
distance 10 metres from the centre of the
wheel. Find:

(a) the speed of a rider in $\mathrm{m\,s^{-1}}$,
(b) the acceleration of a rider.

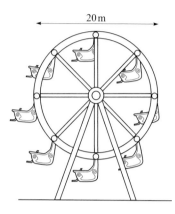

10 A girl is skating around an ice skating rink with a constant speed of
$9\,\mathrm{m\,s^{-1}}$. She first of all makes perfect circles of radius 5 metres. She then
practises circles of radius 4.5 metres while travelling at the same speed.
By how much has her acceleration changed?

11† Calculate the force of attraction between the Moon and an astronaut of
mass 60 kg standing on its surface, using the following data:

mass of Moon $= 7.34 \times 10^{22}\,\mathrm{kg}$
radius of Moon $= 1\,738\,000$ metres
gravitational constant $= 6.67 \times 10^{-11}\,\mathrm{N\,m^2\,kg^{-2}}$

How would this compare with the gravitational force due to the Earth
that she would experience when standing on the surface of the Earth?

12† A satellite of mass m kg, a distance x km from the centre of the Earth
experiences a gravitational force of $0.16mg$. Find x in terms of r, where
r km is the radius of the Earth.

Intermediate

1 A cyclist on a racing bike of total mass m kg is on a circular race track.
Assume that the cyclist is moving at a constant speed of $u\,\mathrm{m\,s^{-1}}$ on a
circular path of radius r metres.
A cyclist of total mass $2m$ kg goes round the track on the same circular
path at a constant speed of $v\,\mathrm{m\,s^{-1}}$. The frictional force acting on the
first bike is the same as that acting on the second. Find the ratio of
u to v.

2 A car of mass 1200 kg travels on a horizontal road at a roundabout. Assume that it is moving at a constant speed of $12\,\mathrm{m\,s^{-1}}$ on a circular path of radius 20 metres. Find:

(a) the angular speed of the car in $\mathrm{rad\,s^{-1}}$,
(b) the acceleration of the car,
(c) the frictional force acting on the car toward the centre of its circular path,
(d) the coefficient of friction between the car and the road.

*3 A conical pendulum consists of a mass of 0.1 kg which makes horizontal circles attached to a piece of light and inextensible string of length 0.5 m. The mass completes each revolution of a circle in 0.5 s. The situation is shown in the diagram. Find:

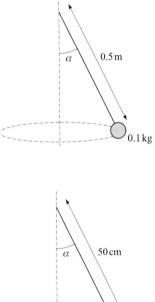

(a) the angle α that the string makes with the vertical through the point at which it is held,
(b) the tension in the string.

4 A conical pendulum has length 50 cm and a bob of mass 0.02 kg. The bob rotates in a horizontal circle of diameter 40 cm with constant angular speed as shown in the diagram. Find:

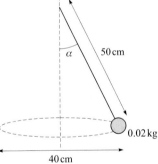

(a) the angle α between the string and the vertical,
(b) the tension in the string,
(c) the linear speed of the bob.

5 A penny is placed on a rough horizontal turntable 0.2 metres from the axis of rotation. A second penny, of the same mass, is placed on the turntable so its speed is half that of the first.

(a) How far is the second penny from the axis of rotation?

The first penny starts to slide when its speed reaches $40\,\mathrm{cm\,s^{-1}}$.
The coefficient of friction between the turntable and each of the pennies can be assumed to be the same.

(b) How fast must the turntable rotate for the second penny to start to slip? (Give your answer in $\mathrm{rad\,s^{-1}}$).

6 A fairground wheel has a diameter of
15 metres. It rotates at a constant speed so
that it makes one complete revolution
every 45 seconds. Model each car as a
particle a distance of 7.5 metres from the
centre of the wheel. Use this model to find:

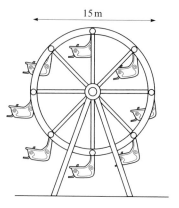

(a) the speed of a car in $m s^{-1}$,
(b) the acceleration of a car.

The cars are actually attached so that they
always hang vertically below their point of
suspension on the wheel. The height of
each car is 1.5 metres.

(c) What effect does this have on the motion?

7 A model aeroplane of mass 3 kg makes
horizontal circles in the air. The resultant
force acting on the plane is 15 newtons
towards the centre of the circle. The radius
of the circle is 50 metres. Assuming that
the aeroplane can be modelled as a
particle, find:

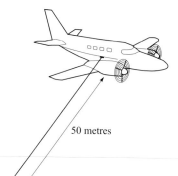

(a) the speed of the aeroplane,
(b) the time taken for each complete circuit.

8 A man is standing on the surface of the Earth north of the equator. His
acceleration due to the rotation of the Earth is $0.02 \, m s^{-2}$. Assuming the
Earth to be a sphere of radius 6400 km, what is the latitude of his
position? (The latitude of a point on the Earth's surface is given by the
angle between the line joining that point to the centre of the Earth and
the equatorial plane.)

9 A conical pendulum has length 27 cm and a bob of mass 0.02 kg. It
rotates in a horizontal circle such that the tension in the string is
0.3 newtons. Find:

(a) the angle between the string and the vertical,
(b) the linear speed of the bob.

10 A conical pendulum is formed from a small bob suspended from a light
inextensible string. The bob is of mass M kg. It rotates in a horizontal
circle of radius r metres with an angular speed of $2 \, rad \, s^{-1}$. Find the
tension in the string in terms of M, g and r.

11[†] A small satellite is put into orbit around the Moon. It has mass 50 kg and is a distance 3480 km from the surface of the Moon. The mass of the Moon can be taken as 7.34×10^{22} kg and its radius as 1740 km. Using $G = 6.67 \times 10^{-11}\,\mathrm{N\,m^2\,kg^{-2}}$, find:

(a) the gravitational force on the satellite,

(b) the speed with which it is travelling.

12[†] An asteroid of mass 20 kg is travelling in orbit round a planet of mass 6×10^{20} kg. It is travelling at a speed of $240\,\mathrm{ms^{-1}}$. The only force acting on the asteroid can be assumed to be due to the gravitational attraction between itself and the planet. Calculate the distance between the centre of the planet and the asteroid assuming that the orbit is circular. Take $G = 6.67 \times 10^{-11}\,\mathrm{N\,m^2\,kg^{-2}}$.

Advanced

1 A conical pendulum is made from a light inextensible string of length x cm with a bob of mass 0.1 kg at the end. The bob rotates in a horizontal circle with an angular velocity of $9\,\mathrm{rads\,s^{-1}}$. The tension in the string is 2 newtons. Find x.

*2 A motorbike and rider of total mass 400 kg travel in a horizontal circle of radius 50 m on a road banked at an angle of $10°$ to the horizontal. The situation is shown in the diagram. The

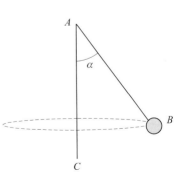

motorbike is travelling at a speed of $20\,\mathrm{ms^{-1}}$. Find the coefficient of friction between the motorbike and the road if the motorbike is just on the point of slipping up the banking.

3 The figure shows a conical pendulum in which a particle of mass m is fixed to the end B of a light inextensible string AB where $AB = x$. The pendulum rotates with constant speed ω about a fixed vertical pole CA. The angle between the string and the vertical is α.

(a) Sketch a diagram showing the forces on the particle.

(b) Show that either $\alpha = 0$ or $\cos \alpha = g/(\omega^2 x)$ where g is the acceleration due to gravity.

(c) The string will break when the tension exceeds $3mg$. Find the maximum value of α possible.

4 A student models the motion of a seat on a fairground chairoplane. He takes the seat to be a particle on the end of a light inextensible string RS. The string is joined to an L-shaped wire PQR as shown in the diagram.

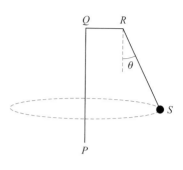

The wire rotates so that R rotates about PQ with constant angular velocity ω. The line PQ is vertical and the points P, Q, R and S all lie in a vertical plane. RS makes an angle of θ with the downward vertical and $QR = RS \sin \theta$.
Show that $RS = \dfrac{g}{(2\omega^2 \cos \theta)}$.

5 A particle P of mass 1 kg is attached to one end of a light inextensible string of length 0.75 metres. The other end of the string is fixed to point O on a smooth horizontal table. The particle moves in a horizontal circle of radius 0.75 metres with a constant angular speed of ω rad s^{-1}. Given that the tension in the string is 24 newtons calculate:

(a) the value of ω,
(b) the speed of the particle.

A particle of mass 2 kg is placed at rest directly in the path of P.

(c) The two particles stick together on impact; calculate the new tension in the string.

6 An engine is travelling around a banked section of track at 60 km h^{-1}. Its motion can be modelled as that of a particle travelling at constant speed around a circular path of radius 350 metres. The distance between the rails is 1.4 metres.
What is the difference in height between the two rails if there is to be no side thrust on the rails?

7 A cyclist in the Tour de France rides his bike at a constant speed of 36 km h^{-1} on a circular path of radius 17 metres around a sharp bend.

(a) Calculate the magnitude of the acceleration of the cycle.
(b) The total mass of the rider and cycle is 72 kg. The magnitude of the friction force between the cycle and the road can not exceed 600 newtons without skidding taking place. Find (in km h^{-1}) the greatest speed at which the cyclist can travel round the bend without skidding.

8   A particle is attached to the end A of a light inextensible string AB of length $2x$ metres. The end B is fixed a distance $2x$ metres above the horizontal ground. The particle describes a horizontal circle with constant velocity at a height of x metres above the ground.

(a) Calculate the steady speed of the particle in terms of x.
(b) The string breaks and the particle falls to the ground. Find the speed of the particle on impact with the ground in terms of x.

9†   An asteroid of mass m kg at the inner edge of an asteroid belt is travelling in orbit round a planet. The mass of the planet is M kg. The asteroid is travelling at a speed of v m s^{-1} at a height of x metres above the centre of the planet and G is the gravitational constant. The only force acting on the asteroid can be assumed to be due to the gravitational attraction between itself and the planet.

(a) Show that $MG = xv^2$.
(b) The asteroid belt is a width of $0.1x$ metres so the furthest asteroid from the centre of the planet is $1.1x$ metres from the centre of the planet. Find the velocity of this asteroid in terms of v.

Revision

1   A children's roundabout has a diameter of 4 metres. It makes one complete revolution every 4π seconds. P is a point on the perimeter of the roundabout.
A plan of the roundabout is shown on the diagram at time $t = 0$.

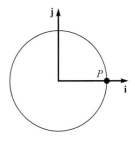

(a) Show that the position of P after t seconds in terms of the axes shown is
$\mathbf{r} = 2\cos(0.5t)\mathbf{i} + 2\sin(0.5t)\mathbf{j}$ metres.
(b) Hence find the acceleration of P after t seconds, in vector form.

2   A model aeroplane is travelling in horizontal circles of radius r metres. The speed of the plane is constant but the resultant force towards the centre of the circle is suddenly doubled while the speed remains unchanged. What effect does this have on the path of the plane and the time it takes to complete a circuit?

3   A particle of mass 0.1 kg moves in a circle with constant speed 2 m s^{-1} and acceleration 5 m s^{-2}. Find:

(a) the radius of the circular path,
(b) the time taken by the particle to make one complete revolution.

4 A watch has a second hand that is of length 1.2 cm, and a minute hand that is 1 mm shorter. Model this situation by assuming that the tip of the second hand of the watch describes a circle of radius 1.2 cm with constant angular speed and the tip of the minute hand describes a circle of radius 1.1 cm also with constant angular speed.

(a) Find the angular speed of any point on the second hand.
(b) Find the angular speed of any point on the minute hand.
(c) Find the magnitude of the velocity of the tip of the second hand.
(d) Find the magnitude of the acceleration of the tip of the minute hand.
(e) Describe how your model would differ from reality.

*5 A small bead runs around the inside rim of a horizontal circular tray. It travels with a constant angular velocity of $2 \, \text{rad} \, \text{s}^{-1}$. The radius of the tray is 20 cm. The bead is modelled as a particle.

(a) How long does it take to complete one circuit of the tray?
(b) Find the acceleration of the bead.
(c) The bead has a diameter of 1 cm. Find a better approximation to the actual acceleration of the bead.

6 A particle travels in a horizontal circle with angular velocity $1.5 \, \text{rad} \, \text{s}^{-1}$ and acceleration towards the centre of the circle of $4.5 \, \text{m} \, \text{s}^{-2}$. Find:

(a) the radius of the circle,
(b) the speed of the particle.

7 A conical pendulum consists of a light inextensible string of length 12 cm and a bob of mass 0.05 kg. It rotates in a horizontal circle such that the tension in the string is 0.75 newtons. Find:

(a) the angle between the string and the vertical,
(b) the radius of the circle,
(c) the linear speed of the bob.

8 A cyclist in a sponsored ride cycles around a sharp bend. Her motion can be modelled by that of a particle travelling at a constant speed of $24 \, \text{km} \, \text{h}^{-1}$ on a horizontal circular path of radius 15 metres.

(a) Calculate the magnitude of the acceleration of the cycle.
(b) Find the minimum value of the coefficient of friction between the cycle and road.

9 A particle P of mass m is attached by a light inextensible thread of length l to a fixed support O. The particle moves with constant angular speed ω in a horizontal circle with centre C vertically below O. The thread is inclined at an angle θ to the vertical as shown in the diagram.

(a) Show that the tension, T, in the thread is $ml\omega^2$.

(b) The greatest tension that the thread can withstand without breaking is 16.2 N. Given that $l = 0.25$ m and $m = 0.2$ kg,

    (i) show that $\omega \leq 18$ radians per second,

    (ii) find the greatest possible value of θ, giving your answer to the nearest degree.

[NEAB]

10[†] Although the motion of each of the planets around the Sun is elliptical, it can be modelled as circular. The following table gives data about the motion of three of the planets

Planet	Mass (kg)	Period of revolution round Sun (years)	Average speed (m s^{-1})	Mean distance from the Sun (m)
Mercury	0.33 x 10^{24}	0.241	V	5.79 × 10^{10}
Earth	5.98 x 10^{24}	1	29 800	14.96 × 10^{10}
Neptune	103 x 10^{24}	T	5430	449.7 × 10^{10}

Assume that the universal gravitational constant is $G = 6.67 \times 10^{-11}\,\mathrm{N\,m^2\,kg^{-2}}$.

(a) Use this information to calculate the mass of the Sun.

(b) Hence or otherwise calculate:

    (i) the average speed of Mercury (V),

    (ii) the period of revolution of Neptune around the Sun (T).

11 The figure shows a railway engine of mass m kg travelling round a curved track. The centre of mass of the engine is moving along the arc of a horizontal circle of radius 500 m. The track is banked at an angle θ to the horizontal.

    (i) Calculate the acceleration of the engine when it travels at a constant speed of 12.5 m s^{-1}.

At this speed, the engine experiences no sideways force from the rails up or down the slope.

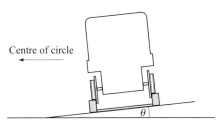

Centre of circle

    (ii) Write down the radial equation of motion and the vertical equilibrium equation. Hence show that θ is approximately $1.8°$.

When the engine is stationary, the magnitude of the sideways force that the rails exert on the engine up the slope is F N.

(iii) Find F in terms of m.

There is a speed limit, V m s^{-1}, for this section of track. It is set such that, at the speed limit, the magnitude of the sideways force exerted by the rails *down* the bank at the speed limit should also be F N.

(iv) Calculate V.

[MEI]

9 Energy, work and power

Kinetic energy; gravitational potential energy; elastic potential energy;[†] conservation of mechanical energy; work done by a force; work/energy principle; power as rate of doing work

Take the acceleration due to gravity to be $g\,\mathrm{m\,s^{-2}}$ where $g = 9.8$.
Give answers to three significant figures unless otherwise stated.

The kinetic energy of a particle of mass m kg, travelling with velocity $v\,\mathrm{m\,s^{-1}}$, is given by $\frac{1}{2}mv^2$. Kinetic energy is measured in joules.

The increase in gravitational potential energy of a particle of mass m kg that is raised a vertical distance of h metres is given by mgh N m (or joules).

The elastic potential energy of a string or spring of natural length l metres and modulus of elasticity λ that has been stretched x metres is given by $\dfrac{\lambda x^2}{2l}$ joules.

Kinetic energy, gravitational potential energy and elastic potential energy are all forms of mechanical energy.

If there are no dissipative forces, such as friction, and no energy is added from outside, then the total mechanical energy of a system is conserved.

The work done by a force is equal to the change in energy produced by the force.

The work done by a constant force $\mathbf{F}$ newtons displaced through $\mathbf{r}$ metres is given by $Fr\cos\theta$, where θ is the angle between the directions of the force and the displacement.

Power is the rate at which a force does work. It is measured in watts.

Basic

1 Find the kinetic energy of the following:

(a) a particle of mass 20 kg travelling with speed $25\,\mathrm{m\,s}^{-1}$,
(b) a centipede of mass 2 grams travelling with a speed of $5\,\mathrm{cm\,s}^{-1}$,
(c) a satellite of mass 1 tonne travelling round the Earth with a speed of $32\,000\,\mathrm{km\,h}^{-1}$.

2 Find the loss in potential energy of the following:

(a) a particle of mass 0.02 grams falling a vertical distance of 23 cm,
(b) a shot of mass 2 kg which is thrown from a height of 1.8 metres above ground level, rises to 2.3 metres and falls to the ground,
(c) a child of mass 25 kg going down a slide. The slide has a length 4 metres and makes an angle of 30° with the horizontal.

3 Find the work done by Susan in the following situations.

(a) She pushes a wheelbarrow of mass 20 kg through a horizontal distance of 100 metres against a resistive force of 40 N. The wheelbarrow starts and finishes at rest.
(b) She lifts a bag of potatoes of mass 5 kg a vertical distance of 1.5 metres. The bag starts and finishes at rest.
(c) She pushes a coin of mass 5 grams in a horizontal straight line for a distance of 1.5 metres across a smooth table. There are no resistive forces. The coin starts at rest and has a speed of $1\,\mathrm{m\,s}^{-1}$ when she stops pushing.
(d) She pushes against a stationary car of mass 1.2 tonnes to stop it rolling back down a slope of angle 3° with the horizontal.

4 A particle of mass 0.2 kg has a velocity $\mathbf{v} = 3\mathbf{i} - 2\mathbf{j}\,\mathrm{m\,s}^{-1}$. Find its kinetic energy.

5 Asif sits at rest at the top of a chute 20 metres above the surface of a swimming pool. His weight is 300 N. He then slides all the way down to the bottom.

(a) Find the potential energy lost by Asif when he reaches the pool.
(b) Assuming that there are no resistive forces present, find his speed when he enters the pool.
(c) Explain why your answer suggests that in reality some resistive forces are present.

6 Anya, whose mass is 32 kg, slides down a playground slide that stands on level ground. It is made from a curved sloping section of metal OA and a horizontal section AB as shown in the diagram. The arc OA is 8 metres in length. O is 3 metres above the ground and A is 0.4 metres above the ground.

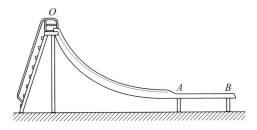

(a) Find the potential energy lost by Anya in sliding:
    (i) from O to A,
    (ii) from A to B.

(b) Use the diagram to estimate, to the nearest 100 J, the potential energy lost by Anya in sliding the first 4 metres along OA.

*7 A car of mass 1500 kg accelerates uniformly from rest along a straight horizontal road. It reaches a velocity of $25\,\mathrm{m\,s}^{-1}$ in a distance of 500 metres against a constant resultant force, due to friction and air resistance, of 200 newtons. Find the work done by the engine.

*8 A girl of mass 55 kg is swimming in a swimming pool of length 50 metres. The resistance due to the drag of water is approximately 40 newtons. All other resistances to her motion can be ignored.

(a) Find the work done by the girl in swimming 50 metres if her speed through the water is a constant $1\,\mathrm{m\,s}^{-1}$.

(b) On another occasion the girl starts from rest and accelerates at $0.05\,\mathrm{m\,s}^{-2}$ for the first 10 metres, and then continues at a constant speed. Find the work she does during the first 50 metres.

(c) Explain why the results of (a) and (b) show that it is reasonable to ignore the initial period of acceleration when finding the work done in swimming the length of a 50-metre pool and to model the motion as one of constant speed.

9 A sports car is travelling at a speed of $40\,\mathrm{m\,s}^{-1}$ along a straight horizontal track. The car and driver have a total mass of 1000 kg. The driver slams on her brakes to simulate an emergency stop and the car stops in a distance of 64 metres.

(a) What is the work done in bringing the car to rest?

(b) Find F, the retarding force, assuming it is considered to be constant.

10 A particle moves through a displacement of $3\mathbf{i} + 4\mathbf{j}$ metres under the action of several forces. Find the work done by one of the forces $\mathbf{F} = 2\mathbf{i} + 4\mathbf{j}$ newtons during this motion.

11 A bead is threaded on a straight rough wire. A force of 10 newtons is applied at an angle of 25° to the wire so that the bead travels horizontally along the wire at a constant speed. Find the work done in moving the bead a distance of 10 cm along the wire.

12 A crane lifts 20 crates, each of mass 100 kg, vertically through a distance of 4 metres. The crates start and finish at rest. What is the total work done by the crane in lifting the crates?

13 A man is running at a constant speed of $5\,\mathrm{m\,s^{-1}}$ along a horizontal road against resistive forces of 2 newtons. Find the work done per second.

*14 What power is required to keep a train of mass 200 000 kg moving along a smooth level track at a uniform speed of $40\,\mathrm{m\,s^{-1}}$ if the resistive force is 0.015% of the weight of the train?

15 A trolley of mass 25 kg has two damaged wheels. These provide a resistive force of 10 newtons. All other resistive forces can be ignored. The trolley is being pushed across a horizontal surface at a speed of $6\,\mathrm{m\,s^{-1}}$. What power is required to cause this motion?

16† Sian is doing an experiment with a light elastic string of unstretched length 1.5 metres. The string's modulus of elasticity is 0.98 N. Find the work done in

(a) stretching the string so its length is 2 metres.
(b) stretching the string so its length is 2.5 metres

17† The work done in stretching a light string, of natural length 2 metres, from 3 metres to 4 metres is 3.6 J. Find the modulus of elasticity of the string.

18† A spring of unstretched length 10 cm has spring constant k N. Find the work done:

(a) in compressing the spring so that it is 5 cm long,
(b) in stretching the spring so that it is 20 cm long,
(c) in stretching the spring from 20 cm to 30 cm in length.

19† The work done in compressing a spring by a distance of 10 cm from its natural length is 0.3 J.

(a) Find its spring constant.
(b) What work must be done to compress it by a further 10 cm?

Intermediate

1 A boy of mass 40 kg slides from rest down a playground slide. The slide is 8 metres long and is inclined at an angle of 40° to the horizontal. Air resistance and friction can be ignored.

(a) Find the potential energy lost by the boy.

(b) Find the speed of the boy at the bottom of the slide.

*2 A motorbike and rider of total mass 120 kg, under a constant resultant force F N, accelerated from 55 km h^{-1} to 70 km h^{-1} over a distance of 30 metres.

(a) What work was done in changing the speed of the motorbike?

(b) Find F.

3 A marble rolls along a smooth track as shown in the diagram. It can be modelled as a particle with no resistive forces acting on it. The marble's journey starts when it is just displaced from rest at point A.

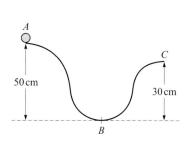

(a) Find the speed of the marble when it passes through points B and C.

(b) Find the height of the marble above B when its speed is 2.5 m s^{-1}.

4 A car including the driver and passengers has a total mass of 1800 kg. When the car was travelling at a speed of 25 m s^{-1} the engine cut out and the car was brought to a halt over a distance of 100 metres. Find the average resistive force over this period:

(a) if the motion took place over horizontal ground,

(b) if the motion took place down a slope of 5° to the horizontal.

5 A diver of mass 60 kg dives from a board that is 5 metres high. After entering the water he continues downward for 2 metres. The only force acting on the diver while travelling through the air is that of gravity. The resistive force, F, acting on the diver in the water is constant. Assuming the diver is at rest when he leaves the diving board and can be modelled as a particle, find:

(a) the constant resistive force, F,

(b) the work done by the water in stopping the diver.

6 A small child of mass 20 kg slides down a waterchute into a swimming pool. The length of the chute is 6 metres and it makes an angle of 30 degrees with the horizontal. There is a constant resistive force of 50 newtons.

(a) Draw a force diagram to show all the forces acting on the child and calculate the work done by each of these forces.

(b) Hence or otherwise find her speed as she reaches the bottom of the slide.

7   A cyclist is pedalling up a slope of $\sin^{-1} 0.05$. If the combined mass of the cyclist and cycle is 90 kg, the cyclist is travelling at a constant speed of $7\,\mathrm{m\,s^{-1}}$ and frictional forces are equal to 10 newtons, find the rate at which the man is working (take $g = 10$).

8   A toy car of mass 0.1 kg travels down a ramp which makes an angle of $\sin^{-1} 0.1$ to the horizontal. It starts from rest and reaches a speed of $2\,\mathrm{m\,s^{-1}}$ after 4 seconds. Calculate:
    (a) the constant resistive force on the car,
    (b) the work done in the first 3 seconds by the resistive force.

9   Three forces, $4\mathbf{i} + 3\mathbf{j}$ newtons, $5\mathbf{i} - 3\mathbf{j}$ newtons and $-7\mathbf{i} + 12\mathbf{j}$ newtons, act on a body of mass 10 kg.
    (a) Find the total work done by the forces in moving the body a distance of 15 metres in the direction $\mathbf{i} + 6\mathbf{j}$.
    (b) The body starts from rest. What is its speed after 15 metres?

10 A body of mass 1 kg is acted on by three forces, $3\mathbf{i} + \mathbf{j}\,\mathrm{N}$, $4\mathbf{i} - 2\mathbf{j}\,\mathrm{N}$ and $k\mathbf{i} + 5\mathbf{j}\,\mathrm{N}$. The body starts from rest and is displaced by $\mathbf{i} + 2\mathbf{j}$ metres in the first second.
    (a) Find k.
    (b) Find the work done by each of the three forces.
    (c) Find the speed of the body after 1 second in surd form.

11 A bus of mass 18 tonnes has a maximum speed of $20\,\mathrm{m\,s^{-1}}$ up a slope of $5°$ to the horizontal when the engine is working at 360 kW. Find the resistance to the motion of the bus.

12 A car of total mass 900 kg is moving against a constant resistance to its motion of 1200 N. It has a maximum power output of 51 kW.
    Find the maximum speed of the car when it is travelling:
    (a) along a horizontal road,
    (b) up a slope of angle $\sin^{-1} 0.12$ to the horizontal,
    (c) down the same slope.

    (d) Explain why your answer to (c) suggests that the resistance to motion of the car is unlikely to be constant for all velocities.

13 A girl pulls her small sister, of weight 270 N, on a sledge of weight 10 N at a constant speed of $1.8\,\mathrm{m\,s^{-1}}$ across a level snow-covered field. She holds the rope so that it is horizontal. The coefficient of friction between the snow and the sledge is 0.05 and the resistive force caused by air resistance can be taken as 45 N. The sledge and passenger can be modelled as a particle P.
    (a) Draw a diagram showing the forces acting on P.
    (b) Show that the rate at which the girl is working is 106.2 W.

14[†] One end of a light elastic string of length 1 metre and modulus of elasticity 0.2 N is fixed to a point *A* on a smooth horizontal table. The other end is fixed to a heavy particle of mass 0.8 kg. The particle is pulled away from *A* so that the string length is doubled and then released. Find the speed of the particle when the string becomes slack.

15[†] A light elastic string of natural length 1.4 metres and modulus of elasticity 28 N is attached to a hook in the ceiling at *P*. A block *Q* of weight 9.8 N is fixed to the other end. The block is held vertically below *P* so that $PQ = 1.4$ metres and then released.

(a) Find the speed of the block when *Q* is 1.8 metres below *P*.
(b) How much further will the block fall before starting to rise again?

16[†] A light elastic string of natural length 1.2 metres has one end fixed to a point *A*. A small bob of mass 100 grams, suspended from the other end as shown in the diagram, hangs at rest at *B*, where *AB* is 1.4 metres. The particle is lifted a distance of 0.2 metres so that the string just becomes slack and then released.

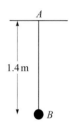

(a) Find the speed of the particle as it passes *B*.
(b) Find the greatest distance below *A* that the particle reaches.

Advanced

1 A large beachball, of mass 100 grams, is thrown vertically upwards with a speed of $7\,\mathrm{m\,s^{-1}}$. It reaches a height of 2 metres above its point of projection.

(a) Find its initial kinetic energy.
(b) Find the loss of mechanical energy due to air resistance during this motion.
(c) Assuming that the air resistance is constant, find the speed of the ball when it returns to its point of projection.

2 A locomotive pulls a train at a steady speed of $25\,\mathrm{m\,s^{-1}}$ along a horizontal section of track. The locomotive engine exerts a power of *P* kW. The total resistance to motion due to air resistance and internal friction on the locomotive can be modelled as a constant force. This force is three times the size of the similar force acting on the train. Find the tension in the coupling between the locomotive and the train in terms of *P*.

3 A car hits a lamp post head-on when travelling in a built-up area. There are skid marks of 5 metres on the road and it is found from impact damage that the car was travelling at about $9\,\mathrm{m\,s^{-1}}$ when it hit the lamp post. A skid test shows that in similar circumstances the car would have been expected to stop in 12 metres if it was originally travelling at $12\,\mathrm{m\,s^{-1}}$.

(a) At what speed was the car likely to have been travelling before it started to skid?

(b) Explain why you think that the car was not breaking the speed limit.

4   A body of mass $2\,\mathrm{kg}$ is projected up a rough inclined plane with an initial speed of $5\,\mathrm{m\,s^{-1}}$. It travels up the slope for some distance and then stops and starts to slide down. The angle of the slope is $10°$ to the horizontal and the coefficient of friction between the slope and the body is 0.1 (air resistance can be ignored).
Calculate:

(a) the work done in bringing the body to rest,

(b) the distance travelled up the slope,

(c) the speed of the body when it returns to its starting point.

5   Paulo is cycling to school. He comes to a straight section of road of length 200 metres sloping downwards and freewheels down it. The slope can be assumed to make a constant angle of $15°$ with the horizontal. His mass is $45\,\mathrm{kg}$ and that of his bicycle is $15\,\mathrm{kg}$.
Assuming Paulo starts from rest, find his speed at the bottom of the slope:

(a) if you assume that no resistive forces act,

(b) if you assume that a constant force of $110\,\mathrm{N}$ opposes his motion.

(c) Explain why the answers to (a) and (b) suggest that the model used in (b) is more realistic.

6   A man can push his car of mass $1250\,\mathrm{kg}$ with a force $F\,\mathrm{N}$ in the direction of motion such that $F = 250 - 5x$ where x metres is the distance pushed from rest along the road. Assume that the car is initially at rest, no resistance forces act and the man pushes the car for a distance of 50 metres.
Find the speed of the car if the road

(a) is horizontal,

(b) is sloping upwards with a constant angle of $\sin^{-1} 0.005$.

7   A car of mass 1.2 tonnes starting from rest experiences a resultant force $F\,\mathrm{N}$. During the first 50 metres of the journey, F can be modelled as $5000 - 3x^2$ where x metres is the distance of the car from its starting point. Find the work done by the force during the first 50 metres of the journey and hence find the speed of the car when $x = 50$.

*8   A body of mass $10\,\mathrm{kg}$ is moving under the action of a force of F newtons. The velocity of the body, $\mathbf{v}\,\mathrm{m\,s^{-1}}$, at time t seconds is given by $\mathbf{v} = (2t + 3)\mathbf{i} + (2 - t^2)\mathbf{j}$ for $0 \le t \le 3$.

(a) Find **F** in terms of t.

(b) Using the fact that $\mathbf{v} = \dfrac{d\mathbf{r}}{dt}$, calculate the work done by the force during the time interval $0 \le t \le 1$.

*9 A lift cage is pulled up and down a shaft by an inextensible cable. The mass of the lift and its occupants must not exceed 3000 kg. A graph of velocity against time for a model of the upward motion of the fully loaded lift is given on the right. Using this model and taking $g = 10\,\mathrm{m\,s}^{-2}$,

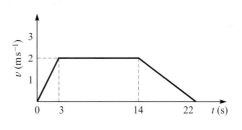

(a) find the power generated by the engine during the time when the lift has constant velocity,

(b) determine the maximum power generated during the lift's ascent,

(c) find the power generated at time $t = 18$.

10 A cyclist, starting from rest, travels along a straight level road. The cycle and cyclist have a combined mass of 80 kg and experience a resultant force of F newtons. During the first 10 metres of the motion, F is related to the distance travelled, x metres, by the relationship $F = 200 - x^2$.

(a) Calculate the work done by the resultant force during the first 9 metres of the motion.

(b) Find the speed of the cyclist after travelling 9 metres.

(c) The cyclist then stops pedalling, puts his brakes on and is brought to rest by a resultant force of 100 newtons. Find the distance travelled from the time he starts to brake until he comes to rest.

11[†] A bungee jumper of mass 60 kg and height 1.8 metres steps off a bridge 80 metres above a river. She has an elastic string, of length L metres and modulus of elasticity 600 N, attached to her ankles. The jumper should just avoid making contact with the water. Model the jumper as a light rod of length 1.8 metres with a mass of 60 kg attached to its midpoint.

(a) Find the length of the string that should be attached to her.

(b) Find her speed when the top of her head is 10 metres above the river.

12[†] A particle of mass 3 kg is attached to one end of a light elastic string of natural length 0.8 metres. The other end of the string is attached to a fixed point O. When the system hangs in equilibrium, the particle is 1 metre below O. The particle is raised to a point 0.8 metres above O and then released from rest.

(a) Show that the modulus of elasticity is 117.6 N.
(b) Find the speed of the particle, u m s^{-1}, as it passes O.
(c) How far below O is the particle when it once again has speed u m s^{-1}.

13[†] An aeroplane of mass 4000 kg lands on the flight deck of an aircraft carrier. Its wheels first touch the deck when it has a speed of 45 m s^{-1}. As the wheels touch down the plane hooks onto the end of an unstretched elastic rope of stiffness 3000 N m^{-1}. The rope immediately begins to stretch. When the extension of the rope is 40 metres, it is released by the plane which then uses its own braking system to bring itself to a complete stop in a further 20 metres. The braking force once the rope is released can be assumed to be constant.

(a) Find the speed of the aircraft when it is released by the rope.
(b) Find the magnitude of the constant braking force.

14[†] A climber is on a rock face. His partner above him has clipped one end of a rope, of natural length 10 metres and stiffness 5000 N m^{-1}, to a piton in the rock. The other end is clipped to the climber's harness. The vertical distance between the piton and the harness clip is 5 metres. The climber, of mass 50 kg, is at rest when he slips and falls.

(a) Find the speed of the climber when the rope first becomes taut.
(b) The climber falls until he is momentarily bought to rest by the rope. The extension of the rope is then x metres.
   (i) Show that $50x^2 - 9.8x - 49 = 0$
   (ii) Hence find the value of x.
(c) Explain why in real life the climber will not immediately bounce back to the point at which he slipped.

Revision

1 A football of mass 0.5 kg is kicked from rest on horizontal ground. It leaves the ground with a speed of 12 m s^{-1} at an angle of 45° above the ground. Calculate the total energy of the ball at any point on its path assuming air resistance can be ignored. Hence find the maximum height above the ground reached by the ball.

2 A boy skims a stone of mass 200 grams across a frozen horizontal lake. The initial speed of the stone is 15 m s^{-1} and it travels for a distance of 50 metres before stopping. The resistive force F acting against the motion of the stone can be assumed to be constant.

(a) Find the work done in stopping the stone.
(b) Find F.

3 A swimmer slides from rest down a waterchute of length 120 metres to enter a pool at a speed of 4 m s^{-1}. The swimmer enters the pool

10 metres vertically below her starting point. A resistive force of 35 N opposes the motion of the swimmer throughout her slide down the chute. Find the mass of the swimmer.

4 A car of mass 600 kg is travelling along a straight horizontal road at a speed of $30\,\mathrm{m\,s^{-1}}$ when its brakes are applied. Find:

(a) the kinetic energy of the car just before its brakes are applied,

(b) the constant force applied to the car if it is brought to rest in 20 metres.

5 A cyclist freewheels down a hill. His speed at the top is $7\,\mathrm{m\,s^{-1}}$ and when he reaches the bottom of the hill he is moving with speed $18\,\mathrm{m\,s^{-1}}$. Assuming that there are no resistance forces acting throughout the cyclist's journey, find the height that he has lost.

6 A child is wheeling a supermarket trolley along at a speed of $1\,\mathrm{m\,s^{-1}}$. When the trolley is at the top of the ramp to the underground car park, the child lets go and the trolley travels down the slope on its own. The trolley and its contents have mass 40 kg and the slope makes an angle of $\sin^{-1} 0.15$ with the horizontal. When the trolley has travelled 16 metres down the slope it has a speed of $6\,\mathrm{m\,s^{-1}}$.

(a) Find the resistive force that opposes the trolley's motion, assuming that it is constant throughout.

(b) A woman tries to stop it at this point before it runs into the cars. What work must she do to bring it to a standstill?

7 A lorry of mass 40 tonnes is travelling along a straight horizontal road. It meets with a constant resistive force equal to 1% of its weight. At a certain instant the power from the engine is 150 kW and the speed of the lorry is $25\,\mathrm{m\,s^{-1}}$.

(a) Find the acceleration of the lorry at this point.

(b) Calculate the maximum possible speed the lorry can attain with this power output if the resistive forces remain unchanged.

8 A car of mass 650 kg is travelling on a straight road which is inclined to the horizontal at $5°$. At a certain point P on the road, the car's speed is $15\,\mathrm{m\,s^{-1}}$. The point Q is 400 m down the hill from P, and at Q the car's speed is $35\,\mathrm{m\,s^{-1}}$.

(i) Assume that the car's engine produces a constant driving force on the car as it moves down the hill from P to Q, and that any resistances to the car's motion can be neglected. By considering the change in energy of the car, or otherwise, calculate the magnitude of the driving force of the car's engine.

(ii) Assume instead that resistance to the car's motion between P and Q may be represented by a constant force of magnitude 900 N. Given that the acceleration of the car at Q is zero, show that the power of the car's engine at this instant is approximately 12.1 W.

(iii) Given that the power of the car's engine is the same when the car is at P as it is when the car is at Q, calculate the car's acceleration at P.

[OCR]

9 A car of mass 1.5 tonnes starts from rest on a horizontal road. The resultant forward force, F, is initially 1500 newtons but this falls in proportion to the distance travelled, x metres, so that after 150 metres its value is zero. It then remains at zero for the rest of the motion.

(a) Find the force in terms of x for $0 \le x \le 150$.

(b) Find the work done by the resultant force during the first **100** metres.

10[†] A light elastic string of natural length 0.75 m is fixed at one end and to the other is attached a mass of 0.80 kg. When the mass hangs in equilibrium the string stretches by 20 cm. The mass is lifted so that it is at the fixed point and then released from rest. Find the distance below the fixed point that the mass first comes to rest.

11[†] A light elastic string of natural length 0.25 m is stretched by 4 cm when a mass of 150 grams is attached to one end and hung freely with the other end of the string fixed. The mass is pulled directly below its equilibrium position by 2 cm and held in this position. The mass is then released.

(a) Show using energy considerations that the mass is next instantaneously at rest when the string has an extension of 2 cm.

(b) If on another occasion the mass is pulled 6 cm below the equilibrium position, find the height through which the mass rises before coming instantaneously to rest.

12[†] A shopkeeper uses light elastic string to hang three toys of masses 100 grams, 200 grams and 400 grams, all at a distance of 50 centimetres below a metal bar as shown in the diagram. The 100 gram toy is attached to a 40 centimetre length of the (unstretched) string.

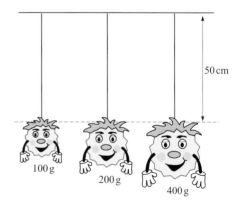

(a) Find the lengths of string used to support the 200 gram and 400 gram toys.

(b) Find the elastic potential energy in each string.

(c) All three toys are pulled down a further 15 cm and then released. Which toy will rise the furthest, and how far from the metal bar will it be at its highest point?

13[†] A restaurant keeps dinner plates warm by storing them in a heated dispenser unit. The unit consists of a circular platform contained in a vertical circular cylinder and supported by three identical springs. The unit is surrounded by a horizontal surface, used as a serving area, as shown in the diagram below. When dinner plates are stacked on the platform, the springs are compressed and the platform and plates descend into the cylinder. There is no friction between the platform and the cylinder and at all times the platform is horizontal.
The springs obey Hooke's law under compression and each of them is of natural length 0.8 m. The mass of the platform is 3 kg.
It may be assumed that $g = 10 \, \mathrm{m \, s^{-2}}$.

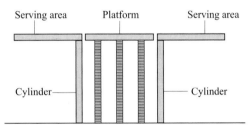

(a) When 16 dinner plates, each of mass 0.75 kg, are stacked on the platform and the system is in equilibrium, the compression of the springs is 0.2 m.
  (i) Show that the modulus of each spring is 200 N.
  (ii) Calculate the elastic potential energy of each of the compressed springs.
(b) A waiter gently places 4 more plates on top of the 16 plates and then releases them. Calculate the distance that the platform descends before coming momentarily to rest.
(c) State one modelling assumption, other than those given in the question, that you have used in your calculation in part (b).
(d) The unit is designed so that when a stack of plates is in equilibrium on the platform the topmost plate is always level with the serving area. Each plate added to a stack increases the height of the stack by 1 cm. Before the waiter added 4 plates to the stack of 16, the topmost plate was level with the serving area. Confirm that when the stack of 20 plates is in equilibrium, the topmost plate will again be level with the serving area.
[NEAB]

Circular motion with variable speed

Motion under gravity restricted to a vertical circle; motion under gravity not restricted to a circular path

Take the acceleration due to gravity to be $g\,\mathrm{m\,s}^{-2}$ where $g = 9.8$. Give answers to three significant figures unless otherwise stated.

Motion in a circle with variable speed

The velocity of a particle travelling on a circular path with varying speed is changing both in magnitude and direction.

Motion in a vertical circle under gravity

If the particle is moving in a vertical circle under gravity, for example on a smooth circular wire, on a light inextensible string or at the end of a light rod, then the total mechanical energy of the system remains constant.

Motion restricted to a vertical circular path

The particle will complete the circle if its speed at the highest point is greater than zero.

Motion not restricted to a vertical circular path

If a particle P is free to rotate in a vertical circle at one end of a light string OP fixed at O, then P will:
   (a) oscillate below the level of O,
   (b) complete the circle if the string never becomes slack, or
   (c) cease to travel in a circle at some point above the level of O and travel as a projectile until the string becomes taut again.

Basic

1   A bead slides on a smooth circular wire of radius 0.5 metres. The wire is fixed in a vertical plane. The speed of the bead at the top of the circle is $2\,\mathrm{m\,s}^{-1}$.

(a) Find the bead's angular speed at the lowest
     point of the wire.

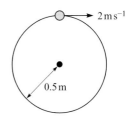

(b) The bead has a mass of 30 grams.
     (i)   Explain why the resultant force acting on
           the bead at the lowest point of the wire
           acts towards the centre of the wire.
     (ii) Find the magnitude of this force.

2 A particle moves under gravity on a smooth vertical circular path, of
   radius 1.5 metres, with a speed of $8 \, \mathrm{m \, s^{-1}}$ at the bottom of the circle.

   (a) Find the velocity of the particle at the top of the circle.
   (b) Find the angle between the line joining the particle to the centre of
        the circle and the vertical when the speed of the particle is $5 \, \mathrm{m \, s^{-1}}$.

3 A bead travelling round a smooth circular wire in a vertical circle has a
   minimum speed of $2.4 \, \mathrm{m \, s^{-1}}$ and a maximum speed of $4.2 \, \mathrm{m \, s^{-1}}$.
   Find the radius of the circle.

*4 A bead is free to travel round a smooth circular wire
   of radius r metres. The wire is fixed in a vertical
   plane. The particle is projected from the lowest point
   on the wire with a speed $v \, \mathrm{m \, s^{-1}}$. Find the minimum
   value of v if the particle is to describe a complete
   circle.

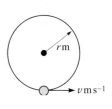

5 A particle, hanging by a light inextensible string d metres
   long, is free to move in a vertical circle. It is held so the
   string makes an angle of 0.8 rad with the vertical, as
   shown, and then released. The speed of the particle at the
   lowest point of its swing is $0.5 \, \mathrm{m \, s^{-1}}$.
   Find the length of the string.

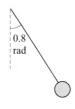

6 A small boy is sitting on a swing. The ropes are
   2 metres long. A girl helps him to swing by pulling
   the seat towards her until the ropes make an angle
   of 25° to the vertical and then letting go.

   (a) Modelling the motion of the boy as that of a
        particle on the end of a 2 metre light
        inextensible string, calculate the maximum speed
        attained by the boy.
   (b) The centre of mass of the boy is actually above
        the seat of the swing. Does this mean that the
        actual maximum speed of the boy is likely to be
        greater or less than that given above? Explain
        your answer.

7 A bead is fixed to the end of a wooden rod which is free to rotatate about one end in a vertical plane. The bead can be modelled as a particle and the wooden rod as being light, inextensible and of length d metres. The rod is held so that it is horizontal and the bead is projected downwards with a speed of $v\,\mathrm{m\,s^{-1}}$. Find v in terms of d if the rod rotates through a complete circle.

8 The track of a roller-coaster ride has one section where the train makes a complete loop with the passengers appearing to hang upside down in their harnesses. This part of the ride can be modelled as a complete circle of radius 10 metres. At the start of the ride the train is winched up to a height of 35 metres above that of the base of the circle and is released to run down a sloping track before it enters the beginning of the loop. Assuming that the train can be modelled as a particle on a smooth wire find:

  (a) the maximum speed of the train as it passes through the loop,
  (b) the minimum speed of the train as it passes through the loop.
  (c) Discuss what effect the modelling assumptions that have been made may have on the answers to (a) and (b).

Intermediate

1 A bead is fixed to the end of a wooden rod which is free to rotate in a vertical plane about the other end. The bead can be modelled as a particle and the wooden rod as a light inextensible rod of length 0.2 metres. The rod is held so that it is vertical with the bead at the top and then it is slightly disturbed from rest. Find the angle between the rod and the upward vertical when the bead has achieved half its maximum speed. Give your answer in radians.

2 A particle of mass 100 grams is suspended from a light inextensible string of length 0.1 metres. It is projected horizontally with a speed of $1.2\,\mathrm{m\,s^{-1}}$.

  (a) Find the maximum angle between the string and the vertical. Give your answer in radians.
  (b) Find the minimum tension in the string.

3 A bead is free to move in a vertical plane on the inside surface of a smooth hollow cylinder of radius r metres whose axis is horizontal. The bead can be modelled as a particle. Find, in terms of r:

  (a) the maximum speed the bead can have at the lowest point in its path if it is not to rise higher than the axis of the cylinder,
  (b) the minimum speed the bead can have at the lowest point of its path if it is to travel in complete circles.

4 A heavy particle is hanging on one end P of a light inextensible string OP of length r metres which is fixed at O. The particle is projected horizontally with velocity $v\,\mathrm{m\,s}^{-1}$ from P so that it reaches a point Q, d metres from its point of projection (where $d < r$). Angle $QPO = \alpha$.

(a) Show that $d = 2r \cos \alpha$.
(b) Hence or otherwise show that $v = d\sqrt{g/r}$.

5 A particle of mass 1.4 kg is suspended from the end of a light inextensible string. It is projected so that it just completes a series of vertical circles. Find the maximum tension in the string during the motion.

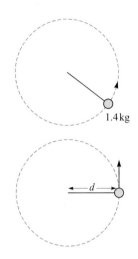

1.4 kg

6 A particle of mass m kg is fixed to the end of a light inextensible string of length d metres. Initially the string is horizontal. Then the particle is projected upwards so that the particle just travels in complete circles.
Show that the tension in the string when the string is next horizontal is $3mg$.

*7 A smooth hollow cylinder of radius a metres, where $a > 1$, is fixed with its axis horizontal. A ball of mass m, lying at the lowest point of the inner surface, is given a horizontal speed of $9a\,\mathrm{m\,s}^{-1}$ so that it travels in a vertical circle in a plane at right angles to the axis of the cylinder.

(a) Assuming the ball can be modelled as a particle, find, in the ensuing motion, the minimum normal reaction between the ball and the cylinder in terms of m, g and a.
(b) Give two reasons why the assumption that the ball is a particle will lead to an overestimate of this reaction.

Advanced

1 A particle of mass 2 kg is fixed to the end of a light inextensible string of length 1 metre. The particle is held so that the string is horizontal and then it is projected downward with speed $u\,\mathrm{m\,s}^{-1}$ so that it just travels in a complete vertical circle.

(a) Find the value of u.
(b) Find the tension in the string when it makes an angle of θ to the downwards vertical, in terms of g and θ.

2 The path of a skateboarder on a track can be modelled as an arc *BC* of a circle with straight-line extensions *AB* and *CD* either side as shown.

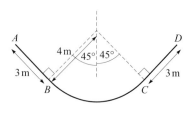

AB and *CD* are of length 3 metres and make an angle of 45° with the vertical. *BC* is in the form of a quadrant of a circle of radius 4 metres. The line joining *B* and *C* is horizontal. The skateboarder starts from rest at *A*.

(a) Modelling the skateboarder as a particle of mass 68 kg sliding on a smooth surface, find the normal reaction between the skateboarder and the track between *A* and *B* in surd form.

(b) Explain why this reaction changes at *B*.

(c) Calculate the maximum reaction between the skateboarder and the track to three significant figures.

3 A smooth hemispherical bowl with centre *O* and internal radius 25 cm is fixed at an angle of 1 rad to the horizontal as shown in the diagram. The bowl rests on a horizontal table. A particle of mass 0.3 kg is released from rest from a point on the inside surface of the bowl that is level with *O*.

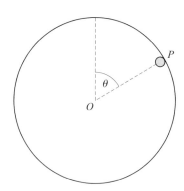

(a) Find the speed of the particle when it leaves the surface of the bowl.

(b) Find the speed of the particle when it hits the table.

(c) Find the magnitude of the resultant force on the particle:
　　(i) just before it leaves the bowl,
　　(ii) just after it leaves the bowl.

4 A particle is free to run smoothly on the inside of a sphere of radius *a* metres. The particle is projected from the lowest point of the sphere with a speed of u m s^{-1} where $2ga < u^2 < 3ga$.

The particle leaves the surface of the sphere at a point *P* where *OP* makes an angle θ with the upward vertical through *O*, the centre of the sphere.

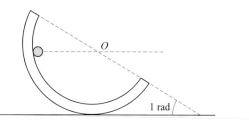

Show that $\cos \theta = (u^2 - 2ga)/3ga$.

*5 A block of mass 0.42 kg is suspended by a light inextensible string of
length d metres from a point O. The block is hanging freely. A pellet of
mass 0.02 kg travelling horizontally at a speed of $55\,\mathrm{m\,s^{-1}}$ strikes the
wooden block and becomes embedded in it. The speed of the pellet and
the block immediately after the impact is $u\,\mathrm{m\,s^{-1}}$. Assume that both the
block and pellet can be modelled as particles.

(a) Calculate u.
(b) Find the minimum value of d if the block and pellet are to remain
below O in the following motion.
(c) Show that for the pellet and block to make complete circles d must
be less than 0.128 to three significant figures.

6 A block of mass 0.6 kg is suspended from a light inextensible string of
length 1.2 metres from a fixed point O.
The string is initially vertical and the block, which can be modelled as a
particle, is given a horizontal velocity of $6\sqrt{2}\ \mathrm{m\ s^{-1}}$.

(a) Show that the block will move in a complete vertical circle.
(b) Find the tension in the string when it is horizontal.

7 A motor cyclist rides over a humpback bridge.
The bike and rider can be modelled as a
particle travelling at constant speed throughout
his motion over the bridge. His path can be
modelled as the arc of a circle of radius
6 metres which subtends an angle of $60°$ at the
centre of the circle.
Find the maximum speed of the rider if he is
not to lose contact with the surface of the
bridge.

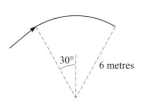

8 A skier starting from rest travels
down a snow slope of angle 0.7 rad
to the horizontal for 25 metres before
entering a horizontal stretch.
Her path then starts to descend
again. This second slope can be
modelled as an arc of a circle of
radius r metres. The skier can be
modelled as a particle travelling on a
smooth surface.
Find r if the skier loses contact with
the ground when the angle between
the tangent to the slope and the
horizontal is 0.5 rad.

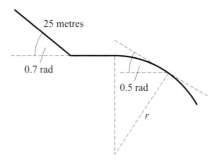

9 The diagram shows the cross-
section of a prism. Its surface is
horizontal between P and Q and in
the form of a quadrant of a circle,
centre O and of radius 1 metre
between Q and R. PQ is of length
2 metres.

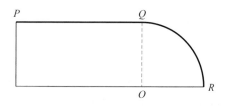

Two identical particles, A and B, are joined together by a light
inextensible string of length 2 metres. They are placed on the horizontal
surface so particle A is at P and particle B is at Q. Particle B is displaced
slightly so it starts to slip down towards R.
Find the angle between OB and the vertical when B loses contact with
the surface.

Revision

1 A particle moves under gravity on a vertical circular path, of radius
0.8 metres, with a speed of $6\,\mathrm{m\,s}^{-1}$ at the bottom of the circle.

(a) Find the velocity of the particle at the top of the circle.
(b) Find the angle in radians between the line joining the particle to the
centre of the circle and the vertical when the speed of the particle is
$3\,\mathrm{m\,s}^{-1}$.

2 A particle of mass 1 gram hanging by a light inextensible
string 0.8 metres long is free to swing through an arc of a
vertical circle like a pendulum. The particle is held so that
the string makes an angle of 0.7 radians with the vertical
as shown and then it is released. Find the speed of the
particle:

(a) at the lowest point of its swing,
(b) when the string makes an angle of 0.5 radians with the vertical.

3 A bead travelling round a smooth circular wire in a vertical circle has a
minimum speed of $6\,\mathrm{m\,s}^{-1}$. The radius of the circle is 2.5 metres. Find the
maximum speed of the bead.

4 A bead is free to travel round a smooth circular wire of radius r metres.
The wire is fixed in a vertical plane. The bead travels so that its speed
$v\,\mathrm{m\,s}^{-1}$ at the lowest part of the path is twice its speed at the highest
point on its path. Find r in terms of v and g.

5 A child is hanging at rest on the end of a rope, directly under the point
of suspension of the rope. He is pushed horizontally so that he has an
initial velocity of $3\,\mathrm{m\,s}^{-1}$. His motion can be modelled as that of a
particle on the end of a light inextensible string of radius r metres. He
reaches a point d metres from his point of projection (where $d < r$).
Show that $d = 3\sqrt{(r/g)}$.

6 A bead of mass of m grams slides on a smooth circular wire of radius
a metres. The wire is fixed in a vertical plane and the bead is set in
motion so that it describes vertical circles, with its speed at the top of the
circle being $u\,\mathrm{m\,s^{-1}}$.

(a) State the two positions of the bead where the resultant force acting
on the bead acts towards the centre of the wire.

(b) Find the two possible values of the difference between the normal
reactions at these two points. Explain clearly the conditions under
which each occurs.

7 A particle of mass 150 grams is suspended from a light inextensible string
of length 0.7 metres. When hanging at rest directly below its point of
suspension it is projected horizontally with a speed of $3\,\mathrm{m\,s^{-1}}$.

(a) Find the maximum angle between the string and the vertical (give
your answer in radians).

(b) Find the minimum tension in the string.

8 The diagram shows the cross-section
of a smooth surface that is in the
form of a hemisphere, centre O and
radius 1.4 metres. A particle is placed
on the surface at point P where the
angle between OP and the vertical is
0.5 radians. The particle starts to
slide and loses contact with the
surface at point Q. Find the length of
the arc PQ.

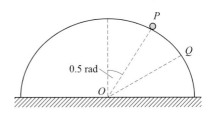

9 A girl is experimenting with a small
ball-bearing of mass m and a smooth
hemispherical bowl of radius a. She
places the bowl upside down
with its rim firmly held on a
horizontal table and holds the
ball-bearing at the highest
point, A, of the outer surface
of the bowl. She then projects
the ball-bearing with a small
horizontal speed u as shown
in the diagram. You may
assume that while it is in
contact with the bowl the
ball-bearing slides down the
surface without rolling.

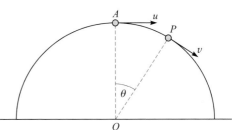

A short time after projection, the ball-bearing is still in contact with the bowl at point P. The speed at P is denoted by v. The point O is at the centre of the circular rim of the bowl and the angle AOP is denoted by θ.

(i) Draw a diagram showing the forces acting on the ball-bearing at P. Explain briefly why mechanical energy is conserved.

(ii) Find an expression for v^2 in terms of u, g, a and θ.

(iii) Show that the reaction R of the bowl on the ball-bearing is given by
$$R = mg(3\cos\theta - 2) - mu^2/a.$$
Verify that this equation is dimensionally correct.

The girl tries different initial speeds and finds that the ball-bearing always leaves the bowl before θ reaches some fixed value α.

(iv) Find the least value of α for which this is true.
[MEI]

*10 A light inextensible rope of length 5 metres is attached at one end O to the ceiling of a gymnasium. A boy of mass 30 kg holds the free end of the rope in one hand and with his other hand he grips a bar fixed to the wall of the gymnasium. The bar is at a height of

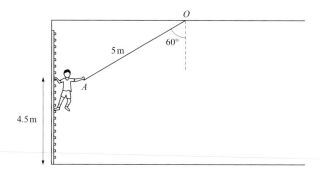

4.5 metres above the floor. The rope is taut and makes an angle of $60°$ with the vertical, as shown in the diagram. It may be assumed that the boy can be modelled as a particle.

(a) The boy releases his hold on the bar and swings down on the end A of the rope.

(i) Show that the speed, $v\,\mathrm{m\,s^{-1}}$, of the boy when the rope makes an angle θ with the downward vertical is given by

$$v^2 = 49(2\cos\theta - 1)$$

(ii) Find the value of v when $\theta = 0°$.

(b) At the instant when $\theta = 0°$, the boy releases the rope and moves under the force of gravity only. Determine his total horizontal distance from the wall when he reaches the floor.

(c) In this question it has been assumed that the boy can be modelled as a particle. Comment on this assumption with reference to your answer to part (b). Do not refer to air resistance.
[NEAB]

Collisions

Elastic and inelastic collisions in one and two dimensions; Newton's law of restitution; oblique impact of a smooth sphere on a smooth plane and of two smooth spheres[†]

Take the acceleration due to gravity to be $g\,\mathrm{m\,s^{-2}}$ where $g = 9.8$.
Give answers to three significant figures unless otherwise stated.

The **principle of conservation of linear momentum** states that, if two bodies collide, their total momentum remains constant.

Impact between two bodies which coalesce is said to be **inelastic**.
Impact between two bodies which separate after the collision is said to be **elastic**.

Newton's law of restitution states that if two objects are in direct elastic impact then the ratio of their speed of separation to their speed of approach is constant. This can be written in the form

$$\frac{\text{separation speed}}{\text{approach speed}} = e$$

where e is called the **coefficient of restitution**.

If $e = 1$ then the collision is said to be perfectly elastic. Mechanical energy is conserved.

If $1 > e > 0$ then the collision is elastic but mechanical energy is not conserved.

If $e = 0$ then the collision is inelastic. Mechanical energy is not conserved.

If a smooth sphere collides **obliquely** with a smooth plane then the component of velocity of the sphere parallel to the plane is unchanged by the impact, while the component of velocity of the sphere normal to the plane satisfies Newton's law of restitution.

> If two smooth spheres collide **obliquely** then the components of velocity of the spheres at right angles to their line of centres are unchanged, while their components of velocity along the line of centres satisfy Newton's law of restitution.

Basic

*1 A smooth ball travels at a constant speed of $4\,\mathrm{m\,s^{-1}}$ across a smooth horizontal table and collides with an identical ball that is stationary. The coefficient of restitution between the balls can be assumed to be 0.8. Find the speed of each ball immediately after the collision.

2 Two smooth balls each of mass 1 kg are approaching each other along a straight line. Each ball has a speed of $5\,\mathrm{m\,s^{-1}}$. The coefficient of restitution between the balls is 0.75.

(a) Find the speed of each ball immediately after the collision.
(b) Find the impulse that each ball receives due to the collision.

3 A curling stone of mass 5 kg is projected over the ice. The stone strikes the small stationary marker with a speed of $4\,\mathrm{m\,s^{-1}}$. The mass of the marker is 0.3 kg and their line of centres lies along the line of motion of the stone. The impact can be assumed to be perfectly elastic.
Calculate the speed immediately after impact of:

(a) the stone,
(b) the marker.

4 A particle A of mass m kg is moving in a straight line with constant speed $u\,\mathrm{m\,s^{-1}}$. A second particle B of mass $2m$ kg is moving in an opposing direction to A with a speed of $ku\,\mathrm{m\,s^{-1}}$. Find the resulting speeds of A and B after they collide in terms of k and u if:

(a) the collision is perfectly inelastic,
(b) the collision is perfectly elastic.

5 Two balls, A of mass 2 kg and B of mass 3 kg, travel with speeds $7\,\mathrm{m\,s^{-1}}$ and $6\,\mathrm{m\,s^{-1}}$ respectively over a smooth horizontal surface. Their direction of motion is along the line of centres of the balls. The coefficient of restitution between the two balls is 0.7.
Find their velocities after they collide if:

(a) the balls are travelling towards each other,
(b) both balls are travelling in the same direction.

6 A smooth ball of mass $2m$ travels at a speed u along a horizontal smooth surface. It collides with another smooth ball of mass $3m$ that is stationary. The coefficient of restitution between the balls is e.

   (a) Find in terms of u and e the speed of each ball immediately after the collision.

   (b) Find in terms of m, u and e the energy lost due to the collision.

7 Two pucks P and Q of masses 60 grams and 80 grams are travelling directly towards each other with speeds of $7\,\mathrm{m\,s^{-1}}$ and $10\,\mathrm{m\,s^{-1}}$ respectively. The coefficient of restitution between the two pucks is 0.4. Calculate the speeds of the two pucks immediately after the impact.

*8 Two bumper cars, A and B, whose masses, including their drivers, are 200 kg and 300 kg respectively, are moving towards each other. Car A is travelling with velocity $4\mathbf{i} + 3\mathbf{j}\,\mathrm{m\,s^{-1}}$ and car B with velocity $-3\mathbf{i} - 4\mathbf{i}\,\mathrm{m\,s^{-1}}$. They strike each other a glancing blow. After the collision A travels off with velocity $2\mathbf{i} + \mathbf{j}\,\mathrm{m\,s^{-1}}$. Find the velocity of car B.

9 A ball of mass 0.2 kg falls from rest at a height of 1 metre, bounces on the floor and rises to a maximum height of 0.6 metres after the bounce.

   (a) Find the coefficient of restitution between the ball and the floor.

   (b) Find the impulse that the ball receives from the floor.

10 A ball of mass 0.5 kg is dropped from rest at a height of 1 metre above a horizontal surface. The ball bounces on the surface and then rises to a height of 0.75 m before coming instantaneously to rest.

   (a) Find the coefficient of restitution between the ball and the surface.

   (b) Find the energy lost by the ball at the bounce.

11 A ball is dropped from rest at a height of h metres above the floor. Given that the coefficient of restitution between the ball and floor is e, find, in terms of h and e, the height to which the ball will rise before coming instantaneously to rest after bouncing on the floor.

Intermediate

1 Two particles, A and B, of equal mass, travel towards each other with speeds of u and $2u$. After collision, A changes direction and they both travel in the same direction with speeds of $5\,\mathrm{m\,s^{-1}}$ and $4\,\mathrm{m\,s^{-1}}$ respectively. Find the value of u and the coefficient of restitution between the two particles.

2 A particle A of mass m is moving with speed $4u$ in a straight line on a smooth horizontal table. It collides with another particle B of mass km which is moving in the same straight line on the table with speed u and in the opposite direction to A. In the collision the particles form a single particle which then moves with a speed $0.25u$ in the original direction of A's motion.

(a) Find the value of k.

(b) Find the work done during the collision in terms of m and u.

*3 A small smooth ball of mass 0.25 kg moves across a horizontal smooth surface with a constant speed of $10\,\mathrm{m\,s^{-1}}$ until it hits a vertical wall. After the collision the ball has a speed of $8\,\mathrm{m\,s^{-1}}$ in the opposite direction to its initial direction of travel.

(a) Find the coefficient of restitution between the ball and the wall.

(b) Find the impulse that is exerted by the wall on the ball.

(c) Find the energy lost by the ball due to the collision.

4 Three particles A, B and C lie in a straight line. They have masses m, $2m$ and $3m$ respectively and are travelling with velocities $8u$, $4u$ and $2u$ along AC.

Describe their motion:

(a) if all the collisions are inelastic,

(b) if their collisions are perfectly elastic,

(c) if the coefficient of restitution between each of the particles is 0.5.

5 A particle A of mass $3m$ is moving in a straight line with speed u. A second particle of mass $2m$ is moving in the same straight line with speed v. The particles coalesce on impact. The combined particle moves in the same direction as A but with speed $0.5u$. Find v in terms of u and use your answer to interpret the motion of the masses.

6 A ball is dropped from rest at a height of 0.8 metres onto a smooth horizontal surface. The coefficient of restitution between the ball and the surface is 0.85.

(a) What height will the ball reach on its first bounce?

(b) How many bounces will it make before the speed of impact is less than half the original speed of impact?

7 Two ice skaters, John and Julie, of equal mass, fall over on the ice and slide along so that their paths intersect. Their velocities just before impact are $2\mathbf{i} + 4\mathbf{j}\,\mathrm{m\,s^{-1}}$ and $3\mathbf{i} - 2\mathbf{j}\,\mathrm{m\,s^{-1}}$ respectively. They cling together as they collide.

(a) Find their velocity immediately after the impact.

(b) Find the ratio of their total kinetic energy just before the collision to that just after the collision.

8 Two particles A and B of masses 4 grams and 6 grams respectively are travelling along the same line when they collide. Their velocities after the collision are $5.2\,\mathrm{m\,s^{-1}}$ and $7.2\,\mathrm{m\,s^{-1}}$ respectively and the coefficient of restitution between the two particles is 0.5. Find their initial velocities.

9 A rock of mass $5m$ slides with speed of $8\,\mathrm{m\,s^{-1}}$ over a smooth sheet of ice. It collides with a stationary stone of mass m. After the collision, the stone moves off with a speed of $8\,\mathrm{m\,s^{-1}}$ in the original direction of motion of the rock.

(a) Find the velocity of the rock.
(b) Find e.

Advanced

1 Two balls of equal size but of masses $0.2\,\mathrm{kg}$ and $0.1\,\mathrm{kg}$ are at rest on a smooth pool table at B and A respectively. The line of centres of the two balls lies along AB and is also at right angles to the smooth cushion at the edge of the table. A is nearest to the cushion.

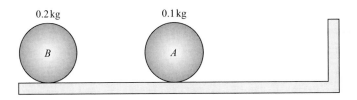

The coefficient of restitution between the two balls and the balls and the cushion is 0.9. The ball at B is projected towards A with a speed of $12\,\mathrm{m\,s^{-1}}$. Describe the subsequent motion of the balls until both balls stop colliding either with each other or with the cushion.

*2† A smooth ball of mass $0.2\,\mathrm{kg}$ is moving across a smooth horizontal surface with a constant speed of $10\,\mathrm{m\,s^{-1}}$ when it collides with a wall. When the ball hits the wall it is moving in a direction that makes an angle of $30°$ with the wall as shown. The coefficient of restitution between the ball and the wall is 0.6.
After the collision the ball moves with speed $v\,\mathrm{m\,s^{-1}}$ in a direction that makes an angle θ with the wall.
Find v and θ (given in degrees).

$10\,\mathrm{m\,s^{-1}}$ $30°$

Before collision

$v\,\mathrm{m\,s^{-1}}$ θ

After collision

3 A large box of mass $1.5\,\mathrm{kg}$ rests on a smooth horizontal surface. A ball hits the box at right angles to the vertical side of the box and then rebounds. It is travelling horizontally with a speed of $7\,\mathrm{m\,s^{-1}}$ when it hits the box.

The ball is of mass 0.5 kg and the coefficient of restitution between the ball and the box is 0.7.

(a) Find the speed of the box after the ball hits it.
(b) The ball is thrown a second time against the box so that it strikes it at the same speed as before. Find the resulting speed of the box.

4 Two particles A and B are moving directly towards each other on a smooth horizontal surface.
A travels with speed $4u$ and B travels with speed $3u$. The masses of A and B are $2m$ and $3m$ respectively and the coefficient of restitution between them is 0.5. When A and B collide, their directions of motion are reversed and they begin to travel with speeds of v and w respectively.

(a) Find v and w in terms of u.

The particle A subsequently strikes a fixed vertical wall at right angles and rebounds from it with speed w.

(b) Find the coefficient of restitution between A and the wall.
(c) Find the magnitude of the impulse on A due to this second collision.

5 A smooth sphere P travels across a smooth horizontal surface with speed u. It collides with another smooth sphere Q which is at rest. They can be modelled as identical particles of mass m. The coefficient of restitution between the spheres is 0.8.

(a) Find in terms of u the speeds of P and Q after impact if the impact is direct.

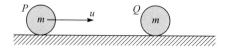

(b) The sphere Q then collides with a wall which is perpendicular to its direction of motion. The coefficient of restitution, e, between the wall and the sphere Q is such that Q now has the same speed as P. Find e.
(c) The diagram below shows a very simple model of the way the magnitude of the force F between the sphere and the wall varies during the time the sphere is in contact with the wall. The force acts for 0.001 seconds. Find the maximum value of the force in terms of m and u.

6† A smooth ball of mass 0.5 kg is travelling at $10\,\text{m}\,\text{s}^{-1}$ across a smooth horizontal surface when it collides with a vertical wall.
The ball is moving in a direction that makes an angle of $60°$ with the wall before the collision. After the collision the ball moves in a direction that makes an angle of $40°$ with the wall. Find:

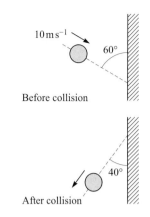

(a) the coefficient of restitution between the ball and the wall,
(b) the energy lost at the collision,
(c) the impulse the ball receives from the wall at the collision.

7 A pellet travelling horizontally at a speed of $150\,\text{m}\,\text{s}^{-1}$ strikes the centre of a wooden block which is initially at rest on a smooth horizontal surface. The mass of the pellet is 0.08 kg and the mass of the block is 4 kg. The pellet becomes embedded in the block and their final common speed is $V\,\text{m}\,\text{s}^{-1}$.
Calculate, correct to two decimal places:

(a) the value of V,
(b) the total work done on the block.

8 A bat is used to hit a ball of mass 0.15 kg. Just before impact the ball is travelling horizontally at speed $20\,\text{m}\,\text{s}^{-1}$. After impact the ball is travelling horizontally with speed $30\,\text{m}\,\text{s}^{-1}$ in the opposite direction.

(a) Find the magnitude of the impulse exerted on the ball.
(b) The force from the bat can be modelled as $F(t) = k \sin(100\pi t)$ where t is the time after the ball first makes contact with the bat. For the case where the bat can be considered to be in contact with the ball for 0.01 s, find k.

9 Two small spheres P and Q move directly towards each other on a smooth horizontal table with speeds $4u$ and $2u$ respectively. The mass of P is $2m$, the mass of Q is m and the coefficient of restitution between the spheres is e. After colliding, P and Q both move in the same direction with speeds v and w respectively.

(a) Find v and w in terms of e and u.
(b) The total kinetic energy of the spheres after the collision is k times their total kinetic energy before the collision. Show that
$k = (2e^2 + 1)/3$.
(c) Comment on the case when $k = 1$.

10[†] A ball is travelling horizontally at $10\,\mathrm{m\,s^{-1}}$ when it leaves a table 1 metre above a horizontal floor. The coefficient of restitution between the ball and the floor can be taken to be 0.8.

(a) Find the horizontal distance the ball has travelled from the edge of the table when it first bounces on the floor.

(b) Find the horizontal distance between the first and second bounces of the ball.

Revision

1 A smooth ball travels at a constant speed of $6\,\mathrm{m\,s^{-1}}$ across a smooth horizontal table and collides with an identical ball that is stationary. The coefficient of restitution between the balls can be assumed to be 0.5. Find the speed of each ball immediately after the collision.

2 Two smooth balls of masses 1 kg and 2 kg respectively are approaching each other along a straight line. Each ball has a speed of $8\,\mathrm{m\,s^{-1}}$. The coefficient of restitution between the balls is 0.9.

(a) Find the speed of each ball immediately after the collision.

(b) Find the impulse that each ball receives due to the collision.

3 Two balls A and B of masses 3 kg and 4 kg travel with speeds $8\,\mathrm{m\,s^{-1}}$ and $7\,\mathrm{m\,s^{-1}}$ respectively over a smooth horizontal surface. Their direction of motion is along the line of centres of the balls. The coefficient of restitution between A and B is 0.6.
Find their velocities after they collide if:

(a) A and B are travelling towards each other,

(b) both A and B are travelling along AB.

4 Two pucks P and Q of masses 70 grams and 55 grams are travelling towards each other with speeds of $8\,\mathrm{m\,s^{-1}}$ and $2\,\mathrm{m\,s^{-1}}$ respectively. The speeds of the two pucks immediately after the impact are $2.28\,\mathrm{m\,s^{-1}}$ and $5.28\,\mathrm{m\,s^{-1}}$. Both pucks are now travelling in the same direction and can be modelled as particles.

(a) Find the coefficient of restitution between the two pucks.

(b) Give one reason why the question stated that the pucks were to be modelled as particles.

5 Two bumper cars A and B, of masses 300 kg and 350 kg including their drivers, collide with each other. Just before the impact car A is travelling with velocity $2\mathbf{i} + 6\mathbf{j}\,\mathrm{m\,s^{-1}}$ and car B with velocity $-4\mathbf{i} - 4\mathbf{j}\,\mathrm{m\,s^{-1}}$. Immediately after the collision, car B travels off with velocity $-\mathbf{i} + 2\mathbf{j}$. Find the velocity of car A.

6 Two particles P and Q of equal masses are travelling along the same line when they collide. Their velocities after the collision are $2.2\,\mathrm{m\,s^{-1}}$ and $3.8\,\mathrm{m\,s^{-1}}$ respectively and the coefficient of restitution between the two particles is 0.4. Find their initial velocities.

*7 Two particles A and B are moving directly towards each other on a smooth horizontal surface.
A travels with speed $3u$, and B travels with speed $7u$. The masses of A and B are $3m$ and m respectively and the coefficient of restitution between them is 0.7. When A and B collide, their directions of motion are reversed and they begin to travel with speeds of v and w respectively.

(a) Find v and w in terms of u.

The particle A subsequently strikes a fixed vertical wall at right angles and rebounds from it with speed $\dfrac{w}{6}$.

(b) Find the coefficient of restitution between A and the wall.
(c) Find the magnitude of the impulse on A due to this second collision in terms of m and u.

8[†] A snooker ball A has mass $0.15\,\mathrm{kg}$. It moves over a horizontal snooker table and collides with the vertical side of the table which you may assume to be smooth. Take unit vectors $\mathbf{i}$ and $\mathbf{j}$ to lie in the plane of the table and to be normal to and in the direction of the side of the table respectively, as shown. Just before collision the ball is moving with velocity $5\mathbf{i} + 8\mathbf{j}\,\mathrm{m\,s^{-1}}$. The coefficient of restitution between the ball and the side of the table is 0.8. Find:

(a) the velocity of the ball just after collision,
(b) the impulse received by the ball at the collision,
(c) the energy lost by the ball as a result of the collision.

9 Two particles A and B, of masses 4 grams and 6 grams respectively, are travelling along the same line when they collide. Their velocities after the collision are $6\,\mathrm{m\,s^{-1}}$ and $8\,\mathrm{m\,s^{-1}}$ respectively and the coefficient of restitution between the two particles is 0.5. Find their initial velocities.

10[†] A ball travels towards a wall. The coefficient of restitution between the ball and the wall is 0.9.
If the ball hits the wall with speed $10\,\mathrm{m\,s^{-1}}$, find its speed of rebound:

(a) if the initial direction of the ball is at right angles to the wall,
(b) if the initial direction of the ball is at $45°$ to the wall.

11† Two smooth spheres A and B, of masses $0.16\,\text{kg}$ and $0.04\,\text{kg}$ respectively, are free to move on a smooth horizontal table. Initially A is at rest and B is moving with speed $10\,\text{m s}^{-1}$. The spheres collide and just before they do so the direction of motion of B makes an angle of $60°$ with the line of centres. After the impact B moves off at right angles to the line of centres as shown in the diagram.

(a) Show that the speed of A after the impact is $1.25\,\text{m s}^{-1}$.

(b) Find the coefficient of restitution between the two spheres.

(c) Find the speed of B.

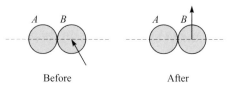

Before   After

12 A smooth puck of mass m is moving with speed $4u$ on a smooth horizontal surface when it collides directly with a smooth block of mass $4m$ which is at rest. After the collision the puck travels in the opposite direction to its initial motion. The coefficient of restitution between the puck and the block is e.

(a) Show that the speed of the block after the collision is $0.8(1+e)u$.

(b) Show that $e > 0.25$.

13 A particle P moving with speed u collides directly with an identical particle Q which is at rest. The coefficient of restitution between the particles is $\frac{1}{2}$. Find, in terms of u, the speeds of P and Q after the impact. [NEAB]

14 Small seed pods, each of mass $0.007\,\text{kg}$, are falling vertically at $2.2\,\text{m s}^{-1}$.

(i) One pod collides with a stationary, hovering fly of mass $0.004\,\text{kg}$ and sticks to it. Calculate the velocity of the fly immediately after the collision.

(ii) Another pod collides with a stationary, hovering fly, also of mass $0.004\,\text{kg}$. In this case the pod moves downwards with a speed of $1\,\text{m s}^{-1}$ immediately after the collision. Find the velocity of the fly immediately after the collision and the coefficient of restitution.

Another small seed pod is falling vertically at a speed of $1.5\,\text{m s}^{-1}$ when it bursts into two parts. One part, P, has a mass of $0.005\,\text{kg}$ and immediately after the pod bursts it has velocity $(2.4\mathbf{i} + 0.7\mathbf{j})\,\text{m s}^{-1}$, where $\mathbf{i}$ and $\mathbf{j}$ are unit vectors with $\mathbf{i}$ horizontal and $\mathbf{j}$ vertically downwards. The other part of the pod, Q, has a mass of $0.002\,\text{kg}$.

(iii) Explain briefly why the two parts of the pod must move in the same vertical plane immediately after the pod bursts.

(iv) Calculate the velocity of part Q immediately after the pod bursts, giving your answer as a vector in terms of $\mathbf{i}$ and $\mathbf{j}$.

[MEI]

12 | Moments, couples and frameworks

Moment of a force; resultant moment; equilibrium of non-concurrent forces; line of action of a resultant force; couples; equilibrium of rigid bodies; stresses and strains in light pin-jointed frameworks

Take the acceleration due to gravity to be $g\,\mathrm{m\,s^{-2}}$ where $g = 9.8$.
Give all answers to three significant figures unless otherwise stated.

> The moment of a force $\mathbf{F}$ about a pivot point O is given by the product of the magnitude of the force and the perpendicular distance between the force and the pivot point O.
>
> The units of a moment are newton metres ($\mathrm{N\,m}$).
>
> A body is in equilibrium when the vector sum of the forces acting on the body is zero and the sum of their moments about any axis is zero. If only three forces act on a body in equilibrium then they either pass through a point or are parallel.
>
> A system of two forces of equal magnitude but opposite direction is called a couple.
>
> Any system of coplanar forces acting on a rigid body can, in general, be replaced by a single force acting at an arbitrary point in the plane of the forces together with a couple. Either the force or the couple may be zero.
>
> To calculate the forces in the members of a light pin-jointed framework, the equilibrium of each joint must be considered as well as the equilibrium of the system as a whole.

Basic

1 In each of the situations (a) to (f) on the next page find the moment of the force $\mathbf{F}$ about the point O. State the direction of the moment.

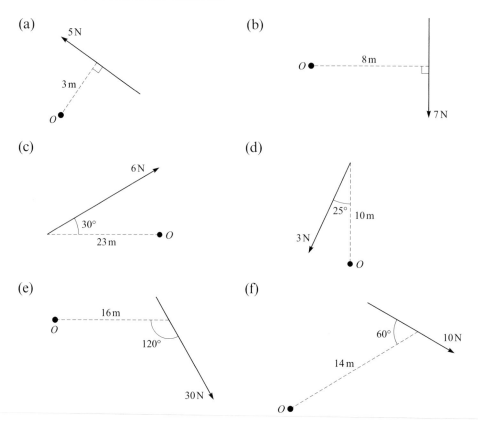

2 For each of the coplanar systems of forces shown below, find their resultant moment about O giving its magnitude and direction.

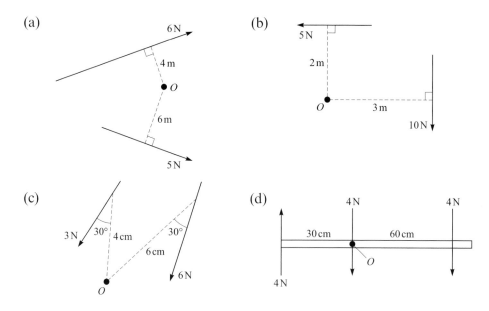

3 The following systems of forces have no resultant moment about the pivot point O. Find the value of **F** in each case.

(a)   (b)

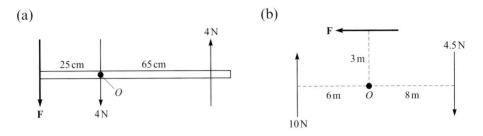

4 A seesaw is made from a uniform plank of wood of mass 30 kg and length 4 metres pivoted at its centre. A small boy and girl sit on the seesaw so that it balances. The boy, of mass 25 kg, sits right at one end of the plank.
  (a) Calculate the distance of the girl, of mass 40 kg, from the other end of the plank.
  (b) What is the total reaction force at the pivot?

5 Carol and Paul are playing on a playground roundabout that is divided into eight equal sections.
Carol pulls one way with a force of 200 N and Paul pulls another with a force of 350 N. The direction of action of each force is shown in the diagram.
  (a) Which way does the roundabout turn?
  (b) With what force should Paul pull to keep the roundabout stationary?

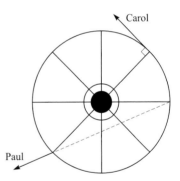

6 Karim puts his computer and printer onto a table top. The mass of the computer is 17 kg and that of the printer 6 kg. The table top is of length 2 metres and mass 15 kg. The computer, printer and table can be modelled as particles A and B resting on a uniform rod PQ. The rod is supported at P and Q. AP is 40 cm and BQ is 60 cm. Calculate the forces at P and Q.

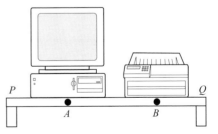

*7   Dianne wants to lift a heavy rock of mass 120 kg. She slides the end of a plank under the rock and then pushes a log of radius 5 cm under the plank to act as a pivot. The plank is 3 metres long and has a mass of 20 kg. Dianne is 158 cm tall and her mass is 60 kg. Discuss where she should place the log.

8   Afsal lifts the handles of a heavy wheelbarrow. It can be modelled as a light horizontal rod of length 0.9 metres pivoted about one end, with a particle of mass 49 kg fixed 25 cm from the pivot. Calculate the force he must exert to lift the handles.

Intermediate

1   In each of the following cases the forces acting on the body can be replaced by a single force **F** acting through O and a couple **C** about O. Find the magnitude of **F** and the magnitude and sense of **C**. Give your answers in surd form.

(a)

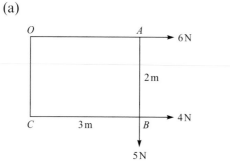

(b)

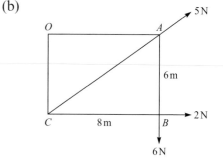

(c) $OABCDE$ is a regular hexagon.

(d) $OC = CA = 2$ metres

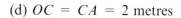

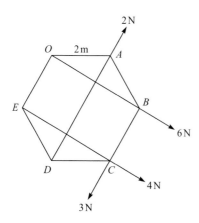

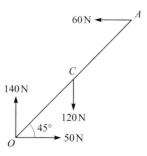

2 A motorcycle has a mass of 230 kg and the distance between the centres of the front and back wheels is 1.5 metres. The centre of mass of the motorcycle lies on a vertical line 1 metre behind the front wheel. Its rider has a mass of 72 kg and the centre of mass of the rider lies on a vertical line midway between the centres of the two wheels. The machine is on horizontal ground and is in equilibrium.
Find the vertical reaction forces on the wheels when:

(a) the rider is not on the machine,
(b) the rider is on the machine.

3 A small boy walks across a plank that is balanced between two supports. The mass of the plank is 25 kg and that of the boy 36 kg. The length of the plank is 3 metres. The plank can be modelled as a uniform rod AB supported at A and B and the boy can be modelled as a particle P a distance x from A.
Find, in terms of x, an expression for the reaction forces $\mathbf{Q}$ and $\mathbf{R}$ at A and B as the boy moves across the bridge.

*4 For each of the following cases the diagram shows a uniform horizontal beam AB of weight W supported on two smooth supports P and Q. In each case an object of weight $2W$ is suspended by a light inextensible string from point C. The systems are in equilibrium. In each case find the exact forces acting at P and Q in terms of W.

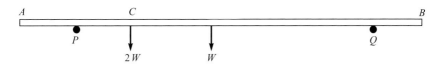

(a) $AB = 4$ metres, $AP = 0.4$ metres, $AC = 1.4$ metres and
$AQ = 3.4$ metres
(b) $AB = 2$ metres, $AP = 0.4$ metres, $AC = 0.2$ metres and
$AQ = 1.8$ metres

5 A rectangular window of mass 10 kg and depth 0.6 m, is freely hinged along its upper edge. It is kept open, so that it makes an angle of 20°, by a horizontal force of P N applied horizontally at the midpoint of the lower edge of the window.
The situation is shown in the diagram.
Assume that the weight of the window acts at the point of intersection of its diagonals.
Find P.

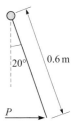

6 A horizontal, uniform plank of length
10 m and weight 100 N is supported at two
points, P and Q, that are 6 m apart so
that the system is symmetrical as shown in
the diagram. A boy of weight 270 N
stands so that he is a distance x m from
P.
Find, in terms of x, the reactions R_P N
and R_Q N at P and Q respectively.

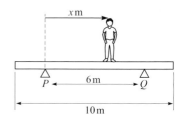

7 A uniform ladder stands on rough, horizontal
ground leaning against a smooth vertical wall.
The ladder has a length of 5 m, mass of 20 kg
and makes an angle of 50° with the horizontal.
The situation is shown in the diagram.
Find the force acting on the ladder:

(a) at the wall,
(b) at the ground.

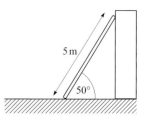

8 A swimmer of mass 60 kg stands on the
edge A of a diving platform AB that is of
length 2 m. The platform is rigid, uniform
and firmly supported at B. The mass of the
platform is 250 kg. The situation is shown
in the diagram.
Find the couple required at the support to
keep the system in equilibrium.

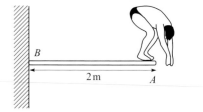

9 A light standard of height 5 metres on a
station platform is hinged at a point 1 metre
above the ground to allow the bulb to be
changed easily. The electrician removes the
locking pin and holds onto the pole at a point
2 metres above the ground as shown. He then
walks backwards supporting the pole in his
hands. The moving section of the light
standard can be modelled as a uniform pole of
length 4 metres and weight 50 N, with a
particle of weight 20 N at the top. Calculate
the vertical force exerted by the electrician:

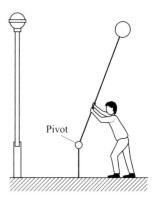

(a) when his hands are 1 metre from the pivot,
(b) when his hands are 4 metres from the pivot.

Advanced

1 Maria is trying to slide a heavy
plank so that it will bridge the gap
over a stream. The stream is 2.4
metres wide and the plank can be
modelled as a uniform rod AB of
weight 300 newtons and length
3 metres. At the start there is an overhang of 1 metre as shown. The
coefficient of friction between the bank and the plank is 0.1. What is the
resultant force Maria must be able to exert at A if the plank is to reach
the other side?

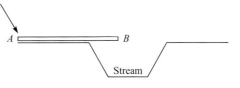

*2 A shop sign is uniform of length 40 cm and
has a total mass of 15 kg. It is freely hinged
at point A on the wall. It is held in position
with AB horizontal, by a light inextensible
wire BC, such that C is 30 cm above A as
shown in the diagram.
Find:

(a) the tension in the wire BC,
(b) the magnitude and direction of the
reaction force of the hinge at A.

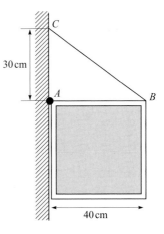

3 The lid of a chest is hinged about one of its long edges. Assume that the
lid is uniform, has length 60 cm, width 25 cm and weight 50 N. The lid is
in limiting equilibrium when it makes an angle α with the horizontal
where $\alpha = 70°$.

(a) Find the maximum resistive couple that the hinge can exert.
(b) The lid of the chest is kept open when $\alpha = 30°$ by applying a
horizontal force P N at the midpoint of the longest *edge* of the chest.
Assuming that the resistive couple still acts, find P.

4 The diagrams on the next page show the simple mechanism by which a
drawbridge over a canal can be raised and lowered by the bridgekeeper.
The bridge OA, of length 3.5 metres and weight 1.5 kN, is hinged at O
and a rope attached to it 1 metre from A is passed over a pulley at B.
OB is vertical and of length 3 metres. A counterweight of weight W is
attached to the end of the rope at C. The first diagram shows the bridge
in the raised position with the rope perpendicular to the bridge. The
bridge is in equilibrium at this point. The second diagram shows the
bridge when it rests on the opposite bank.

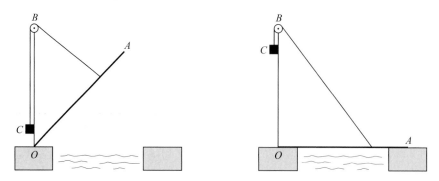

Making suitable assumptions which should be stated:

(a) find the value of W,
(b) find the extra force that needs to be applied to the rope to start raising the bridge from the horizontal,
(c) find the magnitude of the force acting at the pivot point O in each of these cases.

5 A ladder is leaning against a smooth vertical wall. The other end rests on rough horizontal ground. The ladder can be modelled as a uniform rod of length 5 metres and mass M kg. The ladder makes an angle of $60°$ with the horizontal. A man of mass $2M$ kg climbs the ladder. The coefficient of friction between the ladder and the ground is 0.2. The ladder is on the point of slipping when the centre of mass of the man is on a vertical line x metres from the wall.
Find x.

6 Peter and Ann have to put a heavy uniform beam of mass 78 kg and length 2.5 metres onto two trestles a distance 2 metres apart with an equal distance overhanging each end. They discuss how best to lift the beam. Peter knows he can lift 37 kg and Ann can lift a mass of 45 kg without injury. One suggestion is for Peter to lift one end and Ann the other and carry it to the trestles. Another is for one of them to lift one end of the beam while the other moves the trestle underneath and then for them to go round to the other end and lift that end onto the second trestle in the same way. Discuss the two methods of moving the beam, giving the forces and moments involved and any practical difficulties that might occur.

7 The diagram on the next page shows a uniform roof truss. The weight of the truss is 6 kN. It is carrying loads of 8 kN and X kN. The reaction forces are measured as $\mathbf{R}$ kN and $2\mathbf{R}$ kN as shown. Calculate the exact values of $\mathbf{X}$ and $\mathbf{R}$.

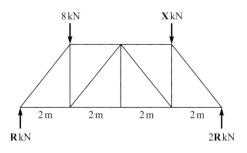

8 The diagram shows a lamina in the form of a regular hexagon *ABCDEF*, with sides of length *a* metres. Forces of magnitude 3 N, 2 N, 2 N, 3N, 2 N and 2 N act along the lines *AB, BC, DC, DE, FE* and *FA* respectively as shown in the diagram.

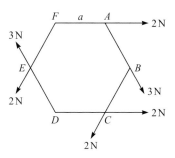

(a) Show that the resultant of these forces is of magnitude 4 N and find its direction.

(b) The lamina is held in equilibrium by a single force **R** applied at *A* and a couple **K**. Find the magnitude of **K** in surd form and indicate its sense.

9 The framework shown in the diagram consists of a series of light pin-jointed rods. The framework is suspended by light strings from points *A* and *B*. Weights of 300 N and 200 N are suspended from *C* and *D* respectively. *AD = BC = 4* metres.

(a) Show that the tension in the string at *A* is 150 N.

(b) Calculate the magnitudes of the internal forces in the rods *AD* and *AE* stating whether each rod is in compression or tension.

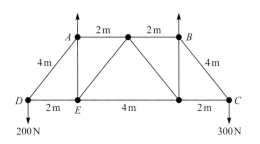

Revision

1   A roundabout in a children's
    playground is in the form of a regular
    hexagon *ABCDEF*. It is free to rotate
    about a vertical axis through centre *O*
    as shown in the diagram. One child
    pushes with a force of 100 N at corner
    D in a direction that makes an angle
    30° with side *CD*.
    Another child pushes with a force *P* N
    along edge *BA* of the roundabout so
    that it does not rotate.
    Find *P*.

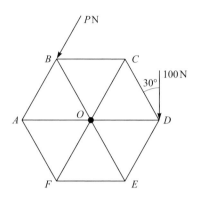

2   A simple bench is made from a uniform plank of mass 24 kg and length
    2.5 m, and two supports *A* and *B*, at 0.5 m from each end of the bench.
    A child of mass 20 kg sits on the bench at *A*. Another person sits at the
    end of the bench furthest from *A* so that the reaction at *A* is zero. The
    situation is represented by the diagram below.

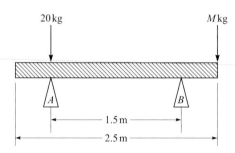

    Find the mass of the person sitting at the end of the bench.

3   A large uniform pole *AB* of weight
    2500 N and length 8 m is freely hinged
    at *A* and lies on horizontal ground. The
    pole is lifted using a rope attached to it
    at end *B*. The rope makes an angle of α
    with the pole as shown in the diagram.

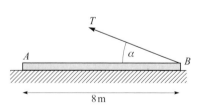

    (a) Find the tension *T* in the rope in
         terms of α when the pole is just
         about to lift off the ground.
    (b) Sketch a graph of *T* against α.
    (c) Explain what your graph suggests
         happens when $\alpha = 90°$.

4 A collapsible shelf is uniform and weighs 40 N. The shelf measures 0.8 m by 0.4 m and is freely hinged along one of its longer edges. It is supported by two cords, one attached to each corner of the shelf opposite the hinged edge. Each cord is of length 0.5 m and is attached to the wall vertically above the hinge.

(a) Draw a diagram to show the forces on the shelf.
(b) What modelling assumptions have you made?
(c) Find the tension in *each* cord.

5 A uniform shop sign of weight 50 N and length 50 centimetres is hinged freely about a point *A*. The centre of mass of the sign is on a vertical line through the midpoint of *AB*. The sign is supported by a light inextensible wire attached to a point *C*, x cm from *A* along the horizontal upper edge *AB* of the sign. The other end of the wire is attached to the wall at *D* where $CD = 2x$ cm. The situation is shown in the diagram. Find:

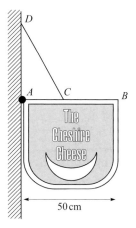

(a) the tension T N in the string in terms of x,
(b) the horizontal and vertical components of the force at the hinge in terms of x.

(c) Explain what this implies about the direction of the force at the hinge.

6 The diagram shows a drawbridge over a canal. The bridge *OA*, of length $4a$ metres and weight $6W$ kN, is hinged at *O* and a rope attached to it a metres from *A* is passed over a pulley at *B*. *OB* is vertical and of length $3a$ metres. A counterweight of weight W is attached to the end of the rope at *C*. The diagram shows the bridge when it rests on the opposite bank. Making suitable assumptions which should be stated:

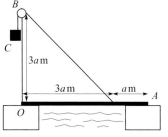

(a) find the extra force, in terms of W, that needs to be applied to the rope to start raising the bridge from the horizontal (give your answer in surd form),
(b) find the magnitude of the force acting at the pivot point *O* at this time in terms of W. Give your answer in surd form.

*7 A ladder is leaning against a smooth vertical wall. The other end rests on rough horizontal ground. The ladder can be modelled as a uniform rod of length 5 metres and mass M kg. The foot of the ladder is 3 metres from the wall, as shown. A man, also of mass M kg, climbs the ladder.
The ladder is on the point of slipping when the centre of mass of the man is on a vertical line 1 metre from the wall.
Find the coefficient of friction between the ladder and the ground.

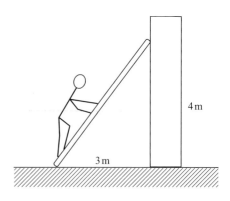

8 An open rectangular door $ABCD$ is smoothly hinged at the points P and Q of the vertical edge AB (see diagram). $AB = 2$ m, $BC = 0.75$ m, $AP = BQ = 0.25$ m, and the weight of the door is 200 N. By modelling the door as a uniform lamina, find the horizontal components of the forces on the door at P and Q.
A wedge is placed between the door and the floor at D, exerting a vertical upward force of magnitude F newtons on the door. Given that the horizontal components of the forces on the door at P and Q are now both zero, calculate F.
[UCLES]

9 A uniform ladder, of mass m, leans against a vertical wall with its base on horizontal ground. The length of the ladder is 6 m. Assume that the wall is smooth and that the ground is rough, with the coefficient of friction between the ladder and the ground equal to 0.5.

(a) If the angle between the ladder and the ground is θ, show that the ladder remains at rest if θ is greater than or equal to 45°.

A person of mass M climbs the ladder.

(b) Show that when the person is at a distance x m from the bottom of the ladder

$$\tan \theta \geq \frac{3m + Mx}{3(m + M)}$$

if the ladder is to remain at rest.

(c) How far up the ladder can the person climb if $\theta = 45°$?

(d) Now assume that $\tan \theta = 2$.

  (i) Show that $x \le 6 + \dfrac{3m}{M}$, if the ladder remains at rest.

  (ii) Use this result to make a prediction about the mass of a person who can reach the top of the ladder.

[AEB]

10

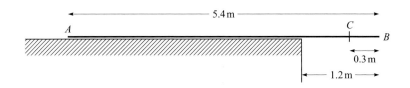

A plank of wood AB has length 5.4 m. It lies on a horizontal platform, with 1.2 m projecting over the edge, as shown in the diagram. When a girl of mass 50 kg stands at the point C on the plank, where $BC = 0.3$ m, the plank is on the point of tilting. By modelling the plank as a uniform rod and the girl as a particle,

(a) find the mass of the plank.

The girl places a rock on the end of the plank at A. By modelling the rock also as a particle,

(b) find, to 2 significant figures, the smallest mass of the rock which will enable the girl to stand on the plank at B without it tilting.

(c) State briefly how you have used the modelling assumptions that the
  (i) plank is uniform,
  (ii) the rock is a particle.

[Edexcel]

Centres of mass

Centres of mass of uniform laminae, compound bodies and uniform solids (including the use of calculus); toppling and sliding[†]

Give answers to three significant figures unless otherwise stated.

> If a body can be modelled as a number of rigidly connected point masses m_1, m_2, m_3, m_4 ... located at points (x_1, y_1), (x_2, y_2), (x_3, y_3), (x_4, y_4), ... then the centre of mass will be located at $(\bar{x}, \bar{y})$ where
>
> $$\bar{x} = \frac{\sum mx}{\sum m}, \quad \bar{y} = \frac{\sum my}{\sum m}$$
>
> Under normal circumstances the position of the centre of gravity is independent of the gravitational force per unit mass and hence is the same as the position of the centre of mass and can be calculated in the same way.
>
> Where a body cannot be divided into a finite number of parts whose masses and position of centres of mass are known then it may be divided into a large number of very small parts whose masses and position of centres of mass are known. The position of the centre of mass of the whole body can then be found by integration.
>
> $$\bar{x} = \frac{\int mx \, dx}{\int m \, dx}, \quad \bar{y} = \frac{\int my \, dy}{\int m \, dy}$$

Basic

1 A non-uniform beam AB has a mass of 4 kg and is of length 4 metres. A mass of 2 kg is attached to the beam at B, as shown in the diagram on the next page. The beam is horizontal and in equilibrium when supported at point C which is 1 m from B.

Find the distance of the centre of mass of the beam from A.

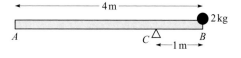

2 A light rod AB of length 1 metre has a mass of 3 kg attached to end A and a mass of 4 kg attached to end B. Find the distance of the centre of mass of the system from end A.

3 Three particles A, B and C, of masses $2m$, $3m$ and $4m$ respectively, are attached to a light rod of length $2a$. A is attached to one end, B is attached to the other and C is attached to the rod's midpoint. Find, in terms of a, the distance of the centre of mass of the system from A.

4 A thin uniform lamina in the shape of a 'T' is made from two rectangles measuring 30 cm by 10 cm, as shown in the diagram. AB is the line of symmetry of the shape. Find the distance of the centre of mass of the shape from A.

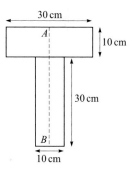

*5 A system of masses m, $2m$ and $3m$ has the masses situated at $i + j$, $2i + j$ and $-3i + j$ respectively. Find the position of the centre of mass of the system.

6 A television aerial can be modelled as a uniform metal rod of length 1.5 m and mass 4 kg to which is attached a second uniform metal rod made of the same material and of length 1.2 m. The two rods are perpendicular to each other and their point of intersection, O, is such that each rod has 20 cm on one side of O, as shown in the diagram. Find the distance of the centre of mass of the aerial from O.

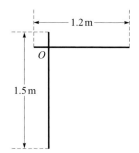

7 A shop sign is made from a uniform circular lamina of diameter 90 cm from which a square of side 20 cm has been punched. The centre of the square lies at the midpoint of a radius of the circle and is positioned so that a diagonal lies on this radius as shown in the diagram. Find the position of the centre of mass of the sign.

8 An empty perfume bottle can be modelled as a cylinder joined to a spherical cap as shown in the diagram. The cylinder has length 15 cm, diameter 10 cm and mass 100 grams. The cap has diameter 4 cm and mass 25 grams. Find the height of the centre of mass of the bottle above its base.

Intermediate

1 A thin uniform wire forms a framework in the shape of a right-angled triangle ABC. $AB = 9$ cm, $BC = 12$ cm and angle $B = 90°$. Find the distance of the centre of mass from B.

2 A child's building brick system contains square cuboid interlocking bricks of side length 2 cm. An 'L' shape is made of 10 bricks with one side one brick longer than the other as shown in the diagram. Assume that each brick is uniform. Find the distance of the centre of mass of the system from point O.

3 A uniform square lamina $ABCD$ of side length a and mass $4m$ has masses $4m$, $2m$, $4m$ and $6m$ placed at A, B, C, D respectively, as shown in the diagram. Find, in terms of a, the distance of the centre of mass of the system from:

(a) AD,
(b) AB.

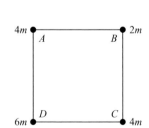

*4 A framework consists of three uniform rods of lengths 6 cm, 8 cm and 10 cm. The mass of a 1 cm length of rod is 10 grams.
The rods are joined at the vertices with pins of mass 10 grams to form a right-angled triangle *LMN* as shown in the diagram.
Find the distance of the centre of mass of the structure from point *M*.

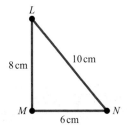

5 Masses 2*m* and 3*m* are situated at $2\mathbf{i} + \mathbf{j}$ and $3\mathbf{i} - 2\mathbf{j}$ respectively. A third mass 4*m* is situated so that the centre of mass of the entire system is at $5\mathbf{i} + 4\mathbf{j}$. Find the position of the 4*m* mass.

6 A shop sign is made from a rectangle of thin uniform card from which a circular hole is punched. The rectangle has dimensions 100 cm by 50 cm and the hole has diameter 40 cm. The hole lies on the longer line of symmetry of the rectangle such that its centre is 30 cm from one of the shorter edges of the rectangle. Find the distance from this edge that a cord should be attached to the sign so that it will hang with the longer edge horizontal.

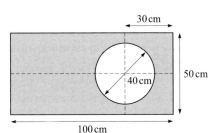

7 A shop sign is made from a thin uniform material. It can be considered to comprise two rectangles *A* and *B* as shown in the diagram. Rectangle *A* has dimensions 6*h* by 3*h*. Rectangle *B* has dimensions 2*h* by *a*. Find *a* in terms of *h* if the centre of mass of the sign lies along the edge where *A* and *B* meet.

8 A uniform lamina *ABCDE* is a pentagon that can be considered to comprise a square of side 50 cm joined to an equilateral triangle also of side 50 cm, as shown in the diagram.
Find the distance of the centre of mass from the edge *CD*.

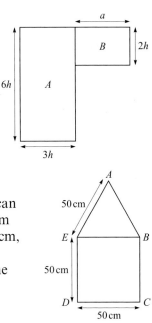

9 A framework of uniform rods is in the form
of a right-angled triangle ABC.
Angle $A = 90°$, AB is of length 30 cm and AC
is of length 40 cm. Masses of 2 kg, which may
be modelled as particles, are placed at each
corner of the framework. The system is as
shown in the diagram.
Find the distance of the centre of mass of the
system from sides AB and AC:

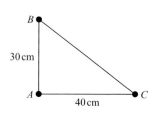

(a) assuming that the rods are light,
(b) assuming that the rods are of mass 10 kg/m.

10 A semi-circular lamina is made of uniform material and has radius 10 cm.
Find, using integration, the distance of its centre of mass from its straight
edge.

11 A uniform lamina is made in the shape
of the area enclosed by the curve
$y = 4 - x^2$ and the x-axis, as shown in
the diagram. Find the coordinates of its
centre of mass.

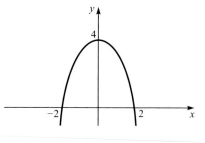

12 A uniform solid cone of height 10 cm
and base radius 4 cm is formed by
rotating the area enclosed by the lines
$y = 4 - \frac{2}{5}x$ $(0 \le x \le 10)$, $y = 0$ and
$x = 0$ about the x-axis, as shown in
the diagram. Find, using integration
techniques, the distance of the centre
of mass of the cone from its base.

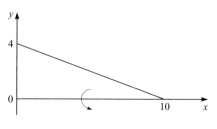

13 A uniform solid hemisphere is formed by rotating the
positive quadrant of a circle whose equation is
$x^2 + y^2 = 16$, referred to Cartesian axes, about the
x-axis as shown in the diagram. Find, using integration,
the distance of the centre of mass of the hemisphere
from its plane face.

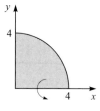

14 A uniform metal plate is made from a rectangle $ABCD$ where AB has length a and BC has length $20\,\text{cm}$. When the plate is suspended by the corner A, AB makes an angle of $43.1°$ with the vertical. Find a.

Advanced

1 A non-uniform rod LM is of length $4a$ and mass $8m$. It is at rest horizontally on two supports A and B such that $LA = BM = a$.

   (a) A mass of $3m$ is placed at L so that the rod is on the point of rotating about A.
   Find, in terms of a, the distance of the centre of mass of the system from A.

   (b) With the $3m$ mass remaining in place at L find, in terms of m, the mass that should be placed at M so that the rod is now on the point of rotating about B.

2 A uniform straight wire is bent into an 'L' shape ABC where $AB = 3a$ and $BC = a$, as shown in the diagram.
The 'L' shape is suspended freely from A.
Find the angle that the limb AB makes with the vertical.

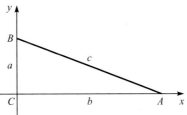

3 The area enclosed by the curve $y^2 = 4x$, the x-axis and the line $x = 4$, which lies in the positive quadrant, is rotated through one revolution about the x-axis. Find the coordinates of the centre of mass of the uniform solid that is formed.

4 A right-angled triangle ABC is right-angled at C and positioned with C at the origin of Cartesian axes, A on the x-axis and B on the y-axis, as shown in the diagram. A and B lie on the line $y = a - \dfrac{ax}{b}$.

   (a) Show, using integration, that the centre of mass of the triangle is at $\left(\dfrac{b}{3}, \dfrac{a}{3}\right)$.

   (b) A right-angled triangle is such that its sides are of length $5\,\text{cm}$, $12\,\text{cm}$ and $13\,\text{cm}$. It is freely suspended from the corner opposite its shortest side. Find the angle that its hypotenuse makes with the vertical.

   (c) A second right-angled triangle is such that the right angle is at C, $AC = 6\,\text{cm}$ and $BC = 8\,\text{cm}$. This triangle has a weight of $10\,\text{N}$ and is suspended by two vertical light strings attached to the triangle at B and C so that BC is horizontal. Find the tensions in the strings supporting the triangle.

5 (a) A semi-circular lamina has radius a. Its straight edge is aligned with the y-axis of Cartesian axes, and the x-axis is its line of symmetry, as shown in Figure 1. Show, using integration, that the centre of mass of the lamina is a distance $\dfrac{4a}{3\pi}$ from its straight edge.

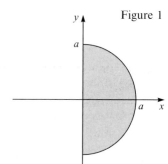

Figure 1

(b) A shop sign is in the form of a uniform semi-circular lamina of diameter 1 metre from which a semi-circle of diameter 75 cm has been removed such that the resulting figure retains one line of symmetry.
The sign is suspended from one corner, marked as A in Figure 2.
Find the angle that AB makes with the vertical.

Figure 2

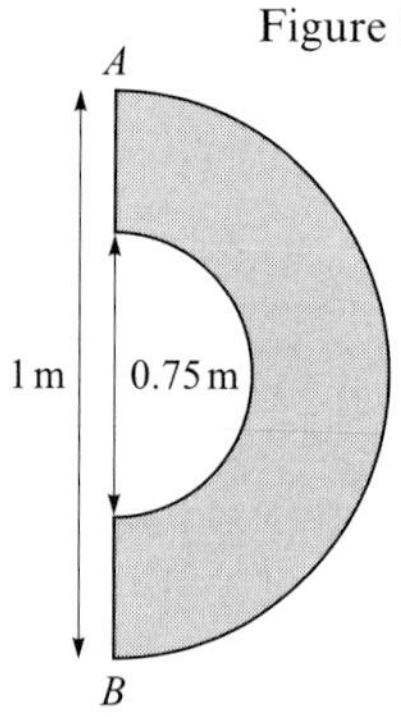

*6 A uniform metal plate is made by cutting a square of side 10 cm from one corner of a larger square of side 20 cm. The resulting plate is suspended from O as shown in the diagram so that one side of the square makes an angle α with the vertical.
Find α.

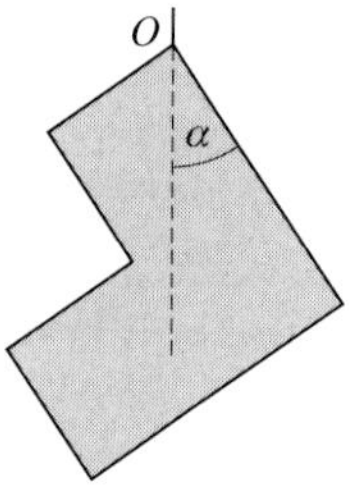

7 A composite solid is formed by joining at their circular faces a uniform right circular cone of radius a and height $2a$, and a uniform cylinder of radius a and length a. The density of the cylinder can be taken to be ρ. If the centre of mass of the composite body is at the intersection of the cylinder and cone find, in terms of ρ, the density of the cone.

8 A uniform lamina $ABCDEF$ is formed by removing a rectangle of dimensions 8 cm by 12 cm from a square of side length 20 cm, as shown in the diagram. Find the distance of the centre of mass of the lamina from its edges:

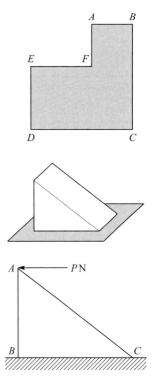

(a) AF,
(b) FE.

9[†] A prism of weight 18 N lies at rest on a rough horizontal plane.
Its cross-section is in the shape of a right-angled triangle ABC where $AB = 3$ cm, $BC = 4$ cm and $CA = 5$ cm. AB is vertical. Model the prism as a triangular lamina.

(a) Find the horizontal and vertical distances of the centre of mass of the prism from B.

A horizontal force of P N is applied to the point A as shown.

(b) The coefficient of static friction between the plane and the prism is 0.5. Find the value of P at which the prism moves, stating whether it slides or topples.

10[†] (a) Show, by integration, that the centre of mass of a uniform hemisphere of radius a is at a distance $\dfrac{3a}{8}$ from its plane face.

(b) A uniform solid body is formed by sticking the plane face of a solid hemisphere of radius a to one plane face of a solid cylinder of radius a and height $2a$.
  (i) Find the distance of the centre of mass of this body above its circular face.
  (ii) The body is at rest on a rough plane with its plane face in contact with the plane. The plane makes an angle of θ with the horizontal. The angle of the plane is gradually increased. Show that for the body to slide before it topples the coefficient of static friction $\mu \leq 0.744$.

11[†] A uniform cylinder of diameter $2a$ and height h rests on a rough surface that slopes at an angle θ to the horizontal as shown in the diagram.

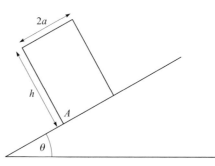

The coefficient of friction between the cylinder and the slope is $\frac{4}{5}$. The cylinder is both on the point of sliding down the slope and toppling about point A. Show that $h = 2.5a$.

Revision

1 Masses of $3m$, $4m$ and $5m$ are attached to a light rod at distances $3a$, $4a$ and $5a$ respectively from one end O. Find, in terms of a, the distance of the centre of mass of the system from O.

2 A framework of light rods forms a right-angled triangle ABC with angle $B = 90°$, $AB = 4$ cm and $BC = 3$ cm. Equal point masses are placed at each of A, B and C. Find the distance of the centre of mass of the system from B.

3 A uniform lamina is in the form of a 'T' shape with both rectangular limbs of width 5 cm. One limb is of length 25 cm. The other limb is of length h cm, such that the centre of mass of the shape is on its line of symmetry at the point A, where the two rectangles join, as shown in the diagram. Find h.

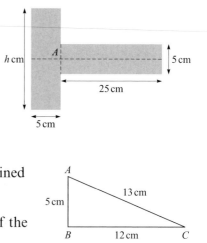

4 A framework consists of three uniform rods of lengths 5 cm, 12 cm and 13 cm, joined together to make a right-angled triangle ABC, as shown in the diagram. Find the distance of the centre of mass of the framework from point B.

5 Particles of masses m, $2m$ and $2m$ are placed at points with coordinates $(1, 2)$, $(-2, 3)$ and $(2, -1)$ respectively.

(a) Find the coordinates of the centre of mass of this system.

A fourth particle of mass $3m$ is placed such that the centre of mass of the system shifts to the origin, $(0, 0)$.

(b) Find the coordinates of the point at which the $3m$ mass is placed.

6 A body is formed by removing a hemisphere from a uniform metal cylinder. The cylinder has radius $2a$ and length $4a$. The hemisphere has radius a and its plane face lies in one of the circular faces of the cylinder. The solid formed has one plane of symmetry.

Find, in terms of a, the distance of the centre of mass of the body from the circular face of the cylinder that remains complete.

*7 A solid uniform plinth for a trophy is formed by rotating the area bounded by the curve $y = \dfrac{x^2}{5} + 10$, the x- and y-axes and the line $x = 5$ about the x-axis. Find the cordinates of the centre of mass of the plinth.

8 (a) Show, using integration, that the centre of mass of a uniform solid right circular cone of vertical height h and base radius a is a distance $\dfrac{h}{4}$ from its base.

(b) A uniform composite body is formed by attaching the plane face of a cone of radius a and height h to a cylinder of radius a and length a. If the centre of mass of this body is at the face of the intersection of the cylinder and cone, find h in terms of a.

9 A piece of wood can be prepared as a stand for a pencil. The piece of wood shown in the photograph can be considered as a prism whose cross-section is a parallelogram. The pencil fits through a cylindrical hole which is drilled through the piece of wood. A side view of the situation is shown in Fig. 1 in which the cross-section of the wood is replaced by the parallelogram $ABCD$. The centre of mass of the pencil and the piece of wood together must then be vertically above AB.

Model the situation so that the piece of wood has no thickness so that it can be represented by BC as shown in Fig. 2. The mass of the pencil is 20 grams and its centre of mass is at its mid-point which is 2 cm to the

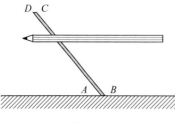

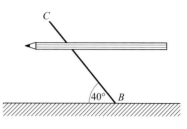

Figure 1   Figure 2

right of the vertical through B. The mass of the piece of wood is 10 grams and it is inclined at $40°$ to the horizontal.

(a) Find the position of the centre of mass of the piece of wood.

The piece of wood is now used to support a pencil of mass m grams.

(b) Find the horizontal distance, x centimetres, of the line of action of the weight of the pencil from B.

(c) Sketch a graph showing how x varies with m.

(d) State where the centre of mass of a very heavy pencil must lie if the system is to remain in equilibrium with the pencil horizontal.

[OCR]

10[†] A uniform solid is composed of a cylinder of radius 10 cm and length 20 cm attached to a cuboid of square cross-section of side 30 cm and height 10 cm. Each of the two bodies is made from the same material and the composite body has one axis of symmetry.

(a) Find the distance of the centre of mass of the composite body from the square face of the cuboid to which the cylinder is *not* attached.

(b) The body is placed on a sloping surface with
   (i) the cuboid,
   (ii) the cylinder in contact with the surface as shown in the diagrams.

For each case find the angle θ that the surface makes with the horizontal when the body topples, given that the body does not slide.

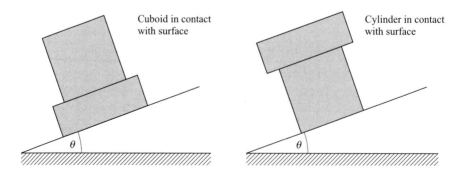

Cuboid in contact with surface

Cylinder in contact with surface

11[†] A uniform solid, S, is placed with its plane
face on horizontal ground. The solid consists
of a right circular cylinder, of radius r and
height r, joined to a right circular cone of
radius r and height h.
The plane face of the cone coincides with one
of the plane faces of the cylinder, as shown in
the diagram.

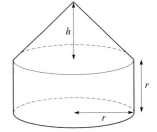

(a) Show that the distance of the centre of
mass of S from the ground is

$$\frac{6r^2 + 4rh + h^2}{4(3r + h)}$$

The solid is now placed with its plane face on a rough plane which is
inclined at an angle α to the horizontal. The plane is rough enough to
prevent S from sliding. Given that $h = 2r$, and that S is on the point of
toppling,

(b) find, to the nearest degree, the value of α.

[Edexcel]

14

Simple harmonic motion

Force, acceleration, velocity and displacement associated with simple harmonic motion; simple harmonic motion of objects attached to springs and elastic strings; simple harmonic motion of simple pendulum

Take the acceleration due to gravity to be $g \text{ ms}^{-2}$ where $g = 9.8$.
Give answers to three significant figures unless otherwise stated.

An object that moves in a straight line so that its acceleration is always directed towards a fixed point and is always proportional to its displacement from that point moves with simple harmonic motion (SHM).

$$\frac{d^2x}{dt^2} = -\omega^2 x$$

If the displacement of a particle P from an origin O is x then its acceleration is given by

$$\frac{d^2x}{dt^2} = -\omega^2 x,$$

where ω^2 is the constant of proportionality.
The **displacement**, x, of the particle is given by

$$x = a\cos(\omega t + \varepsilon)$$

where a is the amplitude (maximum displacement of the particle from O) of the motion and ε depends on the displacement of the particle when $t = 0$.
The **velocity**, v, of the particle is given by

$$v = -a\omega\sin(\omega t + \varepsilon)$$
$$v^2 = \omega^2(a^2 - x^2)$$

The **period**, T (time for one complete oscillation), is given by

$$T = \frac{2\pi}{\omega}$$

Basic

*1 A particle performing simple harmonic motion makes 4 oscillations per second with amplitude 10 centimetres. Calculate the maximum acceleration of the particle.

2 A particle performs simple harmonic motion, with amplitude a, about a fixed point O. The period of one complete oscillation is T. The particle is at a point P, $\dfrac{T}{12}$ seconds after passing through O. Find, in terms of a, the distance OP.

3 A particle performs simple harmonic motion such that $\ddot{x} = -16x$. Find x in terms of t given that, when $t = 0$, $\dot{x} = 0$ and $x = 2$.

4 The motion of a particle is such that $x = 5\sin(\pi t)$ where x metres is its displacement from O at time t seconds.
   (a) Show that $\ddot{x} = -\pi^2 x$.
   (b) State (i) the amplitude, (ii) the period of the particle's motion.

5 A particle moves with simple harmonic motion about O. When it is 2 metres from O its speed is $4\,\mathrm{m\,s^{-1}}$ and its acceleration is $8\,\mathrm{m\,s^{-2}}$. Calculate:
   (a) the period,
   (b) the amplitude,
   (c) the maximum speed,
   of the particle.

6 A particle is moving with simple harmonic motion about O so that it makes 5 oscillations per second and its greatest acceleration is $25\,\mathrm{m\,s^{-2}}$. Find, in centimetres, the amplitude of the motion of the particle.

7 At the entrance to a harbour the depth of water at high tide is 25 metres and at low tide 5 metres. The time between successive high tides is 12 hours. Assume that the tide rises and falls with simple harmonic motion. Find, in centimetres per second, the maximum rate of change of the depth of water.

8 A particle is performing simple harmonic motion with amplitude 0.5 metres. Its speed when it is 0.25 metres from its mean position, O, is $1\,\mathrm{m\,s^{-1}}$. Find:
   (a) the period of the oscillations,
   (b) the speed of the particle as it passes through O,
   (c) the maximum acceleration of the particle.

9 A simple pendulum is displaced from rest by an angle of 0.08 radians and then released. The subsequent oscillations have time period 0.5π seconds.

(a) Calculate the length of the pendulum.
(b) Find the maximum speed of the bob.
(c) What assumptions have you made in modelling this situation?

10 A particle of mass 5 grams is suspended on a light spring and hangs in equilibrium. The particle is pulled downwards a distance of 2 centimetres and then released. Its equation of motion is given by $x = 0.02 \cos 3t$ where t seconds is the time from release and x metres is its displacement from the equilibrium position.

(a) Find its period.
(b) Find the velocity of the particle after 4 seconds.
(c) Find the resultant force acting on the particle when it reaches its highest point.

11 A body moves so that its equation of motion is $x = 5 \cos \pi(t + 0.05)$ where x metres is its displacement from a fixed point A after t seconds.

(a) Find x when $t = 0$.
(b) Find its velocity and acceleration at time t.
(c) Hence show why this motion can be described as simple harmonic motion.
(d) How many oscillations will the body complete in one minute?

Intermediate

1 A particle performs simple harmonic motion about O. When passing through a point 1 metre from O the particle has a speed of $2\,\mathrm{m\,s^{-1}}$, and when passing through a point 2 metres from O it has a speed of $0.5\,\mathrm{m\,s^{-1}}$. Find:

(a) ω,
(b) the amplitude of the particle's motion.

*2 A light elastic string of natural length 0.5 metres is fixed at one end and attached to its other end is a mass of 0.25 kilograms hanging freely in equilibrium so that the string is extended by 0.1 metres. The mass is pulled down 5 centimetres below its equilibrium position and released so that it performs simple harmonic motion.

(a) Show that the motion can be described by the equation $\ddot{x} = -10gx$.
(b) Find the maximum speed of the mass.

3 A particle oscillates with an amplitude of 4 metres and a time period π. Its motion can be modelled as simple harmonic motion. Find the distance from the centre of oscillation and the magnitude of its acceleration when the body is travelling at a speed of $4\,\mathrm{m\,s^{-1}}$.

4   A particle of mass m is attached to one end of a light elastic string of natural length l and modulus of elasticity $2mg$. The other end of the string is fixed and the particle hangs in equilibrium.
(a) Find, in terms of l, the extension e of the string.
(b) The particle is pulled down a further distance a, where $a < e$, and then released. By considering the forces acting on the particle when it is a distance x vertically below its equilibrium position, show that the particle executes simple harmonic motion with period $T = 2\pi\sqrt{\dfrac{l}{2g}}$.

5   A boat is anchored in a harbour. Its keel is a height h metres above the seabed at time t where t is measured in hours. The graph shows how h varies with time.

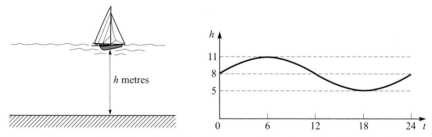

The motion can be described by the equation $h = d + A\cos(\omega t)$.
(a) Find A, d and ω.
(b) Find, in metres per second, the maximum rate of change of height of water in the harbour.

6   A particle of mass $0.5\,\mathrm{kg}$ is attached to one end of a light elastic spring of natural length $0.5\,\mathrm{m}$ and modulus $50\,\mathrm{N}$. The other end of the spring is fixed to a point on a smooth horizontal surface. The particle is held at a point on the surface so that the length of the spring is $0.4\,\mathrm{m}$ and then it is released. Calculate:
(a) the period of the resulting oscillations,
(b) the speed of the particle when the spring is unstretched.

*7   A heavy bob swings on the end of a light inextensible string. Its angle of displacement to the vertical, ϕ, is always small. The bob has mass 200 grams and the string is of length $80\,\mathrm{cm}$.
(a) Draw a force diagram and by using Newton's second law tangentially to the path of the bob's motion find $\dfrac{\mathrm{d}^2\phi}{\mathrm{d}t^2}$ in terms of ϕ.
(b) Show this can be approximated to SHM and find its period to three significant figures.

8 A body of mass m kg is suspended by a Hookian spring and allowed to oscillate freely. It makes two complete oscillations per second and its amplitude is 0.3 metres.

    (a) Find its acceleration in terms of its displacement from its mean position.

    (b) How many oscillations per second would it make if the mass were doubled?

9 A body of mass 5 kg moves along a line OA with simple harmonic motion. When it is 50 cm from the centre of oscillation the acceleration and velocity of the body are $-50\,\mathrm{m\,s^{-2}}$ and $7\,\mathrm{m\,s^{-1}}$ respectively. Calculate:

    (a) the amplitude of the motion,

    (b) the force on the body when it is furthest away from the centre of oscillation.

10 A particle of mass 0.8 kg is attached to one end of a light elastic spring of natural length 0.25 m and modulus 100 N. The particle lies at rest with the spring unstretched on a smooth horizontal table and with the other end of the spring fixed to a point on the table. The particle is held so that the spring is stretched by 0.1 m and it is at rest. The particle is then released and executes simple harmonic oscillations. Find the period of the oscillations.

11 In a storm in 1994 a lamp post on the M62 motorway started to oscillate. Its maximum angular displacement from the vertical was 0.2 radians. The height of the post was 10 metres. What was the maximum speed of the lamp? Model its motion as that of a simple pendulum.

12 A particle moves on the line OX so that after time t seconds its displacement from O is x metres. Its equation of motion can be modelled by $\ddot{x} = -9x$. After 1 second it is 2 metres from O travelling with speed $1\,\mathrm{m\,s^{-1}}$. Find:

    (a) the time for a single oscillation,

    (b) the amplitude of an oscillation.

    (c) The motion is actually that of a mass of 10 kg hanging on a spring.

        (i) What assumptions have been made when modelling the motion in this way?

        (ii) How is the actual motion likely to vary from that of the model?

Advanced

1 A particle moves on the line OX so that after time t seconds its displacement from O is x metres and $\ddot{x} = -9x$. When $t = 0$, $x = 4$ and $\dot{x} = 5$. Find:

    (a) the maximum displacement of the particle from 0,

    (b) the position and velocity of the particle when $t = 1$.

2 A small ball of mass 0.2 kg is attached to a light elastic string of natural length 0.75 m and modulus 10 N. The ball is at rest on a smooth horizontal table and the other end of the elastic is fixed to a point on the table. The ball is held so that the elastic is stretched by 0.1 m and then released. Find:

(a) the speed of the ball when the string becomes slack,

(b) the time taken for the ball to first return to its initial position.

3 A particle of mass m kg is fixed between two identical springs, each of natural length l metres and spring constant k N m^{-1}, which rest on a smooth horizontal table.

The other ends of the springs are fixed to points A and B on the table, $3l$ metres apart. The springs can be assumed to be Hookian.

The particle is displaced from its equilibrium position O towards A so that it is l metres from A, and then released. Find:

(a) the magnitude of the particle's velocity when it returns to O,

(b) the time taken for the particle to first return to O after its release.

4 Two light elastic strings each of natural length 0.6 m and modulus 8 N are attached at one of their ends to a particle of mass 0.5 kg. The free ends of the strings are attached to points A and B on a smooth horizontal table where $AB = 2.0$ m. The particle P lies at C, the midpoint of AB at rest. It is then displaced 0.4 m along AB towards B, held at rest and then released. By considering P at a point x m from C show that the motion of P is simple harmonic and find the period of its motion.

5 A particle of weight 20 N is attached to the free end of a light elastic spring of natural length 0.5 m and modulus 100 N which hangs vertically from a fixed point. The particle is pulled downwards a further 0.1 m and then released. Show that the period of the resulting oscillation is

$$\frac{2\pi}{\sqrt{10g}} \text{ seconds.}$$

6 Points A and B are on a smooth horizontal plane a distance $4a$ apart. A light elastic string of natural length a and modulus λ is fixed to A. A second light elastic string of natural length a and modulus $\dfrac{\lambda}{2}$ is fixed to B.

A particle P of mass m is attached to the free end of each string and the system lies in equilibrium.

(a) Find the distance of P from A.

The particle is now displaced a distance $\dfrac{a}{3}$ along the line AB towards B and held at rest before being released.

(b) Show that the subsequent motion of P is simple harmonic with

$$\text{period } T = 2\pi\sqrt{\frac{2ma}{3\lambda}}.$$

7 A particle of mass m is attached to one end of a light elastic string of modulus $5mg$ and natural length l. The other end of the string is held fixed at point O on a smooth surface inclined at $30°$ to the horizontal. The string is parallel to the line of greatest slope of the surface and the system is in equilibrium as shown in the diagram.

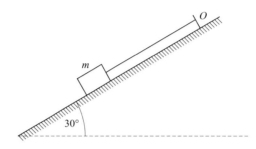

(a) Find, in terms of l, the extension of the string.

The string is pulled a distance $\dfrac{l}{20}$ further down the line of greatest slope and released from rest.

(b) Find the period of the resulting simple harmonic motion.

8 A mass of $0.6\,\text{kg}$ hangs in equilibrium attached to one end of a light elastic string of natural length $0.8\,\text{m}$ and modulus $24\,\text{N}$. The mass is pulled down a further $25\,\text{cm}$ and released. For one complete oscillation calculate the time for which the string is:

(a) taut,
(b) slack.

9 A scale pan of mass 400 grams is hung from a light extensible spring causing it to extend a distance of $4\,\text{cm}$. A 500 gram mass is held in the pan and released. The pan and mass then oscillate freely with simple harmonic motion.

(a) Find the distance through which the pan falls before rising again.
(b) Calculate the maximum tension in the spring.
(c) Calculate its period of oscillation.

10 A particle is describing simple harmonic motion about a fixed point A. At time T_1 its velocity is v_1 and its displacement from A is x_1 and at time T_2 its velocity is v_2 and its displacement from A is x_2.

Show that the period of oscillation of the motion is $T = 2\pi\sqrt{\dfrac{x_2^2 - x_1^2}{v_1^2 - v_2^2}}$.

11 A particle on the end of a spring completes 45 oscillations a minute. The velocity at a point 2.5 cm away from the mean position is $30 \, \text{cm} \, \text{s}^{-1}$.

    (a) Calculate the amplitude of the motion.
    (b) If P and Q are two points 2.5 cm and 5 cm respectively from the centre of motion, find how long it takes for the particle to travel from P to Q.

12 A particle is travelling with simple harmonic motion. While travelling from one extremity of its path to the other its distances from its mean position at three consecutive seconds are found to be 2 metres, 3.5 metres and 4.5 metres.

    (a) Find the time of a complete oscillation.
    (b) Find the amplitude of the motion.

Revision

1 A particle moves with simple harmonic motion about O such that its displacement, x metres, from O is given by $x = 2 \cos(10\pi t)$. Find the number of oscillations of the particle per second.

2 A piston performs simple harmonic motion such that it has a maximum speed of $1.5 \, \text{m} \, \text{s}^{-1}$ and takes 3 seconds to make a complete oscillation. Find:

    (a) the amplitude of the piston's motion,
    (b) the maximum acceleration of the piston.

3 A particle describes simple harmonic motion. Its equation of motion can be given as $\ddot{x} = -0.25x$ and its maximum velocity is $0.8 \, \text{m} \, \text{s}^{-1}$. Find the amplitude of the motion.

4 The graph below is of a particle that executes simple harmonic motion in a straight line such that at time t its displacement from O is x. State:

    (a) an equation for x in the form $x = A \cos \omega t$,
    (b) an equation for the motion in the form $\ddot{x} = -\omega^2 x$.

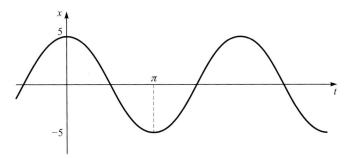

5 A simple pendulum describes simple harmonic motion of amplitude
0.05 radians and period $\frac{\pi}{4}$ seconds. Its displacement from the vertical
after t seconds is ϕ radians.

(a) Find an expression for the angular acceleration of the pendulum in
terms of its angular displacement from the vertical.
(b) What is its maximum angular velocity?
(c) What is its angular displacement 0.5 seconds after it passes its point
of maximum displacement?

6 A particle of mass m is attached to one end of a light elastic spring of
natural length l and modulus λ. The other end of the spring is fixed to a
point on a smooth horizontal surface. The particle is held on the surface
so that the spring is compressed by a distance a and then released so that
the system oscillates. By considering the particle when it is at a point so
that the spring has extension x, show that the oscillations have period

$$T = 2\pi\sqrt{\frac{ml}{\lambda}}.$$

7 A particle is moving in a straight line with simple harmonic motion
centred at O. The particle has speeds $4\,\mathrm{m\,s^{-1}}$ and $6\,\mathrm{m\,s^{-1}}$ when at points
$2\,\mathrm{m}$ and $1\,\mathrm{m}$ from O respectively. Find:

(a) the amplitude,
(b) the period,

of the motion.

8 A simple pendulum swings at a rate of 2 oscillations per second. How
many oscillations a second would it make if allowed to swing with simple
harmonic motion on the Moon? (Assume gravity on the Moon is one
sixth that on the Earth.)

9 A particle of mass m is attached to one end of a light elastic string, the
other end of which is held fixed so that the system hangs freely in
equilibrium. The string has natural length l and modulus $4mg$.

(a) Find, in terms of l, the equilibrium extension of the string.

The string is pulled down by a further distance $\frac{l}{8}$ and released from rest.

(b) Show that in the ensuing motion the particle performs simple

harmonic motion with period $T = \pi\sqrt{\dfrac{l}{g}}.$

10 A particle of mass 0.2 kg performs simple harmonic motion in a horizontal straight line centred at O. At a certain instant the displacement of the particle from O is 1.5 m, its acceleration has magnitude 30 m s^{-2} and it has kinetic energy 2 J. Find the amplitude of the particle's motion.

11 One end of a light elastic string of natural length a and modulus $3mg$ hangs freely with one end attached to a fixed point O. Two particles of masses m and $\dfrac{m}{2}$ are attached to the free end of the string and the system hangs in equilibrium. If the particle with mass $\dfrac{m}{2}$ falls off, find the amplitude and period of the ensuing motion.

12 An elastic rope has natural length 20 cm and modulus of elasticity 40 N. One end of the rope is attached to a fixed point, and a particle of mass 200 grams hangs from the other end. Take $g = 10$.

(a) Find the extension of the rope when the mass is at rest.

Assume that, when the mass moves, it always travels along a vertical line that passes through the point of suspension.

(b) At time t seconds, the displacement of the mass from its equilibrium position is x metres. Find the tension in the rope in terms of x, and show that $\dfrac{d^2x}{dt^2} = -1000x$.

(c) The mass is set into motion from its equilibrium position, so that it has an initial upward speed of U m s^{-1}. Find the maximum value of U for which simple harmonic motion will take place.

(d) Explain why in reality
   (i) the mass could be set in motion with a greater initial speed without the rope becoming slack,
   (ii) an even greater initial speed could be used if the mass initially moves downwards.

[AQA]

Answers and solutions

Chapter 1 Motion in one dimension

Basic

1 60.0 metres

*2 (a) In the vertical direction (upwards)
$$u = 10\,\mathrm{m\,s^{-1}}$$
$$a = -g\,\mathrm{m\,s^{-2}}$$
At the maximum height $v = 0$.
Using equations of motion for
constant acceleration
$$v = u + at$$
$$0 = 10 - gt$$

$$t = \frac{10}{g} = \frac{10}{9.8} = 1.0204$$

When $t = 1.0204$, using
$s = ut + \frac{1}{2}at^2$
gives
$$s = 10 \times 1.020 - \frac{9.8}{2} \times 1.020^2$$
$$= 5.10 \text{ metres}$$
(b) When the particle returns to its
point of projection $s = 0$.
Using $s = ut + \frac{1}{2}at^2$ gives

$$0 = 10t - \frac{g}{2}t^2$$

$$t\left(10 - \frac{g}{2}t\right) = 0$$

$$t = 10 \times \frac{2}{g} = \frac{20}{g}$$

$$= 2.04 \text{ seconds}$$

3 (a) $11\,\mathrm{m\,s^{-1}}$ (b) 30 metres

4 (a) 25 metres   (b) 10 seconds

5 (a) $2.67\ (= 2\frac{2}{3})\,\mathrm{m\,s^{-1}}$

(b)

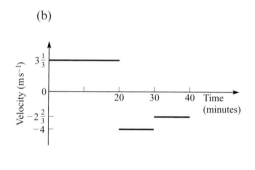

6 (a) 44.4 $(= 44\frac{4}{9})$ seconds
      (b) 494 metres

7 (a) $x = \frac{3}{2}t^2 - t;\ a = 3$
      (b)

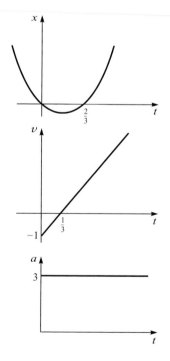

8 (a) 300 metres   (b) 25 metres

9 (a) $7.92\,\mathrm{m\,s^{-1}}$ (b) 1.62 seconds

Intermediate

1 (a) 4.9 metres; $9.8\,\mathrm{m\,s^{-1}}$
(b) 14.7 metres; $19.6\,\mathrm{m\,s^{-1}}$
(c) $14.7\,\mathrm{m\,s^{-1}}$

2 (a) $\dfrac{u}{a}$ seconds   (b) $\dfrac{u^2}{a}$ metres

3 (a) $1.5\,\mathrm{m\,s^{-2}}$ (b) 7 metres
(c) 1.33 $(\tfrac{4}{3})$ seconds   (d) $7\,\mathrm{m\,s^{-1}}$

4 4.16 s

5 (a) 1125 metres   (b) 30 s

6 (a)

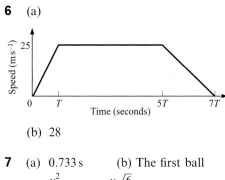

(b) 28

7 (a) 0.733 s   (b) The first ball

8 (a) $\dfrac{u^2}{2g}$ (b) $\dfrac{u\sqrt{6}}{6}$

9 (a) 20 s   (b) $0\,\mathrm{m\,s^{-2}}$

*10 (a) $x = -t^2 + 7t - 10$
When $t = 0$,
$$x = -0^2 + 7 \times 0 - 10$$
$$= -10$$
Displacement $= -10$ metres.
(b) When the particle is at O, $x = 0$
i.e. $-t^2 + 7t - 10 = 0$
Factorising the quadratic, we get
$(-t + 2)(t - 5) = 0$
$t = 2$ or $t = 5$
So the particle is first at O when
$t = 2$
(c) $x = -t^2 + 7t - 10$
Differentiating gives
$v = -2t + 7$

and differentiating again
$a = -2$
so when $t = 2$
$v = -2 \times 2 + 7 = 3\,\mathrm{m\,s^{-1}}$
$a = -2\,\mathrm{m\,s^{-2}}$

11 (a) $3.75\,\mathrm{m\,s^{-1}}$ (b) 10.4 metres
(c) According to the model, when
$t = 20$ the distance travelled is 66.7
metres. However, the velocity at that
point is zero and after that the
sprinter runs back towards the start.
So the finish line is never reached.

Advanced

1 3.90 seconds

2 (a)

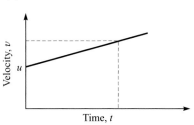

(b) Distance is area under graph.
(c) Acceleration is rate of change of
velocity, i.e. the gradient of the graph,
$$a = \frac{v - u}{t}.$$

(d) Distance is equal to the area of
the rectangle (ut) + the triangle
$(\tfrac{1}{2}at \times t)$.

*3 (a)

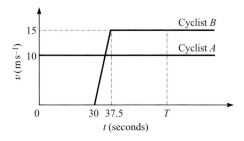

(b) Note that cyclist B reaches a speed of $15\,\mathrm{m\,s^{-1}}$ after 7.5 seconds because her acceleration is $2\,\mathrm{m\,s^{-2}}$. When $t = T$ the area under the graph of each, i.e. the distance travelled, is the same i.e.

$$10T = \tfrac{1}{2} \times 7.5 \times 15 + (T - 37.5)$$
$$\times 15$$
$$10T = 56.25 + 15T - 562.5$$
$$506.25 = 5T$$
$$T = 101\,\text{seconds}$$

(c) $a = \dfrac{-t}{2}$

(Note t is now defined as the time in seconds after the cyclist first applies her brakes.)
Integrating gives

$$v = \dfrac{-t^2}{4} + c$$

When $t = 0$, $v = 10$ so $c = 10$

$$v = \dfrac{-t^2}{4} + 10$$
$$= 10 - 0.25t^2$$

(d) (i) When $v = 0$

$$0 = \dfrac{-t^2}{4} + 10$$
$$\dfrac{t^2}{4} = 10$$
$$t = \sqrt{40} = 6.32\,\text{s}$$

(ii) Integrating gives

$$x = \dfrac{-t^3}{12} + 10t + k$$

When $t = 0$, $x = 0$ so $k = 0$

$$x = \dfrac{-t^3}{12} + 10t$$

When $t = \sqrt{40}$

$$x = \dfrac{-\left(\sqrt{40}\right)^3}{12} + 10\sqrt{40}$$
$$= 42.2\,\text{metres}$$

4   (a) $v = \dfrac{t^2}{4} + t - 2$

(b) -1.59 metres

5   (a) $t = 2$; $t = 3$
(b) $3t^2 - 10t + 6$

(c) When $t = \tfrac{4}{3}$,
acceleration $= -2\,\mathrm{m\,s^{-2}}$,
and when $t = 2$,
acceleration $= 2\,\mathrm{m\,s^{-2}}$

6   (a) $v = 2.2$; $s = 2.13$
(b) $v = 11.2$; $s = 22.2$
(c) $v = 11.2$; $s = 78.2$

7   (a) $18.6\,\mathrm{m\,s^{-1}}$ (b) 39.3 metres

Revision

1   (a)

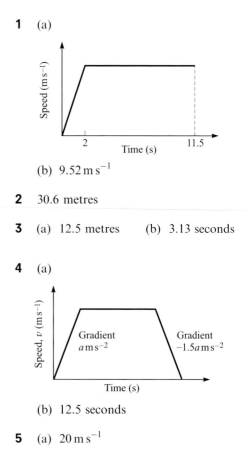

(b) $9.52\,\mathrm{m\,s^{-1}}$

2   30.6 metres

3   (a) 12.5 metres   (b) 3.13 seconds

4   (a)

(b) 12.5 seconds

5   (a) $20\,\mathrm{m\,s^{-1}}$

(b)

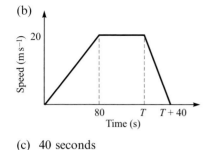

(c) 40 seconds
(d) 330 seconds

6 (a) $t^2 - 2t - 1$ (b) $\dfrac{t^3}{3} - t^2 - t$

(c) $1 + \sqrt{2}$ seconds, (d) $3\frac{1}{3}$ metres
$1 - \sqrt{2}$ seconds

7 (a) 27 metres (b) $-12.7\,\mathrm{m\,s}^{-2}$
(c) 243 metres

8 1.30 seconds

9 -0.653 metres, i.e. 0.653 metres below
the point of projection

10 (a) $\frac{1}{3}$ seconds
(b) (i) $\frac{2}{3}$ seconds (ii) 0.148 metres

11 (a) $\dfrac{u}{g}$ seconds (b) at O

12 $88\frac{1}{3}$ seconds

13 (a) $4\,\mathrm{m\,s}^{-1}$ (b) $t = 3$ seconds
(c) $6\frac{3}{4}$ metres

14 (i) 20 seconds (ii) $\frac{1}{2}\,\mathrm{m\,s}^{-2}$
(iii) $10\,\mathrm{m\,s}^{-1}$

Chapter 2 Projectiles

Basic

1 (a) 1.02 seconds
   (b) 6.10 metres

2 (a) 1.75 seconds
   (b) $17.1 \, \text{m s}^{-1}$

*3 *Solution using equations of motion*
   (a) Consider motion vertically downwards for the ball from the edge of the table to the floor: at $t = 0$,
   speed $v = 0$
   displacement $s = 0$
   Throughout the motion:
   acceleration $a = g = 9.8$
   After t seconds $s = 0.75$
   Since $a = 9.8$, by integration
   $$v = 9.8t + c$$
   Substituting initial conditions $t = 0$,
   $v = 0$ gives $c = 0$
   $\therefore v = 9.8t$
   By integration $s = 4.9t^2 + k$
   Substituting initial conditions $t = 0$,
   $v = 0$, gives $k = 0$
   $\therefore s = 4.9t^2$
   When the ball lands, $s = 0.75$ so

   $$0.75 = 4.9t^2$$

   $$t = \sqrt{\frac{0.75}{4.9}}$$

   $$= 0.391$$

   (b) Horizontally the motion has constant speed, so horizontal displacement, x, is given by
   $$x = 5t$$
   so $x = 5 \times 0.3912 = 1.96$ metres

Solution using vectors
Consider unit vectors $\mathbf{i}$ and $\mathbf{j}$ to be horizontal and vertically upward respectively with an origin at the point where the ball leaves the table.
At $t = 0$,

$$\mathbf{r} = \begin{pmatrix} 0 \\ 0 \end{pmatrix}, \mathbf{v} = \begin{pmatrix} 5 \\ 0 \end{pmatrix}, \mathbf{a} = \begin{pmatrix} 0 \\ -9.8 \end{pmatrix}$$

After t seconds,

$$\mathbf{v} = \begin{pmatrix} c_1 \\ -9.8t + c_2 \end{pmatrix} \text{ where } c_1 \text{ and } c_2$$

are constants of integration.

Substituting $\mathbf{v} = \begin{pmatrix} 5 \\ 0 \end{pmatrix}$ when $t = 0$
gives
$c_1 = 5$ and $c_2 = 0$, so $\mathbf{v} = \begin{pmatrix} 5 \\ -9.8t \end{pmatrix}$.

Integrating gives

$$\mathbf{r} = \begin{pmatrix} 5t + c_3 \\ -4.9t^2 + c_4 \end{pmatrix}$$

Substituting $\mathbf{r} = \begin{pmatrix} 0 \\ 0 \end{pmatrix}$ when $t = 0$
gives
$c_3 = 0$ and $c_4 = 0$,

so $\mathbf{r} = \begin{pmatrix} 5t \\ -4.9t^2 \end{pmatrix}$

(a) When the ball lands,

$$\mathbf{r} = \begin{pmatrix} 5t \\ -4.9t^2 \end{pmatrix} = \begin{pmatrix} R \\ -0.75 \end{pmatrix}$$

where R is the horizontal distance travelled before the ball hits the floor.

So
$4.9t^2 = 0.75,$

$$t = \sqrt{\frac{0.75}{4.9}} = 0.391 \text{ seconds}$$

(b) $R = 5t = 5 \times 0.3912 = 1.96$ metres

4 (a) 40 metres   (b) 19.6 metres

5 (a) 0.125 seconds
     (b) 0.0766 metres

6 (a) $19.6 \, \text{m s}^{-1}$ downwards
     (b) $31.8 \, \text{m s}^{-1}$

7 (a) 2.33 seconds   (b) 4.37 seconds

8 (a) 0.765 seconds   (b) 19.9 metres

9 11.1 metres

10 25.0 metres

11 29.7 metres

Intermediate

1 (b) 0.613 metres

*2 **Solution using equations of motion**
(a) Vertically upward $a = -g$.
Integrating gives $v = -gt + c$.
Substituting initial conditions:
when $t = 0$,

$$v = 19.6 \sin 45° = \frac{19.6}{\sqrt{2}}$$

so $c = 9.8\sqrt{2}$
$\Rightarrow v = 9.8\sqrt{2} - gt$

At the highest point, $v = 0$ so
$t = \sqrt{2}$ seconds.

(b) Integrating v gives
$y = 9.8\sqrt{2}t - 4.9t^2 + k$
When $t = 0$, $y = 0$, $k = 0$
so $y = 9.8\sqrt{2}t - 4.9t^2$
When $t = \sqrt{2}$,
$y = 9.8\sqrt{2} \times \sqrt{2} - 4.9 \times 2$
    $= 9.8$ metres
(c) The ball lands after it has
travelled for twice the time it takes to
reach its highest point, i.e. after
$2\sqrt{2}$ seconds.
Horizontally the component of
velocity remains constant at

$$19.6 \cos 45° = \frac{19.6}{\sqrt{2}} \, \text{m s}^{-1}$$

So distance travelled is
$9.8\sqrt{2} \times 2\sqrt{2} = 39.2$ metres

Solution using vectors
Assume the ball can be modelled as a
particle. This means that air resistance
can be ignored.
Assume its acceleration is **a**:

$$\mathbf{a} = \begin{pmatrix} 0 \\ -9.8 \end{pmatrix} \text{m s}^{-2}$$

Its velocity is $\mathbf{v} \, \text{m s}^{-1}$ and its
displacement is **r** metres, t seconds
after it is hit, relative to horizontal
and vertical axes.
By integration

$$\mathbf{v} = \begin{pmatrix} 19.6 \cos 45° \\ 19.6 \sin 45° - 9.8t \end{pmatrix}$$

since

$$\mathbf{v} = \begin{pmatrix} 19.6 \cos 45° \\ 19.6 \sin 45° \end{pmatrix} \text{ when } t = 0$$

and

$$\mathbf{r} = \begin{pmatrix} x \\ y \end{pmatrix} = \begin{pmatrix} 19.6t \cos 45° \\ 19.6t \sin 45° - 4.9t^2 \end{pmatrix}$$

since $\mathbf{r} = 0$ when $t = 0$.
(a) The ball reaches its highest point
when the vertical component of
velocity is zero, so
$19.6 \sin 45° = 9.8t$
$\Rightarrow t = \sqrt{2}$

(b) At the highest point $t = \sqrt{2}$, so substituting for t in $\mathbf{r}$ gives
$$y = 19.6\sqrt{2}\sin 45° - 4.9 \times 2$$
$$= 9.8$$
The maximum height reached is 9.8 metres.
(c) Its range is the horizontal distance travelled (i.e. when $y = 0$ again)
$$0 = 19.6t\sin 45° - 4.9t^2$$
so $t = 0$ or $t = 2\sqrt{2}$
($t = 0$ is when the golf ball is struck)
Substituting $t = 2\sqrt{2}$ in the horizontal component of $\mathbf{r}$
$$x = 19.6 \times 2\sqrt{2}\cos 45°$$
$$= 39.2$$
The range is 39.2 metres.

3 (a) 1.5 seconds   (b) 19.1 metres

4 (a) 3.02 seconds   (b) 1.51 seconds
(c) 11.2 metres

5 (a) $\frac{2}{3}$ seconds   (b) 6.48 metres

6 19.6 m s^{-1}

7 (a) 4.52 seconds   (b) 54.2 metres

(c)

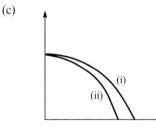

(d) The ball is a particle.
Air resistance can be ignored.
g is constant.
The sea is flat (waves can be ignored).

8 20.2 metres

9 3.91 metres

10 (a) The ball has no size.
The mass acts at the centre of gravity.
g is constant.

Air resistance can be ignored.
(b) Only the fact that g is constant is really justified. The other assumptions can be made but one must remember that the answers given will be very inaccurate.
(c) The range of the ball is likely to be an overestimate.

11 17.5 m s^{-1} at angle of 53.1° above the horizontal $(10.5\mathbf{i} + 14\mathbf{j})$ m s^{-1}

12 29.6 m s^{-1}

Advanced

*1 Model the ball as a particle where the only force acting is the constant gravitational force.
Let θ be the angle of projection and x and y be horizontal and vertical displacements from the origin at time t.
Using the equations of motion for constant acceleration, vertically
$$y = 30t\sin\theta - 4.9t^2$$
and horizontally
$$x = 30t\cos\theta$$
The projectile lands when $y = 0$
so $30t\sin\theta - 4.9t^2 = 0$
$$\Rightarrow t = 0 \text{ or } t = 6.122\sin\theta$$
($t = 0$ is when it leaves the ground)
It must also land 60 metres away so, when $t = 6.122\sin\theta$, x must be 60.
Therefore $60 = 30 \times 6.122\sin\theta \times \cos\theta$
Simplifying gives $4 = 6.122\sin(2\theta)$
(remember $2\sin\theta \times \cos\theta = \sin(2\theta)$)
So $\sin(2\theta) = 0.666\,66$
As $0 \le \theta \le 90°$ you must consider
$0 \le 2\theta \le 180°$
$2\theta = 40.8°$ or $139.2°$
$\theta = 20.4°$ or $69.6°$
The angle of projection must be 20.4° or 69.6° (note that these add to 90°).

2 (a) 22.0 m s^{-1} (b) 63.0°

3 (a) The ball is a particle. The distance between the two people is the same as the distance between the two

hands. Air resistance can be ignored.
g is constant.
(b) 18.4 metres
(c) 1.15 metres

4   (a) 1.70 metres   (b) 0.590 seconds
(c) The ball lands at 17.7 metres so is
within the service line.

5   (a) $17.4 \,\mathrm{m\,s^{-1}}$
(b) The ball would have a radius of
around 0.2 metres. This would mean
that it should reach a height of
4.2 metres if it is to clear the wall.
Also the air resistance would slow the
ball down and thus the initial speed
should be increased.

6   (a) $13.9 \,\mathrm{m\,s^{-1}}$ (b) 8.32 metres

*7   If h metres is the height of release
and ϕ is the angle of projection (in
degrees) then
$$h = 3.14 \sec^2 \phi - 12 \tan \phi + 1$$
This gives the graph

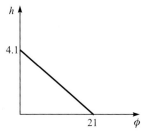

Assuming the boy is of normal height,
the possible release heights lie between
2.4 metres at an angle of 9° and
1.0 metres at 16° to the nearest
degree.

8   (a) The ball has no size. The mass
acts at the centre of gravity. g is
constant. Air resistance can be
ignored.
(b) 52.5° and 28.0°
(c) The ball has no size. Air
resistance can be ignored.

10 25.9 metres

Revision

Section A
1   (a) 11.0 metres
(b) Assumptions include: the only
force acting is due to gravity; the
speed of light is infinite; the speed of
release of the ball is zero.

2   (a) 1.23 metres
(b) $4.9 \,\mathrm{m\,s^{-1}}$ vertically downwards
(c) $5.29 \,\mathrm{m\,s^{-1}}$
(d) 1 metre

3   (a) 2.11 seconds   (b) 81.6 metres

4   (a) 0.714 seconds   (b) 21.4 metres

5   (a) 3.87 metres   (b) 21.5 metres

6   (a) 6.81 metres   (b) $22.2 \,\mathrm{m\,s^{-1}}$

7   0.260 metres

Section B
*1   (a) By integration,
$$\mathbf{v} = 10\mathbf{i} + (12 - 9.8t)\mathbf{j}$$
since $\mathbf{v} = 10\mathbf{i} + 12\mathbf{j}$ when $t = 0$. The
particle reaches its highest point when
the vertical component of velocity is
zero.
So $12 - 9.8t = 0$
$$t = 1.22$$
It reaches its highest point after
1.22 seconds.
(b) By integration,
$$\mathbf{r} = 10t\mathbf{i} + (12t - 4.9t^2)\mathbf{j}$$
taking the origin to be at the point of
projection.
(i) When $t = 2$,
$$\mathbf{r} = 20\mathbf{i} + (12 \times 2 - 4.9 \times 2^2)\mathbf{j}$$
$$= 20\mathbf{i} + 4.4\mathbf{j}$$
(ii) When $x = 15$,
$10t = 1.5$ so $t = 1.5$ hence
$$y = 12 \times 1.5 - 4.9 \times 1.5^2$$
$$= 6.98$$
(iii) When $x = 15$, $t = 1.5$,
$$\mathbf{v} = 10\mathbf{i} + (12 - 9.8 \times 1.5)\mathbf{j}$$
$$= 10\mathbf{i} - 2.7\mathbf{j}$$

The velocity has magnitude

$$v = \sqrt{(10^2 + (-2.7)^2)}$$
$$= 10.36$$

and direction

$$\tan^{-1}\left(\frac{2.7}{10}\right) \text{ or } 15.1°$$

The velocity is therefore
$10.4\,\mathrm{m\,s^{-1}}$ at an angle of $15.1°$
(downward) to the horizontal.

2   3.27 metres

3 $u = 39.2$, $\mathbf{r} = \begin{pmatrix} 100 \\ 78.4 \end{pmatrix}$ metres

4   (a) $\mathbf{v} = \begin{pmatrix} 4 \\ 6 - 9.8t \end{pmatrix}$, $\mathbf{r} = \begin{pmatrix} 4t \\ 6t - 4.9t^2 \end{pmatrix}$

(b) Maximum height $= 1.84$ metres
(c) When $t = 0.5$, height is
1.78 metres. Distance from origin is
3.40 metres.

5   44.7 metres; $50.3\,\mathrm{m\,s^{-1}}$

6 $a = 2.77$; initial speed $= 6.61\,\mathrm{m\,s^{-1}}$

7 $\begin{pmatrix} 8.95 \\ 15.3 \end{pmatrix} \mathrm{m\,s^{-1}}$

Section C
1   (b) (i) 9.1 metres   (ii) 141.4 metres
(iii) 0.27 seconds

2   (i) 62.5 metres
(ii) 56.8 metres; shell is falling
(iii) Earliest; 2.05 seconds; latest;
4.99 seconds
(iv) For shell 1 $H_1 = 4.9T_1^2$.
For shell 2 $H_2 = 4.9T_2^2$, so if
$T_1 = T_2$,
$H_1 = H_2 = 4.9T_1^2 = 4.9T_2^2$
(v) Let the maximum heights reached
by the two shells be H_1 and H_2, and
the time taken to reach these heights
be T_1 and T_2.
Thus $H_1 = 4.9T_1^2$ and $H_2 = 4.9T_2^2$.
The two shells explode at the same
time so $T_1 = T_2$ and hence
$4.9T_1^2 = 4.9T_2^2$.
Thus $H_1 = H_2$.

3   (iii) $2.7\,\mathrm{m\,s^{-1}}$, $3.6\,\mathrm{m\,s^{-1}}$
(iv) 0.27 metres
(v) 0.309 metres

Chapter 3 Resultant and relative velocity

Basic

1 (a) $1\,\mathrm{m\,s^{-1}}$ due north
(b) $6.40\,(=\sqrt{41})\,\mathrm{m\,s^{-1}}$ on a bearing of $38.7°\,(=\tan^{-1}\frac{4}{5})$
(c) $8.32\,\mathrm{m\,s^{-1}}$ on a bearing of $19.9°$

*2 Resultant velocity of boat is
$\mathbf{v}_r = \mathbf{v}_{\text{boat}} + \mathbf{v}_{\text{river}}$,
where $\mathbf{v}_{\text{boat}}$ is the velocity of the boat in still water and $\mathbf{v}_{\text{river}}$ is the velocity of the river.

$v_r^2 = 5^2 + 0.4^2$
$\quad = 25.16$
(a) Considering the component of velocity in the direction directly across the river gives time taken to cross the river,

$T = \dfrac{20}{0.4} = 50\ \text{seconds}$

(b) Distance travelled by boat:
$d = 5.016 \times 50 = 251\ \text{metres}$

3 $125\,\mathrm{m}$

4 (a) $4.47\,(=\sqrt{20})\,\mathrm{km\,h^{-1}}$ at an angle of $26.6°$ with the downstream bank
(b) $50\,\mathrm{m}$

5 $34.6\,(=20\sqrt{3})\,\mathrm{km\,h^{-1}}$

6 Speed lies between
$31.6\,(=10\sqrt{10})\,\mathrm{m\,s^{-1}}$ and
$41.2\,(=10\sqrt{17})\,\mathrm{m\,s^{-1}}$

7 $17.2\,\mathrm{m\,s^{-1}}$

8 $66\frac{2}{3}$ metres

9 (a) The shortest time occurs when the canoe heads straight across the river.
(b) $200\,\mathrm{s}$, $1.04\,\mathrm{km}$

*10 Velocity of passenger on ship, $\mathbf{v}_A$:

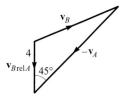

Velocity of second ship (B) relative to A
$\mathbf{v}_{B\,\text{rel}A} = \mathbf{v}_B - \mathbf{v}_A$

Using the cosine rule:
$v_B^2 = 10^2 + 4^2 - 2 \times 10 \times 4 \times \cos 45°$
$\quad = 116 - 56.569$
$v_B = 7.71\,\mathrm{m\,s^{-1}}$
Using the sine rule:
$\dfrac{10}{\sin\alpha} = \dfrac{7.709}{\sin 45°}$
$\alpha = 113.5°$

Ship is on bearing 066.5° sailing with speed 7.71 m s^{-1}.

11 Wind appears to be on bearing 308°.

12 $2\mathbf{i} - 16\mathbf{j}$ m s^{-1}

Intermediate

1 (a) 18 km h^{-1} on bearing 124°; B is 2.5 km east of O
(b) 25 km h^{-1} on bearing 127°; B is $1\frac{2}{3}$ kilometres east of O.

2 (a) $v_A = 1$ m s^{-1} upstream

$v_B = 1.32\left(=\dfrac{\sqrt{7}}{2}\right)$ m s^{-1} downstream

at 40.9° to the bank;
$v_C = 1.20$ m s^{-1} upstream at 62.1° to the bank
(b) 1.57 m s^{-1} upstream at 7.11° to the bank

*3

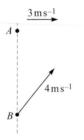

As the aircraft collide, the velocity of B relative to A must be due north:

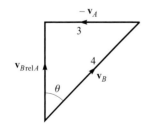

$\theta = \sin^{-1}\left(\frac{3}{4}\right) = 48.6°$

$v_{B\,\mathrm{rel}A} = \sqrt{4^2 - 3^2} = \sqrt{7} = 2.646\,\mathrm{m\,s}^{-1}$

Therefore time taken to travel 100 metres is

$$T = \frac{100}{2.646} = 37.8 \text{ seconds}$$

4 18.9 knots on a bearing of 191°

5 (a) 25 s   (b) 32.0 s

6 (a) 8.07 m s^{-1} on a bearing of 142°
(b) 50 m

7 3 m s^{-1}

8 15.6 m s^{-1} at an angle of 59.0° to his final direction of travel.

*9

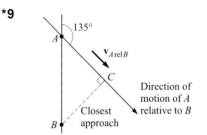

Distance of closest approach is BC,
$BC = 5\sin 45°$
    $= 3.54$ km
    $= 3540$ metres
$BC = AC = 3540$ metres
Time taken to travel distance AC at speed 2 m s^{-1},

$$t = \frac{3540}{2} = 1767 \text{ seconds}$$

$= 29$ minutes

Advanced

1 (a) 24.2 m s^{-1} on bearing 071.9°

2 (a) 11.3°   (b) 0.816 seconds

3 (a) $3\frac{1}{3}$ km   (b) 12.11 p.m.

4 (a) 30 kilometres
(b) 261 m s^{-1} at 116° to OP
(c) 21.6 km; P is 16.0 kilometres past O; Q is 10.1 kilometres from O

5 (a) $10 \, \text{m s}^{-1}$
(b) 173 metres or 548 metres

6 (a) 12.19 p.m., 2 kilometres
(b) 25 minutes

7 12 minutes

8 (a) $\mathbf{r} = (-1 + t)\mathbf{i} + (-2 + 0.5t)\mathbf{j}$
(b) $t = 1.6$ seconds, 1.34 metres

10 (a) 63.5 metres   (b) 62.3 metres
(c) $t = 3.21$ metres

11 (a) 3.70 kilometres
(b) 333 seconds

Revision

1 $36.1 \, \text{m s}^{-1}$ on bearing 146°

2 (a) 75.5° with the upstream bank
(b) 12.9 s

3 $763 \, \text{km h}^{-1}$ on bearing 302°

4 (a) $178 \, \text{m s}^{-1}$ on bearing 277°
(b) $178 \, \text{m s}^{-1}$ on bearing 097.5°

5 (a) $13 \, \text{m s}^{-1}$
(b) (i) At right angles to his path
(ii) $9.22 \, \text{m s}^{-1}$ at an angle of 49.4° to his path

6 (a) $37.7 \, \text{m s}^{-1}$ at 83.4° with the vertical

(b) $32.8 \, \text{m s}^{-1}$ at 82.4° with the vertical

7 $1.56 \, \text{m s}^{-1}$

8 $18.1 \, \text{m s}^{-1}$, bearing 054.0°

9 046.1°

10 (a) $14 \, \text{m s}^{-1}$ at 142° to the direction of motion of the first rider
(b) 3 m

11 (a) 30 m   (b) 23.1 m

12 1.74 seconds

13 43.9 seconds

14 (a) $(50 - 200t)\mathbf{i} + (30 + 60t)\mathbf{j} + 10\mathbf{k}$;
$(-10 + 160t)\mathbf{i} + 240t\mathbf{j} + (70 - 60t)\mathbf{k}$

15 (a)

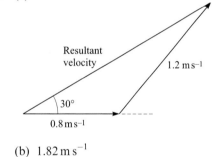

(b) $1.82 \, \text{m s}^{-1}$

Chapter 4 Momentum

Basic

*1 Let original direction of motion of A be taken as positive and velocity of B after the collision be V.

Before A B

After

Momentum of A before impact is $8mu$.
Momentum of B before impact is $-8mu$.
Momentum of A after impact is $-4mu$.
Momentum of B after impact is $2mV$.
Momentum is conserved so
$$8mu - 8mu = -4mu + 2mV$$
$$V = 2u$$
Velocity of B is $2u$ in original direction of A.

2 P: $1.25\,\mathrm{m\,s^{-1}}$; Q: $3.75\,\mathrm{m\,s^{-1}}$

3 $1.43\,\mathrm{m\,s^{-1}}$

4 $1.75\,\mathrm{m\,s^{-1}}$

5 (a) $0.182\,(=\frac{2}{11})\,\mathrm{m\,s^{-1}}$
  (b) $0.0727\,(=\frac{4}{55})\,\mathrm{m\,s^{-1}}$
  (c) $0.291\,(=\frac{16}{55})\,\mathrm{m\,s^{-1}}$

6 $30\,000\,\mathrm{N\,s}$

7 $5\,\mathrm{N\,s}$

8 $3.75\,\mathrm{m\,s^{-1}}$

9 (a) $0.25\,\mathrm{m\,s^{-1}}$
  (b) $0.025\,\mathrm{N\,s}$ in opposite directions

10 (a) $6.67\,(=6\frac{2}{3})\,\mathrm{m\,s^{-1}}$
  (b) $6.67\,m\,\mathrm{N\,s}$

11 $10\,\mathrm{m\,s^{-1}}$

Intermediate

*1 (a) Let speed of stone on impact be $v\,\mathrm{m\,s^{-1}}$.
  Then $v^2 = 2gh$
  $v = 22.136$
  Momentum before impact is given by mv
  $mv = 0.2v = 4.4272$
  Momentum $= 4.43\,\mathrm{N\,s}$
  (b) Momentum after impact $= mu$
  $= 0.4427\,\mathrm{N\,s}$
  Change in momentum
  $= 4.4272 - 0.44272 = 3.9845$
  Impulse from water $= 3.98\,\mathrm{N\,s}$

2 $2m$

3 (a) 0
  (b) Mv

4 $7500\,\mathrm{kg}$

5 $\dfrac{1}{249}$

6 $0.154\,\mathrm{kg}$

7 $20\,\mathrm{m\,s^{-1}}$

8 (a) $12.5\,\mathrm{kg}$ (b) $75\,\mathrm{N\,s}$

Advanced

1 1300 s
This is a very long time: over 20 minutes. The astronaut would have to throw away a larger object or throw the same object at a greater speed to reach the spacecraft more quickly.

3 8.76 N s

4 (a) Let speed of A and B after the string becomes taut be V.
Initial momentum $= 2mu + 0$
Final mom. $= 2mV + mV = 3mV$
Momentum is conserved so $V = \frac{2}{3}u$
(b) Impulse in string is change in momentum of $B = \frac{2}{3}mu$

5 (a) 0.2v N s   (b) 0.5(3.13 − v)
(c) 2.24 m s^{-1}

6 39.1m N s

7 (a) 0.0722 N s vertically upwards
(b) 4 grams

*8

Before impact

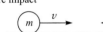

After impact

Let velocity of B after impact be V.
Momentum is conserved so
$(m − M)v = MV − 1.5mv$
$MV = (2.5m − M)v$ in direction shown. v is positive as A reverses direction. But B travels in direction shown so V must be positive.
Thus $2.5m > M$.

9 (a) 0.48u in the direction of the string connecting A and B at the instant it becomes taut, i.e. on a bearing of 307°
(b) 0.768u

Revision

1 (a) 2u in opposite direction to its motion before collision
(b) 6mu in direction of its final motion

2 9.69 m s^{-1}

3 12 m s^{-1}

4 $\frac{8}{9}$ kg

5 (a) 2.5   (b) $\frac{7}{4}$

6 9 m s^{-1}

7 16.3 N s

*8 Let the velocity of block just before impact be $+V$ m s^{-1}.
$V^2 = 2gh$ so $V = 4.427\sqrt{h}$
Momentum before impact is mV.
Block rises to 3 metres so speed just after impact is $\sqrt{6g} = 7.6681$ m s^{-1}.
Momentum after impact is $−61\,345$ N s.
But impulse $=$ change in momentum so $35\,418\sqrt{h} − −61\,345 = 132\,000$
$\sqrt{h} = 1.99$
Height $= 4$ m to nearest metre

9 (a) 2.50 m s^{-1} (b) 3.76 N s

10 6.62 m s^{-1}

11 $w = 6$, $x = 3.5$, $z = 3.5$, $y = 3.8$
B travels faster than C at this point, so it will catch C up and collide with it.

12 (a) 1.2u in original direction of motion of A
(b) 2.8mu N s in opposite direction to motion of A

13 (a) 0.433u m s^{-1} $\left(= \dfrac{\sqrt{3}}{4}u\right)$ in the direction of the string connecting A and B at the instant it becomes taut, i.e. on a bearing of 120°
(b) 0.661u m s^{-1} $\left(= \dfrac{\sqrt{7}}{4}u\right)$

Chapter 5 Forces at a point

Basic

1 (a) $-3.83\mathbf{i} + 3.21\mathbf{j}$
   (b) $4.50\mathbf{i} - 5.36\mathbf{j}$
   (c) $5.64\mathbf{i} + 2.05\mathbf{j}$
   (d) $-1.27\mathbf{i} - 2.72\mathbf{j}$
   (e) $4.33\mathbf{i} + 2.5\mathbf{j}$
   (f) $8.66\mathbf{i} + 5\mathbf{j}$

2 (a) 9.27 N at an angle of 27.2° with
       the 4 N force
   (b) 11.2 N at an angle of 63.4° with
       the 5 N force
   (c) 8.73 N at an angle of 20.1° with
       the 3 N force
   (d) 7.52 N at an angle of 20° with
       both the 4 N forces

3 (a) $0.5\mathbf{i} - 0.33\mathbf{j}$
   (b) $-0.660\mathbf{i} - 6.43\mathbf{j}$

*4 Forces are in equilibrium so form the
    sides of a triangle as shown.

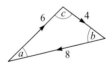

Using cosine formula,

$$\cos a = \frac{64 + 36 - 16}{96}$$

$a = 28.955°$
Using sine rule,
$\sin b = 1.5 \sin a$
so $b = 46.567°$
Angles add up to 180° so
$c = 104.478°$
Hence angles are
151° between 6 N and 8 N forces,

76° between 6 N and 4 N forces,
133° between 4 N and 8 N forces.

5 151° between 21 N and 28 N forces,
   76° between 21 N and 14 N forces,
   133° between 14 N and 28 N forces

6 106 N

7 0.611

8 $r = 3, s = -5$

9 13

10 $-12\mathbf{i} + 5\mathbf{j}$ newtons

Intermediate

1 (a) $3.76\mathbf{i} + 1.37\mathbf{j}$
   (b) $-5.07\mathbf{i} + 10.9\mathbf{j}$

2 (a) $(P - mg\sin\theta)\mathbf{i} + (N - mg\cos\theta)\mathbf{j}$
   (b) $(P\cos\theta - mg\sin\theta)\mathbf{i}$
       $+ (N - mg\cos\theta - P\sin\theta)\mathbf{j}$

*3 (Method 1)

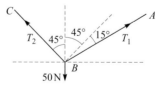

Forces are in equilibrium so resolving
at right angles to BC
$T_1 \cos 15 + T_2 \cos 90 = 50 \cos 45$
$T_1 = 36.6$ N
Resolving horizontally
$T_2 \cos 45 = T_1 \cos 30$
$T_2 = 44.8$ N

(Method 2)

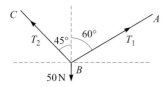

Forces are in equilibrium so resolving horizontally and vertically

$T_2 \sin 45° = T_1 \sin 60°$ (1)
$T_2 \cos 45° + T_1 \cos 60° = 50$ (2)

Substituting for T_2 in (2)

$0.5T_1(\sqrt{3} + 1) = 50$

$T_1 = 36.603$

Substituting in (1) gives $T_2 = 44.829$

Ans. $T_1 = 36.6$ N, $T_2 = 44.8$ N

4   8.39 N

5 $P = 11.5$ N, $N = 23.1$ N

6 $\theta = 82.1°$

7   Dario: 222 N
    Mia: 240 N

Advanced

1   (a) All the matter of the object is assumed to be at a single point in space. The particle is said to have the mass of the object but no dimensions.
(b) 42.8° and 26.5°
(c) 23 kN and 19 kN

*2

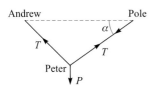

The situation is shown in the diagram. If Peter pulls at right angles to the line between Andrew and the pole as shown, then the tension in both parts of the rope is equal.
Let the maximum pull Peter can manage be P and let the rope make an angle α with the line between Andrew and the pole as shown. The pull on Andrew, T, is given by

$$T = \frac{P}{(2 \sin \alpha)}$$

so, as long as $\sin \alpha < 0.5$ ($\alpha < 60°$), then the pull on Andrew is greater than that exerted by Peter.
If $\alpha < 5°$ then the pull on Andrew is over 5 times that exerted by Peter.

3   (a) 43 N   (b) 28 N
(c) If the bag weighed less than 30 N it would give the correct weight. If it weighed more then, no matter what the weight of the bag was, the readings of both meters would be 30 N.

4   (a) The friction force between the two surfaces is small enough, relative to any other forces present, to be ignored.
(b)

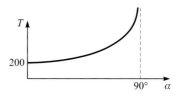

As α approaches 90° the tension becomes infinitely great. Thus the rope would break before it became horizontal.
(c) 4.76 metres.

5   45.2 N

6   (a) 36.9°   (b) $W = (3\sqrt{3} + 4)T$
(c) The mass of the rope is sufficiently small compared with all other masses to be ignored. The rope remains the same length no matter what force acts on it.
(d) If the rope is heavy then some of the reading shown on the gauges is due to the weight of the rope so the expression is an overestimate of W.

7   (a) $T = 0.25W$ (b) $T = 0.3W$

Revision

1 (a) 6.77 N at an angle of 17.2° with the 3 N force
(b) 8.46 N at an angle of 17.7° with the 5 N force

2 82.8°, 138.6°, 138.6°

3 (a) The angle between the wires is 120°
(b) The tension in each of the other wires must increase by 20 newtons.

4 LH wire is 7.23 N
RH wire is 6.39 N

5 (a) 20.6 N   (b) 14.0°

6 (a) (i) C should hold the middle rope, B the rope that makes an angle of 20° to this, and A the rope that makes an angle of 30° to the middle rope.

(ii) The resultant force is 2028 newtons.
(b) 2003 N

7 25.7° and 21.7 N

8 (a) $\cos \alpha = \dfrac{x}{\sqrt{x^2 + 1}}$ and
$\sin \alpha = \dfrac{1}{\sqrt{x^2 + 1}}$

(b) $P = \dfrac{W\sqrt{x^2 + 1}}{(x - 1)}$ $Q = \dfrac{\sqrt{2}W}{(x - 1)}$

(c) Both P and Q must be less than the breaking strain of the rope, a positive finite quantity. Thus $(x - 1)$ must be positive so $x > 1$.
(d) The rope between the window and the packing case breaks first, when $x = 1.44$ metres

9 24.2° and 3.80 N

Chapter 6 Force models

Basic

1   31.4 N

2   The maximum friction force that can act is 137.2 N so the box accelerates.

*3   Resolving in perpendicular and parallel directions to the slope:

$$4g\cos 25° = R$$
$$4g\sin 25° = F$$

But $F = \mu R$ as slipping is about to occur, so

$$4g\sin 25° = \mu \times 4g\cos 25°$$
$$\mu = \tan 25° = 0.466$$

4   (a)   26.8 N   (b)   42.0°

5   5.20 kg

6   20 cm

7   31.3 N

8   (a)   2.45 N   (b)   6.13 cm

9 $\frac{2}{5}$ of natural length

10   6.25 N

11   17 cm

12 6.67×10^{-5} N

13   9.77 N

14 3.53×10^{22} N

Intermediate

*1

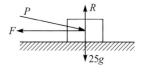

The crate is on the point of sliding so

$$F = \mu R = 0.45R$$

Resolving horizontally and vertically

$$P\cos 12° = F = 0.45R \tag{1}$$
$$P\sin 12° + 25 \times 9.8 = R \tag{2}$$

Substituting for R in (1)

$$P(\cos 12 - 0.45\sin 12) = 0.45 \times 25\,g$$
$$P = 125\,\text{N}$$

2   (a)   0.700   (b)   225 N

3   169 N

4   (a)   12.3 N   (b)   196 N

5   (a)   26.5 N   (b)   41.9 N

6   39.2 cm

7 $\dfrac{m}{2}$

8   43.9 N

9   (a)   42.4 N   (b)   60°

10   (a)   20 cm
     (b)   (i)   70.5°   (ii)   55.4 N

11   (a)   0.667 N   (b)   0.25F
     (c)   4F

12 (a) $5.98 \times 10^{24}\,\text{kg}$
(b) $2.64 \times 10^{6}\,\text{m}$

13 $3.90 \times 10^{-5}\text{degrees}$

14 $g' = 0.997g$

15 1.62 N; at the surface of the Earth the force of attraction would be approximately 9.8 N which is about six times greater.

Advanced

2 $0.8l$

3 (b) (i) $P = \dfrac{mg}{(\sin\theta - \mu\cos\theta)}$

4 (a) 0.626   (b) 13.6 N

*5 The tension T is the same in both parts of the string. Let the extensions in the strings be x_1 and x_2 respectively.

$$T = mg = \frac{\lambda x_1}{l} = \frac{3\lambda x_2}{2l}$$

$$x_1 = \frac{mgl}{\lambda} \quad \text{and} \quad x_2 = \frac{2mgl}{\lambda}$$

but $x_1 + x_2 = \dfrac{5l}{6}$

so $m = \dfrac{5\lambda}{18g}$

6 (a) 26.6°   (c) 0.547l

7 (a) 10mg (b) 1.1$\sqrt{3}\,l$

8 $\frac{2}{3}d$

Revision

*1

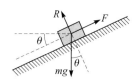

Resolving along and perpendicular to the plane.

$F = mg\sin\theta$ (1)
$R = mg\cos\theta$ (2)

But the block is on the point of slipping so $F = \mu R$. Substituting for F in (1) and dividing (1) by (2) gives $\mu = \tan\theta$

2 $\dfrac{0.6mg}{(\cos\theta + 0.6\sin\theta)}$

3 22.5 N

4 (a) 0.75   (b) 351 N

5 (a) 0.35
(b) The normal reaction, N, between the boat and the slipway is $300g\sin 10°$ whether the boat is being pulled up or down the slipway as the tension in the rope is parallel to the direction of the slipway.
The boat is moving, so friction is limiting and equal to $\mu N = \mu 300g\sin 10°$. Thus friction is the same in both cases.
(c) 1520 N

6 11.8 N

7 2.45 cm

8 (a) 49 N m^{-1} (b) 34 cm
(c) 16 cm

9 3 cm

10 (i) 6.86 N
(ii) 2.94 tan θ
(iii) 35.0°

11 4.98×10^{16} N

12 16F

13 2.00×10^{7} m (20 000 km)

Chapter 7 Newton's second law

Basic

1 3 kN

2 $4.9\,\mathrm{m\,s^{-2}}$

3 $0.857\,\mathrm{m\,s^{-2}}$

4 (a) $25\,\mathrm{m\,s^{-2}}$ (b) $250\,\mathrm{m\,s^{-1}}$
(c) 1250 metres

5 (a) 492 N   (b) 352 N

6 $7.69\,\mathrm{m\,s^{-2}}$

*7

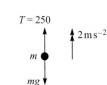

By Newton's second law
$250 - mg = 2m$
$250 = 11.8m$
$m = 21.2\,\mathrm{kg}$

8 (a) $4.42\,\mathrm{m\,s^{-2}}$ (b) 55.3 metres

9 $4.16\,\mathrm{m\,s^{-2}}$

10 $\sqrt{34}\,\mathrm{m\,s^{-2}}\,(5.83\,\mathrm{m\,s^{-2}})$

11 $5\mathbf{i} - 4.5\mathbf{j}$ newtons

Intermediate

1 100 N

2 $1.09\,\mathrm{m\,s^{-2}}$

3 $2.29\,\mathrm{m\,s^{-2}}$ at an angle of 70.9° to 4 N
force

4 0.204

5 (a) $0.156\,\mathrm{m\,s^{-2}}$ (b) 194 N

*6 (a)

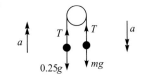

By Newton's second law

$mg - T = ma$ (mass m)
$T - 0.25g = 0.25a$ (mass of 0.25 kg)

but $a = 2$ so $T = 0.5 + 2.45 = 2.95$
Tension $= 2.95$ N
(b) $9.8\,m - T = ma = 2m$
$7.8\,m = 2.95$
$m = 0.378$

7 1270 N

8 (a) 29.5 N   (b) 32.2 N

9 (a) 3150 N   (b) $2.13\,\mathrm{m\,s^{-2}}$

10 (a) $3.5\,\mathrm{m\,s^{-2}}$ (b) 25.2 N

Advanced

1 (a) $5.38\,\mathrm{m\,s^{-2}}$ (b) 22.1 N

*2 Using the forces and angles in the
diagram

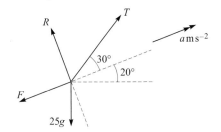

By Newton's second law along and at right angles to the slope,

$T \cos 30° - F - 25g \sin 20° = 25a$
$R = 25g \cos 20° - T \sin 30°$

But $F = \mu R = 0.6R$ and $a = 1$
$T \cos 30° - 15g \cos 20° + 0.6T \sin 30°$
$\qquad - 25g \sin 20° = 25$
$T(\cos 30° + 0.6 \sin 30°)$
$= 15g \cos 20° + 25g \sin 20° + 25$
$1.166T = 246.9$
Tension is 212 N

3 (a) 11.9° with the 750 N force and 18.1° with the 500 N force
(b) 4.74 m s^{-2}

4 (a) 2.45 m s^{-2} (b) 7.35 N
(c) 2.45 N

5 (a) 0.549 N
(b) The train starts to slow down and momentarily stops. The component of the force due to gravity which acts down the slope is 0.299 N. The resistive force is 0.245 N, so the train then starts to go back down the slope, accelerating as it does so.

6 (a) 1.28 m s^{-2} (b) 13.9 N

7 (a) 1.96 m s^{-2}
(b) 39.2 N in string joined to 5 kg mass;
35.3 N in string joined to 3 kg mass

8 (a) 1390 N   (b) 721 N

9 (a) 2 kg mass pulled up the slope then $M = 3.01$ kg
2 kg mass travels down the slope then $M = 0.511$ kg
(b) 21.1 N and 4.09 N respectively.

Revision

1 2 or -14

2 4.48 m s^{-2}

3 (a) 4.40 N   (b) 0.407 kg

4 0.557 m s^{-2} at an angle of 51.1° to 6 N force

5 625 N

6 (a) 1.70 m s^{-2} (b) 23.0 N

*7 (a)

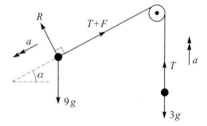

$T = 35$ so, using Newton's second law, for 3 kg mass:
$35 - 29.4 = 3a$
$a = 1.866\,66$
Acceleration is 1.87 m s^{-2}.
(b) For 9 kg mass
$R = 9g \cos \alpha$ and $F = \mu R = 0.25R$
Resolving down the slope gives
$9g \sin \alpha - 2.25g \cos \alpha - 35 = 9a$
$9.8 \sin \alpha = 2.45 \cos \alpha + 5.755$
Squaring both sides and substituting
$1 - \cos^2 \alpha$ for $\sin^2 \alpha$ gives
$102.0 \cos^2 \alpha + 28.20 \cos \alpha - 62.92 = 0$
so $\cos \alpha = 0.6590$ ($\cos \alpha$ not negative)
$\alpha = 48.8°$

8 (a) 0.165   (b) 15.3 N

9 (a) (ii) 0.45 N
(b) The only forces acting are resisitive forces so the train and carriage will slow down and stop. These forces only resist motion so, once the train stops, the forces will no longer act and the train will remain at rest.

10 (i) 0.933 N   (ii) 0.748 m s^{-1}

Chapter 8 Circular motion with constant speed

Basic

1 (a) (i) $4 \, \mathrm{rad \, s^{-1}}$
(ii) $8 \, \mathrm{m \, s^{-2}}$ towards the centre of the circle
(b) $24 \, \mathrm{N}$ towards the centre of the circle

2 (a) $7.5 \, \mathrm{m \, s^{-1}}$ tangentially
(b) $3.75 \, \mathrm{m \, s^{-2}}$ towards the centre of the circle

3 (a) $2\sqrt{2} \, \mathrm{m \, s^{-1}}$
(b) $0.4 \, \mathrm{N}$ towards the centre of the circle

*4 (a) Angular speed $= \dfrac{v}{r} = \dfrac{24}{80} = 0.3$
Angular speed is $0.3 \, \mathrm{rad \, s^{-1}}$
(b) Acceleration of car is $\dfrac{v^2}{r} = \dfrac{242}{80} = 7.2$
Acceleration is $7.2 \, \mathrm{m \, s^{-2}}$ towards centre of path
(c) Force $= ma$ by Newton's second law so $F = 800 \times 7.2$
Force is 5760 newtons

5 (a) $9 \, \mathrm{m \, s^{-2}}$ towards the centre of the circle
(b) $10.5 \, \mathrm{s}$

6 $0.0338 \, \mathrm{m \, s^{-2}}$ towards the centre of the Earth

7 (a) 3 metres   (b) $1.5\pi \, \mathrm{m \, s^{-1}}$
(c) $7.40 \, \mathrm{m \, s^{-2}} \; (3\pi^2/4)$
(d) 4 seconds

8 (a) 10 metres
(b) $-4\sin(0.4t)\mathbf{i} + 4\cos(0.4t)\mathbf{j}$
(c) $-1.6\cos(0.4t)\mathbf{i} - 1.6\sin(0.4t)\mathbf{j}$
(d) $4 \, \mathrm{m \, s^{-1}}$
(e) $1.6 \, \mathrm{m \, s^{-2}}$

9 (a) $2.09 \, \mathrm{m \, s^{-1}}$
(b) $0.439 \, \mathrm{m \, s^{-2}}$ towards the centre of the wheel

10 Increased by $1.8 \, \mathrm{m \, s^{-2}}$

11 $97.2 \, \mathrm{N}$, approx 6 times less

12 $x = 2.5r$

Intermediate

1 $u : v$ is $\sqrt{2} : 1$

2 (a) $0.6 \, \mathrm{rad \, s^{-1}}$
(b) $7.2 \, \mathrm{m \, s^{-2}}$
(c) $8640 \, \mathrm{N}$
(d) 0.735

*3 (a) Particle rotates once in $0.5 \, \mathrm{s}$ so angular speed is $4\pi \, \mathrm{rad \, s^{-1}}$
Resolving vertically and horizontally

By Newton's second law
$$T \cos \alpha = mg \qquad\qquad (1)$$
$$T \sin \alpha = m\omega^2 l \sin \alpha$$
$$T = m\omega^2 l \text{ as } \alpha \text{ is not equal to zero.}$$

Substituting for T in equation (1)
gives $\omega^2 l \cos\alpha = g$

so $\cos\alpha = \dfrac{9.8}{0.5 \times 16 \times \pi^2}$

$\cos\alpha = 0.1241$

so α is 1.45 rad (82.9°)
(b) From equation (1)

$T = \dfrac{mg}{\cos\alpha}$

$T = \dfrac{0.1 \times 9.8}{0.1241}$

$= 7.896$
so tension is 7.90 newtons

4 (a) 0.412 rad (= 23.6°)
   (b) 0.214 N
   (c) 0.925 m s^{-2}

5 (a) 0.1 metres   (b) 2.83 rad s^{-1}

6 (a) 1.05 m s^{-1} (b) 0.146 m s^{-2}
   (c) The path of any point on the car
   is still a circle of diameter 15 metres
   but the centre of the circle would be
   displaced downwards. The speed and
   acceleration are unchanged.

7 (a) 15.8 m s^{-1} (b) 19.9 seconds

8 53.8°

9 (a) 0.859 rad (49.2°)
   (b) 1.52 m s^{-1}

10 $M\sqrt{(g^2 + 16r^2)}$ newtons

11 (a) 8.98 N   (b) 968 m s^{-1}

12 695 km

Advanced

1 24.7 cm

*2 Acceleration is $400 \times 20^2/50 = 3200$ N
horizontally towards the centre of the
circle.

The bike is on the point of slipping
up the bank so friction acts down.
The force diagram is

Let the coefficient of friction be μ.
$F = \mu R$
Resolving vertically
$R\sin 80° = 400g + \mu R\cos 80°$ (1)
Resolving horizontally
$R\cos 80° + \mu R\sin 80° = 3200$ (2)

From (1) $R = \dfrac{400g}{(\sin 80° - \mu\cos 80°)}$

From (2) $R = \dfrac{3200}{(\cos 80° + \mu\sin 80°)}$

So $9.8(\cos 80° + \mu\sin 80°) =$
   $8(\sin 80° - \mu\cos 80°)$
Collecting coefficients gives
$11.04\mu = 6.1767$
Coefficient of friction is 0.559

3 (a)

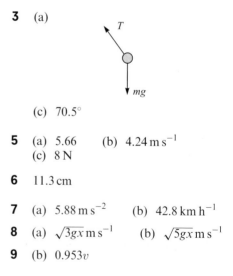

(c) 70.5°

5 (a) 5.66   (b) 4.24 m s^{-1}
   (c) 8 N

6 11.3 cm

7 (a) 5.88 m s^{-2} (b) 42.8 km h^{-1}
8 (a) $\sqrt{3gx}$ m s^{-1} (b) $\sqrt{5gx}$ m s^{-1}
9 (b) 0.953v

Revision

1   (b) $-0.5\cos(0.5t)\mathbf{i} - 0.5\sin(0.5t)\mathbf{j}$

2   The plane describes a circle of radius $\dfrac{r}{2}$ metres. The centre of the circle is therefore displaced by $\dfrac{r}{2}$ metres. The time taken to complete one circuit is halved.

3   (a) 0.8 metres   (b) 0.8π seconds

4   (a) $0.105\,\text{rad s}^{-1}$
       (b) $0.001\,75\,\text{rad s}^{-1}$
       (c) $0.001\,26\,\text{m s}^{-1}$
       (d) $3.35 \times 10^{-8}\,\text{m s}^{-2}$
       (e) If the hands were 1.2 cm and 1.1 cm long respectively then the circles traced out by the tips would have radii less than that as the axle would have to go through the hands. This means that the answers given to (c) and (d) are overestimates. Also the hands of a clock or watch rotate in steps and do not travel smoothly so the magnitude of the actual velocity would vary from zero to a figure larger than that given, as would the acceleration.

*5   (a) One circuit is 2π radians. Angular speed is $2\,\text{rad s}^{-1}$. Time taken is $2\pi/2 = \pi$ seconds.
       (b) Acceleration is $\omega^2 r$
            $= 4 \times 0.2 = 0.8\,\text{m s}^{-2}$
       (c) Path should be at centre of gravity of the bead so radius of path is 19.5 cm.
            Acceleration $= 4 \times 0.195 = 0.78\,\text{m s}^{-2}$

6   (a) 2 metres   (b) $3\,\text{m s}^{-1}$

7   (a) 0.859 rad (49.2°)   (b) 9.08 cm
       (c) $1.02\,\text{m s}^{-1}$

8   (a) $2.96\,\text{m s}^{-2}$ (b) 0.302

9   (b) (ii) 82° (must be less than 83°)

10 (a) $1.99 \times 10^{30}\,\text{kg}$
       (b) (i) $47\,900\,\text{m s}^{-1}$
            (ii) 165 years

11 (i) $0.313\,\text{m s}^{-2}$
       (ii) Radial: $R\sin\theta = 0.313\,m$
            Vertical: $R\cos\theta = mg$
       (iii) $F = 0.312m\,\text{N}$
       (iv) $17.7\,\text{m s}^{-1}$

Chapter 9 Energy, work and power

Basic

1   (a) 6250 J   (b) 2.5×10^{-6} J
     (c) 3.95×10^{10} J

2   (a) 4.15×10^{-5} J   (b) 35.3 J
     (c) 490 J

3   (a) 4 kJ   (b) 73.5 J
     (c) 0.0025 J   (d) 0 J

4   1.3 J

5   (a) 6 kJ   (b) $19.8 \, \mathrm{m \, s^{-1}}$
     (c) This speed (approximately
     45 mph) is far too high for a child to
     enter the water from a chute safely.
     Thus some resistive forces such as air
     resistance and friction must be present
     to slow the child down.

6   (a) (i) 815 J   (ii) 0 J
     (b) 600 J

*7   The acceleration is constant so using
     the equation of motion $v^2 = u^2 + 2ax$
     $25^2 = 2 \times a \times 500$
     so $a = 0.625 \, \mathrm{m \, s^{-2}}$
     The force required to give this
     acceleration is
     $F = ma = 1500 \times 0.625$
     $= 937.5 \, \mathrm{N}$
     The total force required is $937.5 + 200$
     $= 1137.5 \, \mathrm{N}$
     Work done $= 1137.5 \times 500$
     $= 568\,750 \, \mathrm{N \, m}$
     or 569 kJ to the nearest kJ

*8   (a) The work done $= 40 \times 50 = 2 \, \mathrm{kJ}$
     (b) Constant acceleration so the final
     speed v is given by
     $v^2 = u^2 + 2ax$
     $v^2 = 2 \times 0.05 \times 10$

so $v = 1$
The force required to give acceleration
is
$F = ma = 55 \times 0.05 = 2.75 \, \mathrm{N}$
The total force required during first
10 metres is
$40 + 2.75 = 42.75 \, \mathrm{N}$
Total work done
$= 42.75 \times 10 + 40 \times 40 = 2.03 \, \mathrm{kJ}$
(c) (a) models the motion as constant
speed of $1 \, \mathrm{m \, s^{-1}}$. (b) is a more realistic
model for a swimmer, starting from
rest, having a period of acceleration
for the first 10 metres followed by a
constant speed of $1 \, \mathrm{m \, s^{-1}}$. In both
cases most of the swim is carried out
at $1 \, \mathrm{m \, s^{-1}}$. The difference between the
calculations for the two, 27.5 J is an
error of only 1.4%. This suggests that
the simpler model gives a good
approximation.

9   (a) 800 kJ   (b) 12.5 kN

10 22 J

11 0.906 J

12 78.4 kJ

13 10 J

*14 Since the speed is constant, the only
     work done is that in overcoming the
     resistive force.
     Resistive force is
     $200\,000 \times 9.8 \times 0.000\,15 = 294 \, \mathrm{N}$
     Power is work done in 1 second.
     Power $= 294 \times 40 = 11\,760$
     Power is 11.8 kW

15 60 W

16 (a) 0.0817 J   (b) 0.327 J

17 4.8 N

18 (a) 0.001 25 k joules
  (b) 0.005 k joules
  (c) 0.015 k joules

19 (a) 60 N   (b) 0.9 J

Intermediate

1 (a) 2020 J   (b) 10.0 m s^{-1}

*2 (a) 70 km h^{-1} = 19.444 m s^{-1}
  55 km h^{-1} = 15.278 m s^{-1}
  Gain in KE = $\frac{1}{2}m(v^2 - u^2)$
  = 60(278.09 − 233.41)
  = 8681
  Work done = change in KE
  = 8.68 kJ
  (b) Work done = force × distance
  Force = 289 N

3 (a) 3.13 m s^{-1}, 1.98 m s^{-1}
  (b) 18.1 cm

4 (a) 5630 N   (b) 7160 N

5 (a) −2060 N   (b) 4.12 kJ

6 (a)

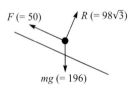

Work done by R is 0
Work done by F is −300 J
Work done by mg is 588 J
(b) 5.37 m s^{-1}

7 385 W

8 (a) 0.048 N   (b) 0.108 J

9 (a) 182 J   (b) 6.04 m s^{-1}

10 (a) −5   (b) 5 J, 0 J, 5 J
  (c) $\sqrt{20}$ m s^{-1}

11 2630 N

12 (a) 42.5 m s^{-1} (b) 22.6 m s^{-1}
  (c) 360 m s^{-1}
  (d) The car will never reach this sort
  of velocity. Air resistance increases as
  the velocity increases and at high
  speeds cannot be ignored.

13 (a)

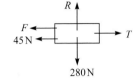

14 0.5 m s^{-1}

15 (a) 2.15 m s^{-1} (b) 0.58 metres

16 (a) 1.4 m s^{-1} (b) 1.8 metres

Advanced

1 (a) 2.45 J   (b) 0.49 J
  (c) 5.42 m s^{-1}

2 10P N

3 (a) 11.9 m s^{-1}
  (b) This is around 26 mph, well under
  the speed limit of 30 mph in built-up
  areas.

4 (a) 25 J   (b) 4.69 metres
  (c) 2.63 m s^{-1}

5 (a) 31.9 m s^{-1} (b) 16.8 m s^{-1}
  (c) The first answer gives a speed of
  over 60 mph. He is unlikely to reach
  this as air resistance is not small at
  high velocities. Even if he could, he
  would be well over the speed limit.

6 (a) 3.16 m s^{-1} (b) 2.26 m s^{-1}

7 125 kJ; 14.4 m s^{-1}

*8 (a) Differentiation gives $\mathbf{a} = 2\mathbf{i} - 2t\mathbf{j}$
  $\mathbf{F} = m\mathbf{a} = 20(\mathbf{i} - t\mathbf{j})$
  (b) Work done = $\int \mathbf{F}.d\mathbf{x} = \int \mathbf{F}.\mathbf{v}dt$
  = $\int 20(\mathbf{i} - t\mathbf{j}).((2t + 3)\mathbf{i} + (2 - t^2)\mathbf{j})dt$
  = 20 $\int(2t + 3 - 2t + t^3)dt$

Work done in first second
$$= 20[3t + 0.25t^4]_0^1 = 65\,\text{J}$$

*9   (a) If T is the tension in the cable at any point, v is the velocity of the lift at that point and P is the power generated then

$Tv = P$

When the lift is travelling with constant speed, $T = 3000g = 30\,000$ v is 2 so P is 60 kW.
(b) The maximum power occurs when the product of the tension in the cable and the velocity is greatest.
This occurs at $t = 3\,\text{s}$.
The upward acceleration of the lift at this point is $\frac{2}{3}\,\text{m s}^{-2}$.
But $T - mg = ma$ (Newton's second law)
$T = 3000\,(10 + 0.667) = 32001$
So the maximum power generated is 64.0 kW to three significant figures.
(c) When $t = 18$, $v = 1(\text{m s}^{-1})$ and $a = -0.25$. The lift is travelling upward still, so

$T - mg = -0.25m$
$T = 3000(10 - 0.25)$
    $= 29\,250$ newtons

Velocity $= 1\,\text{m s}^{-1}$ so the power generated at that point is 29.3 kW to 3 significant figures.

10 (a) 156 kJ   (b) 6.24 m s^{-1}
    (c) 15.6 metres

11 (a) 20.9 metres   (b) 17.4 m s^{-1}

12 (b) 3.96 m s^{-1} (c) 1.6 metres

13 (a) 28.7 m s^{-1} (b) 82 500 N

14 (a) 9.90 m s^{-1} (b) (ii) 1.09
    (c) The rope is built to stretch so that there isn't a dangerous jerk when it becomes taut. It does not regain its initial length. In addition some energy will be lost through air resistance. Note: good climbers always replace a rope after a long fall as it will have lost some of its elasticity.

Revision

1   36 J; 3.67 metres

2   (a) 22.5 J   (b) 0.45 N

3   46.7 kg

4   (a) 270 kJ   (b) 13 500 N

5   14.0 metres

6   (a) 15.1 N   (b) 720 J

7   (a) 0.052 m s^{-2} (b) 38.3 m s^{-1}

8   (i) 257 N   (iii) 0.707 m s^{-2}

9   (a) $F = 1500 - 10x$ (b) 100 kJ

10 1.53 metres

11 (b) 12.5 cm

12 (a) 200 grams: 33.3 cm
            400 grams: 25 cm
    (b) 0.049 J, 0.163 J, 0.49 J
    (c) The 100 gram toy will be 33.8 cm from the bar.

13 (a) (ii) 5 J   (b) 0.08 m
    (c) The waiter doesn't depress the plates when he places the new ones on top. All the plates are at rest when he lets go.

Chapter 10 Circular motion with variable speed

Basic

1 (a) $9.72\,\mathrm{rad\,s^{-1}}$
(b) (i) The wire is smooth so the only reaction force is towards the centre of the circle. The only other force is that due to gravity acting in a vertical direction, i.e. towards the centre of the circle.
(ii) 1.42 newtons towards the centre of the circle.

2 (a) $2.28\,\mathrm{m\,s^{-1}}$ horizontally
(b) 1.24 rad with the downward vertical

3 0.303 metres

*4 Bead is fixed to wire so in limiting case velocity at top equals zero.
At lowest point $KE = 0.5mv^2$
$$PE = 0$$
At highest point $KE = 0$
$$PE = 2mgr$$
Energy is conserved.
$$2mgr = 0.5\,mv^2$$
$$4gr = v^2$$
so $v > 2\sqrt{gr}$

5 0.0421 metres

6 (a) $1.92\,\mathrm{m\,s^{-1}}$
(b) The speed will be less. As the centre of mass of the boy is above the seat then the radius of the path of the centre of mass of the boy will be less than that given. So the potential energy lost will be less and hence the kinetic energy gained will also be less.

7 $v > \sqrt{2gd}$

8 (a) $26.2\,\mathrm{m\,s^{-1}}$ (b) $17.1\,\mathrm{m\,s^{-1}}$
(c) Assumption that the train is a particle: air resistance will slow the train down as it travels along. The centre of gravity of the train will be above the track. This means that when it goes round the circle, the actual radius of the path of the centre of gravity will be less. Not only that but the length of the train means that the centre of gravity of the train when it is on the curved track is probably outside the train itself.

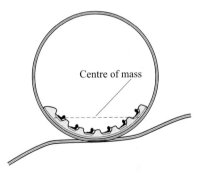

Centre of mass

Hence the difference between the potential energy of the train at the top of the loop and the bottom of the loop is less than that calculated above and so the difference between the maximum and minimum velocities is also less. Assumption that the track is a smooth wire: there will also be friction between the wheels of the train and the track. Once again this will lead to a loss of energy and hence a decrease in speed.

Intermediate

1   1.05 rad

2   (a) 1.30 rad   (b) 0.260 N

3   (a) $\sqrt{2gr}$ m s^{-1} (b) $\sqrt{5gr}$ m s^{-1}

5   82.3 N

*7   (a) The minimum reaction is at the highest point of the cylinder. Let the velocity there be v and the reaction between the ball and cylinder be R.

Initial KE $= 81\dfrac{ma^2}{2}$, PE $= 0$

Final KE $= \dfrac{mv^2}{2}$, PE $= 2mga$

By conservation of energy
$v^2 = 81a^2 - 4ga$

At this point $R + mg = \dfrac{mv^2}{a}$.

Substituting for v^2,
$R = 81ma - 4mg - mg$
Normal reaction is $m(81a - 5g)$.
(b) (i) If the ball is not a particle, and has radius r, the radius of the path of the centre of mass $(a - r)$ of the ball must be used.
As $a - r < a$ the assumption will lead to an overestimate.
(ii) If the ball is not a particle, it will be liable to air resistance so some energy will be lost and the speed v at the top of the circle will be less.

As $R = \dfrac{(mv^2 - mg)}{a}$ the assumption again leads to an overestimate.

Advanced

1   (a) $\sqrt{3g}$ (b) $6g(1 + \cos\theta)$ N

2   (a) $34g\sqrt{2}$
(b) The track must exert a larger force if the direction of motion of the skateboarder is to change.
(c) 1760 N

3   (a) 2.03 m s^{-1} (b) 2.21 m s^{-1}
(c) (i) 4.95 N   (ii) 2.94 N

*5   (a) For system of block and pellet,
initial momentum is $0 + 0.02 \times 55$
final momentum is $0.44\,u$

By conservation of momentum
$0.44\,u = 1.1$
$u = 2.5$

(b) If the pellet and block remain below the point of suspension, the string stays taut so the motion is circular. In the limiting case the speed of the block and pellet must be zero when the angle between the string and the vertical is $90°$.
By conservation of energy,
$\tfrac{1}{2}mv^2 < mgd$
$2.5^2 < 2 \times 9.8 \times d$
$d > 0.319$

(c) If the pellet and block are to make complete circles then the tension in the string must be greater or equal to zero at the highest point of the circle. Let the velocity of the block and pellet be v at this point.
By Newton's second law

$T + mg = mv^2/d$ (1)

and by the principle of the conservation of energy

$\tfrac{1}{2}mv^2 + mg \times 2d = \tfrac{1}{2}mu^2$
$v^2 = 2.5^2 - 4gd$ (2)

From (1), $T > 0$ so $v^2 > gd$
Substituting in (2) gives
$2.5^2 - 4gd > gd$
so $d < 0.12755$
d must be less than 0.128 to 3 s.f.

6   (b) 24.2 N

7   7.14 m s^{-1}

8   50.9 metres

9 $\dfrac{\pi}{3}$ rad $(60°)$

Revision

1   (a) $2.15\,\mathrm{m\,s^{-1}}$
    (b) 0.764 radians with the upward
    vertical

2   (a) $1.92\,\mathrm{m\,s^{-1}}$ (b) $1.33\,\mathrm{m\,s^{-1}}$

3 $11.6\,\mathrm{m\,s^{-1}}$

4 $r = \dfrac{3}{16g}\,v^{2}$

6   (a) The top and bottom of the circle
    (b) If the normal reaction between
    the wire and the bead acts upwards at
    the top, then the difference is
    $\dfrac{2mu^{2}}{a} + 4mg$. If the normal reaction
    between the wire and the bead acts
    downwards at the top of the wire,
    then the difference is $6mg$.

7   (a) $1.22\,\mathrm{rad}\ (= 69.9°)$ (b) $0.506\,\mathrm{N}$

8   0.624 metres

9   (i)

    The bowl is smooth so no friction
acts, also the ball-bearing is small so
air resistance can be ignored.
Therefore no energy is lost to external
forces.
(ii) $v^{2} = u^{2} + 2ag\,(1 - \cos\theta)$
(iii) Newton's second law radially
gives
$$mg\cos\theta - R = \frac{mv^{2}}{a}$$
$$R = mg\cos\theta - \frac{mu^{2}}{a} - 2mg(1 - \cos\theta)$$

$$R = mg(3\cos\theta - 2) - \frac{mu^{2}}{a}$$

R is measured in N.
mg is measured in N.
$\dfrac{mu^{2}}{a}$ is $\mathrm{kg\,m\,s^{-1}}.\dfrac{\mathrm{m\,s^{-1}}}{\mathrm{m}}$ or $\mathrm{kg\,m\,s^{-2}}$
i.e. N
The expression is dimensionally
correct.
(iv) $\cos^{-1}\left(\tfrac{2}{3}\right)\ (= 48.2°)$

*10   (a) (i) Initial $\mathrm{KE} = 0$,
final $\mathrm{KE} = \tfrac{1}{2}mv^{2}$
Initial $\mathrm{PE} = 0$
Final $\mathrm{PE} = 5mg\cos\theta - 2.5\,mg$
Energy is conserved so
$$\tfrac{1}{2}mv^{2} = 2.5\,mg\,(2\cos\theta - 1)$$
$$v^{2} = 5 \times 9.8 \times (2\cos\theta - 1)$$
$$= 49\,(2\cos\theta - 1)$$
(ii) When $\theta = 0, \cos\theta = 1$ so $v = 7$
(b) Height of ceiling $= 4.5 + 5\cos 60°$
$$= 7\ \text{metres}$$
Length of rope $= 5$ metres
Distance left to floor is
$7 - 5 = 2$ metres
Since $s = \tfrac{1}{2}gt^{2}$,
time taken $= \sqrt{4/g} = 0.6389$
Release point is $5\sin 60° = 2.5\sqrt{3}$
from wall.
Horizontal distance travelled from
release point is
$$vt = 7 \times 0.6389 = 4.472$$

Total distance is 8.80 metres to 3 s.f.
(c) The boy is initially about 1 metre
from the wall because of his own size.
Also when he is at the lowest point of
his swing, his feet are at least 1 metre
below the end of the rope so he only
has 1 metre to fall. This will affect the
answer given so perhaps he should
not be modelled as a particle.

Chapter 11 Collisions

Basic

Before impact   **After impact**

m m m m

$\rightarrow 4$ $\rightarrow v$ $\rightarrow w$

Speed of approach $= 4$
Speed of separation $= w - v$
By Newton's law of restitution,
$4e = w - v$ so $3.2 = w - v$
Momentum is conserved so
$4m = m(v + w)$
$4 + 3.2 = 2w$
$w = 3.6$ and $v = 0.4$
Speeds are $0.4\,\mathrm{m\,s}^{-1}$, $3.6\,\mathrm{m\,s}^{-1}$

2 (a) $3.75\,\mathrm{m\,s}^{-1}$; $3.75\,\mathrm{m\,s}^{-1}$
    (b) $8.75\,\mathrm{N\,s}$

3 (a) $3.55\,\mathrm{m\,s}^{-1}$ (b) $7.55\,\mathrm{m\,s}^{-1}$

4 (a) $\frac{1}{3}u(1 - 2k)$
    (b) $\frac{1}{3}u(1 + 4k)$, $\frac{1}{3}u(2 - k)$

5 (a) A: $-6.26\,\mathrm{m\,s}^{-1}$; B: $2.84\,\mathrm{m\,s}^{-1}$
    (b) A: $5.98\,\mathrm{m\,s}^{-1}$; B: $6.68\,\mathrm{m\,s}^{-1}$

6 (a) $0.4u(1 + e)$; $0.2u(2 - 3e)$
    (b) $0.6mu^2(1 - e^2)$

7 P: $6.6\,\mathrm{m\,s}^{-1}$; Q: $0.2\,\mathrm{m\,s}^{-1}$

*8 Let final velocity of B be $a\mathbf{i} + b\mathbf{j}$.
Before impact, total momentum is
$800\mathbf{i} - 900\mathbf{i} + 600\mathbf{j} - 1200\mathbf{j}$
          $= -100\mathbf{i} - 600\mathbf{j}$
After impact, total momentum is
$400\mathbf{i} + 300a\mathbf{i} + 200\mathbf{j} + 300b\mathbf{j}$
But momentum is conserved.
Equating coefficients gives

$-100 = 400 + 300a$ so $a = -\frac{5}{3}$
$-600 = 200 + 300b$ so $b = -\frac{8}{3}$
Car B has final velocity $-\frac{5}{3}\mathbf{i} - \frac{8}{3}\mathbf{j}\,\mathrm{m\,s}^{-1}$

9 (a) 0.775 (b) $1.57\,\mathrm{N\,s}$

10 (a) 0.866 (b) $1.23\,\mathrm{J}$

11 e^2h metres

Intermediate

1 $u = 9\,\mathrm{m\,s}^{-1}$, $e = 0.0370\,(= \frac{1}{27})$

2 (a) 3
    (b) $9.38\,mu^2\,(= 9\frac{3}{8}mu^2)\,\mathrm{J}$

*3 (a) Speed of approach $= 10$
       Speed of separation $= 8$
       By Newton's law of restitution $e = 0.8$
    (b) Impulse $=$ change in momentum
               $= 0.25\,(10 - (-8))$
               $= 4.5\,\mathrm{N\,s}$
    (c) Energy lost $= 0.125(100 - 64)$
               $= 4.5\,\mathrm{J}$

4 (a) A hits B and they stick together
       and go off with speed $5.333u\,\mathrm{m\,s}^{-1}$;
       then A and B combined hit C and
       stick together. The whole body then
       travels on with speed $3.667u\,\mathrm{m\,s}^{-1}$.
    (b) A and B collide and then A
       travels on with speed $2.667u\,\mathrm{m\,s}^{-1}$ and
       B travels on with speed $6.667u\,\mathrm{m\,s}^{-1}$.
       B then collides with C. After the
       impact, B has speed $1.067u\,\mathrm{m\,s}^{-1}$ and
       C has speed $5.733u\,\mathrm{m\,s}^{-1}$. A will now
       catch up B and there will be another
       collision. A now has speed
       $0.533u\,\mathrm{m\,s}^{-1}$ and B has speed
       $2.13u\,\mathrm{m\,s}^{-1}$. The three balls will not
       collide again.

(c) *A* hits *B*, then *A* has speed $4u$ m s^{-1} and *B* has speed $6u$ m s^{-1}. *B* now catches up *C*. After *B* and *C* collide, *C* has speed $4.4u$ m s^{-1} and *B* has speed $2.4u$ m s^{-1}. This is less than *A* so *A* collides with *B* again. After the collision, *A* has speed $2.4u$ m s^{-1} and *B* has speed $3.2u$ m s^{-1}. Thus no more collisions occur.

5 $v = -0.25u$

The two masses *A* and *B* are travelling in opposite directions at the start of the motion. *B*'s speed is a quarter that of *A*. After the collision they both continue in the same direction as *A* at half the original speed of *A*.

6   (a) 0.578 metres
(b) 5

7   (a) $(2.5\mathbf{i} + \mathbf{j})$ m s^{-1}
(b) $2.28 : 1$

8   8.8 m s^{-1} and 4.8 m s^{-1}

9   (a) 6.4 m s^{-1}
(b) 0.2

Advanced

1

Collision	Velocity of *A* after collision (m s^{-1})	Velocity of *A* after collision (m s^{-1})
B hits *A*	15.2	4.4
A hits cushion	-13.68	4.4
A hits *B*	9.22	-7.05
A hits cushion again	-8.299	-7.05
A hits *B*	-6.72	-7.84

*2   Taking components $\mathbf{i}$ and $\mathbf{j}$ perpendicular and parallel to the wall,
initial velocity is $-5\mathbf{i} + 5\sqrt{3}\mathbf{j}$
final velocity is $v \sin\theta\mathbf{i} + v \cos\theta\mathbf{j}$
Using Newton's law of restitution
$v \sin\theta = 0.6 \times 5 = 3$ and $v \cos\theta = 5\sqrt{3}$
$v^2(\sin^2\theta + \cos^2\theta) = v^2 = 3^2 + (5\sqrt{3})^2$
$v^2 = 84$
Hence $v = 9.17$ m s^{-1}.

$$\tan\theta = \frac{\sin\theta}{\cos\theta}$$
$$= \frac{3}{(5\sqrt{3})}$$
$$\theta = 19.1°$$

3   (a) 2.98 m s^{-1} (b) 4.69 m s^{-1}

4   (a) $v = 2.3u$, $w = 1.2u$
(b) 0.522   (c) $7mu$

5   (a) *P*: $0.1u$; *Q*: $0.9u$ (b) $\frac{1}{9}$
(c) $2000mu$ N

6   (a) 0.484   (b) 14.3 J
(c) 6.43 N s

7   (a) 2.94   (b) 882 J

8   (a) 7.5 N s   (b) 375π

9   (a) $v = 2(1 - e)u$, $w = 2(1 + 2e)u$
(c) $e = 1$ so balls are perfectly elastic.

10   (a) 4.52 metres   (b) 7.23 metres

Revision

1   1.5 m s^{-1}, 4.5 m s^{-1}

2   (a) 12.3 m s^{-1}; 2.13 m s^{-1}
(b) 20.3 N s

3   (a) -5.71 and 3.29 m s^{-1} in original direction of travel of *A*
(b) 7.09 and 7.69 m s^{-1}

4 (a) 0.3

(b) As the pucks are of different sizes the motion might not be along the line of centres.

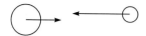

Modelling them as particles ensures that the impact is direct and the pucks do not strike each other a glancing blow.

5 $-1.5\mathbf{i} - \mathbf{j} \, \text{m s}^{-1}$

6 $P : 5 \, \text{m s}^{-1}; \, Q : 1 \, \text{m s}^{-1}$

*7 (a)

Before impact	After impact

3m   m   3m   m

⊕→ 3u   7u ←◯   v ←◯◯→ w

Using conservation of momentum

$9mu - 7mu = mw - 3mv$

$2u = w - 3v$ \hfill (1)

Speed of approach $= 10u$.
Speed of separation $= w + v$.
Using Newton's law of restitution,

$0.7(10u) = w + v$

$7u = w + v$ \hfill (2)

Subtracting (1) from (2) gives

$5u = 4v$

$v = 1.25u$

$w = 5.75u$

(b) Rebound speed of A is $w/6$
$= 0.9583u$

Let the coefficient of restitution between wall and A be e

$0.9583ue = 1.25u$

$e = 0.767$

(c) Impulse = change in momentum
$= 3m(1.25u + 0.9583u)$
$= 3.75mu + 2.875mu$
$= 6.63mu$

8 (a) $-4\mathbf{i} + 8\mathbf{j} \, \text{m s}^{-1}$

(b) $-1.35\mathbf{i} \, \text{N s}$

(c) 0.675 J

9 $9.6 \, \text{m s}^{-1}$ and $5.6 \, \text{m s}^{-1}$

10 (a) $9 \, \text{m s}^{-1}$

(b) $9.51 \, \text{m s}^{-1}$

11 (b) 0.25 \qquad (c) $8.66 \, \text{m s}^{-1}$

13 $P : 0.25u; \quad Q : 0.75u$

14 (i) $1.4 \, \text{m s}^{-1}$

(ii) $2.1 \, \text{m s}^{-1}$, and $e = 0.5$

(iii) As there is no external force present, momentum is conserved so the horizontal component of momentum for the two parts of the pod lies on the same horizontal line. So the velocities are in the same vertical plane.

(iv) $-6\mathbf{i} + 3.5\mathbf{j} \, \text{m s}^{-1}$

Chapter 12 Moments, couples and frameworks

Basic

8 133 N

1 (a) 15 N m anticlockwise
(b) 56 N m clockwise
(c) 69 N m clockwise
(d) 12.7 N m anticlockwise
(e) 416 N m clockwise
(f) 121 N m clockwise

2 (a) 6 N m anticlockwise
(b) 20 N m clockwise
(c) 0.12 N m clockwise
(d) 3.6 N m anticlockwise

3 (a) −10.4 N   (b) 32 N

4 (a) 75 cm   (b) 931 N

5 (a) Anticlockwise   (b) 523 N

6 P: 148 N; Q: 224 N

*7 Let the log be placed x cm from the midpoint of the rod.

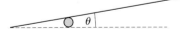

Taking moments about the log,
$120g(150 - x)\cos\theta$
$= 20gx\cos\theta + 60g(150 + x)\cos\theta$
so $9000g = 200gx$. Thus if she uses the whole of her weight she should put the log 45 cm from the centre or 105 cm from the rock. She must push down on the very end of the plank which will be about 30 cm off the ground. If she moves the log nearer to the rock she will not need to exert such a great force and in addition the height of the end of the plank will be greater so it will be easier to push.

Intermediate

1 (a) $F = \sqrt{125}$ N, $C = 7$ N m clockwise
(b) $F = \sqrt{45}$ N, $C = 12$ N m clockwise
(c) $F = \sqrt{101}$ N,
$C = 8 - 4\sqrt{3}$ N m anticlockwise
(d) $F = 10\sqrt{5}$ N, $C = 0$ N m clockwise

2 (a) Front wheel 751 N,
back wheel 1503 N
(b) Front wheel 1100 N,
back wheel 1860 N

3 $\mathbf{Q} = g(48.5 - 12x)$ N,
$\mathbf{R} = g(12.5 + 12x)$ N

*4 (a) Centre of mass of beam is 2 metres from A. Let reaction forces at P and Q be R_P and R_Q respectively.
Taking moments about P:
$2W \times 1 + W \times 1.6 = R_Q \times 3$
$R_Q = 1.2W$
But $R_P + R_Q = 3W$ so $R_P = 1.8W$
(b) Centre of mass of beam is 1 metre from A.
Taking moments about P:
$W \times 0.6 = 2W \times 0.2 + R_Q \times 1.4$
$1.4R_Q = 0.2W$ so $R_Q = \frac{1}{7}W$
But $R_P + R_Q = 3W$ so $R_P = 2\frac{6}{7}W$

5 17.8 N

6 $R_P = 320 - 45x$ and $R_Q = 50 + 45x$

7 (a) 82.2 N horizontally
(b) 213 N at an angle of 67.2° with the ground

8   3630 N m anticlockwise

9   (a) 180 N   (b) 45 N

Advanced

1   456 N at an angle of 80.5° with the ground

*2   (a)

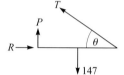

$\sin\theta = 0.6$, $\cos\theta = 0.8$
Taking moments about hinge,
$147 \times 0.2 = T \times 0.4 \times 0.6$
$T = 123$ N
(b) Resolving vertically
$P = 147 - T \times 0.6$
   $= 73.5$
Resolving horizontally
$R = T \times 0.8$
   $= 98.0$
Magnitude of force at hinge is 123 N at an angle of 36.9° to the horizontal.

3   (a) 2.14 N m anticlockwise
(b) 26.2 N

4   Assumptions: the bridge is a uniform rod, with centre of mass 1.75 metres from O. The pivot and pulley are friction free. The rope is light and inextensible.
(a) 0.580 kN   (b) 0.787 kN
(c) 1.27 kN and 0.987 kN

5   1.83 metres

6   (Method 1)
If they both lift at the ends of the beam then they must each lift 39 kg. This is too great for Peter. If Ann lifts nearer the centre of the beam then she can take more of the load. The total mass to be lifted is 78 kg so assume that Ann lifts 43 kg and Peter 35 kg.

Let Ann move x metres from the end. Then, taking moments about Peter's end, $78 \times 1.25 = 43 \times (2.5 - x)$ so $x = 0.233$. Thus if Ann lifts around 23 cm from the end and Peter at the other end they will both be within their limits.
(Method 2)
If only one end is lifted off the ground at a time then the force needed to lift the first end is 382.2 N. This is too much for Peter and well within Ann's limit so Ann must lift the beam and Peter move the trestle and put it under the beam 25 cm from one end.
However, once the beam is on the first trestle, then as Ann lifts the second end she is 2.25 metres from the trestle while the centre of mass of the beam is only 1 metre from the beam.
Taking moments about the trestle, if Ann exerts a force of F newtons, $F \times 2.25 = 764.4 \times 1$, so $F = 340$. Ann will find the second method of lifting the beam easier.

7 $X = 52$ kN; $R = 22$ kN

8   (a) Parallel with AB
(b) $\sqrt{3}a$ clockwise

9   (b) AD: 231 N in tension
        AE: 50 N in compression

Revision

1   115 N

2   96 kg

3   (a) $\dfrac{1250}{\sin\alpha}$

(b)

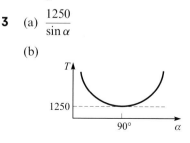

(c) T is a minimum.

4 (a)

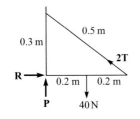

(b) The shelf is a uniform rod of length 0.4 m; there is no couple at the hinge.

(c) 16.7 N

5 (a) $\dfrac{1443}{x}$

(b) $\dfrac{722}{x}$ newtons horizontally,

$50 - \dfrac{1250}{x}$ newtons vertically upwards

(c) When x is very small, the force is downwards and is very great.
As x increases, the angle between the force and the horizontal changes until when $x = 25$ there is no vertical component. The maximum upwards component is 25 N.

6 The bridge is modelled as a uniform rod. The rope is light and inextensible. The pulley is light and friction free.

(a) $(4\sqrt{2} - 1)W$ kN

(b) $2\sqrt{5}W$ kN

*7 Let the forces be as shown in the diagram

Taking moments about the point of contact between the ladder and the wall

$$4F + Mg + 1.5Mg = 3R \qquad (1)$$

Resolving vertically

$$R = 2Mg$$

Substituting in (1)

$$4F = 3R - 1.25R$$
$$F = \tfrac{7}{16}R$$

The coefficient of friction is
$0.438 \ (= \tfrac{7}{16})$.

8 P: 50 N towards door
Q: 50 N away from door
F: 100 N

9 (c) 3 metres
(d) (ii) It doesn't matter how heavy the person is as long as they are not so heavy that the ladder breaks.

10 (a) 30 kg
(b) 3.6 kg to 2 s.f.
(c) (i) The centre of mass is exactly half-way along the plank, i.e. 2.7 metres from one end.
(ii) The rock has no size and can be placed exactly at the end of the plank. The rock would normally be placed so its centre of mass was just inside the end of the plank.

Chapter 13 Centres of mass

Basic

1 2.5 metres

2 $\frac{4}{7}$ metres ($= 0.571$ metres)

3 $\frac{10}{9}a$ metres ($= 1.11a$ metres)

4 15 centimetres

*5 Let the position of the centre of mass
be $a\mathbf{i} + b\mathbf{j}$.
Taking moments about the y-axis,
$a \times 6m = 1 \times m + 2 \times 2m - 3 \times 3m$
$6a = -4$
$a = -\frac{2}{3}$
Taking moments about the x-axis,
$b \times 6m = 1 \times m + 1 \times 2m + 1 \times 3m$
$6b = 6$
$b = 1$
Ans. $-\frac{2}{3}\mathbf{i} + \mathbf{j}$ ($= -0.667\mathbf{i} + \mathbf{j}$)

6 35.4 cm

7 1.51 cm to the left of O along the
diameter on which the diagonal of the
square lies

8 9.4 cm

Intermediate

1 5.41 cm

2 5 cm

3 (a) 0.4a (b) 0.6a

*4 The centres of masses of the rods are
at their midpoints. Total mass of
system is 270 grams.
Taking moments about MN,
$a \times 270 = 3 \times 60 + 3 \times 100 + 6 \times 10$
$\qquad\qquad = 540$
So $a = 2$
Taking moments about LM,
$b \times 270 = 4 \times 80 + 4 \times 100 + 8 \times 10$
$\qquad\qquad = 800$
So $b = 2.9630$
Distance from M is
$\sqrt{a^2 + b^2} = 3.57\,\text{cm}$

5 $8\mathbf{i} + 10\mathbf{j}$

6 56.7 cm

7 $5.20h$ ($= 3\sqrt{3}h$)

8 36.9 cm

9 (a) 13.3 cm; 10 cm
    (b) 14.4 cm; 10 cm

10 4.24 cm

11 (0, 1.60)

12 2.5 cm

13 1.5

14 21.4 cm

Advanced

1 (a) 0.375a (b) 22m

2 52.1°

3 $(2\frac{2}{3}, 0)$

4 (b) 10.9°
   (c) 6.67 N and 3.33 N
      $(= 6\frac{2}{3} N$ and $3\frac{1}{3} N)$

5 (b) 29.3°

*6 Let mass of lamina be $3m$.

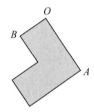

Let centre of mass be x cm from OA.
Taking moments about OA gives

$3mx = 2m \times 5 + m \times 15$

$x = \dfrac{25}{3} (= 8.33)$ cm

Let distance of centre of mass from
OB be y.
Taking moments about OB gives

$3my = 2m \times 10 + m \times 15$

$y = \dfrac{35}{3} (= 11.7)$ cm

But $\tan \alpha = \dfrac{x}{y} = \dfrac{25}{35}$

$a = 35.5°$

7 $\frac{3}{2}\rho$

8 (a) 0.737 cm   (b) 3.89 cm

9 (a) $\frac{4}{3}$ cm; 1 cm   (b) 8 N, topples

10 (b) (i) 1.34a

Revision

1 4.17a $(= 4\frac{1}{6}a)$

2 1.67 $(= 1\frac{2}{3})$ cm

3 125 cm

4 5.22 cm

5 (a) (0.2, 1.2)   (b) $(-\frac{1}{3}, -2)$

6 1.93a

*7 Solid is symmetrical about the x-axis
so the centre of mass lies on the
x-axis. Let centre of mass be at
position $(X, 0)$ and density be ρ.

Mass of solid is $\displaystyle\int_0^5 \rho \pi y^2 \mathrm{d}x$.

Taking moments about the y-axis,

$X \displaystyle\int_0^5 \rho \pi (0.04x^4 + 4x^2 + 100) \,\mathrm{d}x$

$= \displaystyle\int_0^5 \rho \pi x (0.04x^4 + 4x^2 + 100) \mathrm{d}x$

Integrating with respect to x and
simplifying gives

$X[0.008x^5 + 1.333x^3 + 100x]_0^5$

$\qquad = [0.006\,667x^6 + x^4 + 50x^2]_0^5$

$691.67X = 1979.167$
$X = 2.86$
Centre of mass is at (2.86, 0).

8 (b) 2.45a $(= \sqrt{6}a)$

9 (a) 5.22 cm from B along BC

   (b) $x = \dfrac{40}{m}$

   (c)

   (d) Over AB

10 (a) 11.2 cm
   (b) (i) 53.3°
      (ii) 28.0°

11 (b) 48.0°

Chapter 14 Simple harmonic motion

Basic

1   4 oscillations per second

$$\therefore T = \frac{1}{4} = \frac{2\pi}{\omega}$$

$\omega = 8\pi$

Amplitude $= a = 0.1\,\text{m}$.

For SHM

$$\ddot{x} = -\omega^2 x$$

so maximum acceleration occurs when
x is minimum, i.e. $x = -a$

$$\ddot{x} = -(8\pi)^2 \times (-0.1)$$
$$= 6.4\pi^2 \ (= 63.2)\,\text{m s}^{-2}$$

2 $\dfrac{a}{2}$

3 $x = 2\cos(4t)$

4   (b) (i) 5 m   (ii) 2 s

5   (a) π s
     (b) 2.83 $(= 2\sqrt{2})$ m
     (c) 5.66 $(= 4\sqrt{2})$ m s^{-1}

6   2.53 cm

7   0.145 cm s^{-1}

8   (a) 2.72 s   (b) 1.15 m s^{-1}
     (c) 2.67 m s^{-2}

9   (a) 0.613 m   (b) 0.196 m s^{-1}
     (c) The bob of the pendulum is a
particle, the string is light and
inextensible, the amplitude of the
oscillations is small.

10 (a) $\dfrac{2\pi}{3}$ s   (b) $-0.0322\,\text{m s}^{-1}$

     (c) $9 \times 10^{-4}\,\text{N}$

11 (a) 4.94 m
     (b) $v = -5\pi \sin \pi(t + 0.05)\,\text{m s}^{-1}$
       $a = -5\pi^2 \cos \pi(t + 0.05)\,\text{m s}^{-1}$
     (d) 30

Intermediate

1   (a) $1.12 = \dfrac{\sqrt{5}}{2}$ rad s^{-1}

     (b) 2.05 metres

2

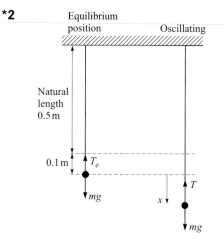

(a) In equilibrium
$T_e = 0.25g$
and by Hooke's law
$T_e = k \times 0.1$
$\therefore k = 2.5g$
When oscillating and mass is x cm
below equilibrium position: (Newton's
second law)

$0.25g - T = m\ddot{x}$
(Hooke's law)
$T = k(0.1 + x)$
$0.25g - 0.1k - kx = m\ddot{x}$

but $0.1k = 0.25g$ (from equilibrium position), so
$-kx = m\ddot{x}$

$\ddot{x} = -\dfrac{k}{m}x$

$= \dfrac{-2.5g}{0.25}x$

$= -10gx$

(b) The string is pulled down $5\,\text{cm}$ so $a = 0.05$.
The mass performs SHM with $\omega^2 = 10g$.
Now $v^2 = \omega^2(a^2 - x^2)$,
so maximum v given, when $x = 0$, by
$v^2 = 10g(0.05^2) = 0.245$
Speed is $0.495\,\text{m s}^{-1}$.

3 $3.46\ (= 2\sqrt{3})$ metres;
$13.9\ (= 8\sqrt{3})\,\text{m s}^{-2}$

4   (a) $\dfrac{l}{2}$

5   (a) $A = 3,\ d = 5,\ \omega = 0.262$
(b) $2.18 \times 10^{-4}\,\text{m s}^{-1}$

6   (a) $0.444\,\text{s}$ (b) $\sqrt{2}\,\text{m s}^{-1}$

*7

Newton's second law applied tangentially to the path of the bob gives
$mg \sin\phi = -m\ddot{s}$
where s is the displacement along the arc of the bob's motion.

$s = l\phi$
so $\ddot{s} = 0.8\ddot{\phi}$
$\therefore\ g \sin\phi = -0.8\ddot{\phi}$
$\ddot{\phi} = -1.25g \sin\phi$

(b) When ϕ is small, $\sin\phi \approx \phi$,
so $\ddot{\phi} = -1.25g\phi$.
This is SHM where $\omega^2 = 1.25g$, so

$T = \dfrac{2\pi}{\omega} = \dfrac{2\pi}{\sqrt{1.25g}}$

Period is 1.80 seconds.

8   (a) $\ddot{x} = -16\pi^2 x$ (b) $\sqrt{2}$

9   (a) $86\,\text{cm}$ (b) $430\,\text{N}$

10 $0.281\,\text{s}$

11 $1.98\,\text{m s}^{-1}$

12 (a) $\dfrac{2\pi}{3}\,\text{s}$ (b) $2.03\,\text{m}$

(c) (i) No energy is lost as heat when the spring compresses and extends. The mass does not overextend the spring. The spring has no mass.
(ii) Energy will be lost so the amplitude of the motion will gradually decrease until the mass hangs at rest in the equilibrium position.

Advanced

1   (a) $4.33\ (= 4\tfrac{1}{3})\,\text{m}$
(b) $x = -3.72\,\text{m}$;
$v = -6.64\,\text{m s}^{-1}$

2   (a) $0.816 = \sqrt{\dfrac{2}{3}}\,\text{m s}^{-1}$ (b) $4.44\,\text{s}$

3   (a) $\sqrt{\dfrac{k}{2m}}l\,\text{m s}^{-1}$ (b) $\dfrac{\pi}{2}\sqrt{\dfrac{m}{2k}}\,\text{s}$

4 $\dfrac{\pi}{2}\sqrt{\dfrac{3}{10}}$ s

6 (a) $\frac{5}{3}a$

7 (a) $\dfrac{l}{10}$ (b) $2\pi\sqrt{\dfrac{l}{5g}}$

8 (a) 0.699 s   (b) 0.224 s

9 (a) 10 cm   (b) 13.7 $(= 1.4g)$ N
(c) 0.602 s

11 (a) 0.0684 metres
(b) 0.0946 seconds

12 (a) 16.5 seconds (b) 4.86 metres

Revision

1 5

2 (a) 0.716 metres   (b) 3.14 m s^{-2}

3 1.6 m

4 (a) $x = 5\cos t$ (b) $\ddot{x} = -x$

5 (a) $\ddot{\phi} = -64\phi$ (b) 0.4 rad s^{-1}
(c) -0.0327 radians

7 (a) 2.53 metres   (b) 2.43 seconds

8 $\dfrac{2}{\sqrt{6}} = 0.816$

9 (a) $\dfrac{l}{4}$

10 1.80 metres

11 $\dfrac{a}{6}$; $2\pi\sqrt{\dfrac{a}{3g}}$

12 (a) 0.001 metres
(b) $T = 200\,(x + 10)$
(c) 0.316
(d) (i) Some of the elastic potential energy in the string will be dissipated in heat rather than turned into kinetic energy. This means that the initial kinetic energy given to the mass can be greater than the difference between gravitational potential energy gained when the string becomes slack and the initial elastic potential energy of the string in its equilibrium position. Thus the initial speed can be greater.
(ii) The amount of energy lost during the motion increases as the distance travelled increases. Thus more energy is lost in travelling down to the lowest point and then back upwards to the top of its oscillation than is lost by just going upwards. Thus the initial kinetic energy, and hence the initial velocity, can be even greater than in the case above.